The
Sacred Power
of
Huna

The
Sacred Power
of
Huna

Spirituality and Shamanism in Hawai'i

Rima A. Morrell, Ph.D.

Inner Traditions
Rochester, Vermont

Inner Traditions
One Park Street
Rochester, Vermont 05767
www.InnerTraditions.com

Library of Congress Cataloging-in-Publication Data

Morrell, Rima A.
  The sacred power of Huna spirituality and shamanism in Hawai'i / Rima A.
Morrell.
    p. cm.
  Summary: "An extensive study of ancient Hawaiian spirituality"--Provided
by publisher.
  Includes bibliographical references (p.   ) and index.
  ISBN 978-159477009-8
  1. Huna. 2. Shamanism. 3. Hawaii--Religion. I. Title.
  BF1623.H85M67 2005
  299'.9242--dc22
                                        2005007810

Printed and bound in the United States by Lake Book Manufacturing, Inc.

10 9 8 7 6 5 4 3 2

Text design and layout by Priscilla Baker
This book was typeset in Sabon, with Temerity and Agenda as display
typefaces

Contents

List of Illustrations

Figures

Tables

All books will become light in proportion
as you find light in them.

Mortimer J. Adler

Acknowledgments

Many thanks to all those who have helped me with my research on Hawai'i and the Pacific. It is impossible to name all those who inspired me along the way, and still do, but you know who you are. You are scattered all over the world and beyond; some of you have already passed along the Road of Tāne into the Leagues of Light of the West; others wish to remain anonymous. I suspect some names are still to be known, and therefore cannot be written. I owe you so much. My thanks to you all is unbounded.

In the academic world of *ao,* or "acknowledged light," my thanks go to Professor Stephen Hugh-Jones, who has done some superb work on the Barasana of South America and gave my original dissertation some excellent input. My thanks to others in the Department of Social Anthropology, Cambridge University, where I always enjoyed learning. To my Cambridge tutor, a lovely woman, Professor Vivien Law, whose linguistic knowledge was breathtaking and who encouraged me to apply for the scholarships that made my trip to Hawai'i possible. To Professor Chris Tilley, at University College London, who supervised my Ph.D. on Hawai'i. So many would have tried to stop me "going my own way" and you never did. For that, I am always grateful. My particular thanks to Polynesian professors Brian Murton and Vili Hereniko at the University of Hawai'i at Mānoa, who inspired me when I was there. Indeed, in later years Brian flew all the way to London to examine my Ph.D. on Huna!

Finally, I would like to dedicate this book to my dear friend and soul-sister Janine, who traveled the world because she loved other cultures and languages. She returned to London only to die in a cycling accident at the age of twenty-seven. Just before she passed, the light shone out of her so strongly she became almost translucent and seemed to float along in beauty. Janine's favorite color was violet and she always wanted to visit Hawai'i, particularly the cliffs of the Nā Pali coast, purpling into the distant light. Perhaps she is dancing there now. I hope this book may, in some small measure, pulse with her eternal light.

Prologue

Even the most timorous journey can disclose the journey
of the mind to God.

MIRCEA ELIADE

One day, in a particular sun-dappled patch of the rain forest on one of
the Hawaiian Islands, I had a powerful experience, one that changed
the way I looked at Hawaiian culture—and myself—forever. I encountered an unexpected portal into the high worlds of Huna, ancient
Hawaiian wisdom, on the slopes of a magic mountain.

I had hitchhiked up the mountain that hot day, wearing my usual
shorts, T-shirt, and flip-flops, intending to spend the day alone in the
coolness of the forest. I came to a sign saying *Kapu,* a tub of rock salt
next to it. I knew it signified the entrance to the remote temple I had
been searching for. I breathed deeply, said a prayer, asked permission,
received the answer that I could pass from the wind, sprinkled some salt
around me, and carefully went past the sign.

I can still remember the colors of that clearing—gray and olive—
and the hot and cold winds that were blowing through it. There were
strangely arresting rocks among the trees. I slowly walked toward them
and felt drawn to one particular arrangement, where a smooth horizontal rock covered several vertical ones. The power in those standing
stones among the trees was so great that when I put my hands on them,
they were hot and vibrating. I didn't know what was going on! It made
no sense to me in terms of how I saw the world, yet my head was clear

and I knew what I was feeling was real. The energy of the temple had such a huge effect on me that I could stay in the clearing for only twenty minutes or so before I knew I had to get back down the mountain to the beach. As I turned to leave, I decided to pick up one of the "skeleton" leaves that covered the clearing (I call them skeleton leaves because, as they decay, the pattern of their lineaments is perfectly preserved). I bent down to put it in my notebook but the decayed leaf was so heavy that I had trouble picking it up. Its great heaviness let me know that *it did not want to be taken away*. So I settled it back in its native earth.

Then the rustling of the wind in the branches turned to eerie murmuring voices that seemed to be coming from the spectral trees around me, the pieces of sky above, and the soft earth below. They said: "You are never alone, you are never alone." I remember thinking "I know that's true, but wish I could always believe it" as I turned and exited rather rapidly!

I found out later that some Hawaiians consider that patch of rain forest near the top of the ancient mountain to be a most sacred temple of the ancient continent of Mū, or Lemuria, now largely submerged. That experience certainly showed me the power of places. It opened me up to taking the legends of the Hawaiians seriously, legends that say trees speak—I have heard them—and that rocks have life—I have felt it, warm and pulsing. Since then, I have never had reason to doubt the ancient stories, and, as you will see, I've had many reasons to believe them, even some of the more "unlikely" stories, such as rainbows appearing on a sudden opening-up of the spirit!

When I first visited Hawai'i in 1990, I had come from Cambridge University to do anthropological fieldwork for my dissertation in a very beautiful part of the world that I had always longed to visit. That was all. I did not dream that the things I would find out would impact every part of my life and send me on a mission I could not resist, resulting in my many years of studying, writing, and eventually teaching about Huna.

It has been a long and often lonely journey, with only my intuition to keep me going. But now I can see that if it had not been this way, I would not have gained the light I am now able to share with you.

When I first encountered instances of the magical energy of Hawaiian spirituality, such as when I visited the ancient temple, my Western belief system was greatly challenged. I had nothing to replace it with, but needed to make sense of what I saw. The autumn mists of Cambridge dissolved as I immersed myself in a study of the Hawaiian language. As my understanding grew, I began to be able to predict the hidden meanings of words and to glimpse the central role of language in Huna. Concurrently, my internal life became richly exciting, as previously disparate elements fit together in a rich pattern of undreamt-of depth and texture.

As the only student to specialize in Polynesia at Cambridge University, I went on to complete my B.A. dissertation—*Into the Night Rainbow, the Hula Dance of Hawai'i as a Technique of Consciousness,* which focused on how the hula dance provides a rich repository of spiritual meanings of great benefit to all who understand even a portion of its kaleidoscopic potential—and receive my honors degree in anthropology. Then I began working on this book. After setting it aside for some time while I completed my Ph.D. in Hawaiian culture, I finally revised it years later.

Most of it was written in another part of Polynesia, in a cottage held between a glittering lake and crystalline mountains on the South Island of New Zealand, at a place called Wanaka. *Wanaka* means "the place where light strikes." It also means "the lore of the *tohunga.*" *Tohunga* is a dialectical form of *kahuna,* or "expert in the sacred" (*ka,* "the one who knows how to strike," and *huna,* "the hidden"). Although I was not in Hawai'i, I was still very much in the same Polynesian cultural context: a Hawaiian can understand the language of the New Zealand Maori eight thousand miles away and shares essentially the same myths, religion, and ritual. As I wrote, I seemed to become lighter and lighter. What I was learning, quite without knowing it, was to grow my light to and through my Higher Self, which guided me in bridging the gap between Western and Hawaiian belief systems.

One of the keys to this process is consciousness: I realized more and more that we need to acknowledge our own influence in creating the world we know.

When we think of "reality," we are thinking not of objective reality in itself, but of how we *experience* what we meet. It is difficult to realize how we each experience the same thing differently. Psychologists say no two people on a busy street see the same thing. One may notice the passing cars; another, people's faces; another, goods in the shops. Some people are so taken up with their thoughts they notice almost nothing at all! In other words, what we notice depends on how much attention we allow it. Or what we see depends on *what is in our mind.*

From the time of Captain Cook until today, visitors to Hawai'i—carrying their own visions of its reality in their minds—have often been unaware of its spiritual and cultural treasures. Similarly, we miss much of the potentials of life; we are out of touch with the dreams, mythology, and magic that lie deep inside ourselves. Yet there are guidelines to help us see more deeply, which make not only Hawai'i clearer and brighter but us brighter too. I have been studying Huna since 1990 and have found it to be the best system I have ever discovered, in all my comparative anthropological studies, for understanding ourselves and the wide world beyond.

Hawaiian culture contains systems of philosophy and psychology far more sophisticated than those found in the West. Certain Hawaiians found the importance of the unconscious long before Freud and Jung. While psychotherapy and psychiatry concentrate on helping us access that knowledge by getting in touch with the past, those sciences remain largely unaware of the effect of the Higher Self, or superconscious. That "Mind of Light" surrounds our mind like a giant aura, knowing, understanding, forgiving all things. Huna contains ways of traveling toward that great light of peace. It's a knowledge that brings greater love, compassion, and understanding: a knowledge that joins, rather than separates. I have written this book to provide some access to this wonderful system, so you can learn about it and share its benefits, if you choose.

One of the first things I was told when I arrived in Hawai'i as a fledging anthropologist from Cambridge University was that I would receive answers only to the questions I asked and that, as a result, *I would never know what I didn't know.* Wise words indeed! Therefore, *The Sacred Power of Huna* is not offered as a definitive book on Hawaiian wisdom (indeed, I do not believe such a thing is possible or even desirable). It is merely the answers I received to the questions I asked. However, those answers shed light not only on the tremendous Hawaiian culture, but also on ways we can all improve the quality of our light and thus our lives. Huna is an amazing system of wisdom, clear and simple, yet complex beyond all human understanding. I apologize for all errors and omissions, aware that I can represent only what I see, and am able to see only a portion of the amazing hologram of light that some call Huna.

Throughout my journeys to Hawai'i I was guided. For example, after I had first reached O'ahu in 1990, my original plan was to visit the island of Moloka'i. But then—one evening in the youth hostel in Honolulu—it came to me very clearly that I should go to Kaua'i instead, so I changed my plans. On that green island I met some kahuna and my encounters with them enabled me to figure out that the system of shamanism I had been looking for had been there under my nose all along, in the bright guise of the hula dance.

Once that realization came, I was surprised to discover that no one else had written about it before. The Hawaiians who knew were keeping mum, safeguarding this precious knowledge from being taught to those who were not ready to learn. And other anthropologists studying Hawai'i hadn't discovered it yet. After being led to ask the questions, I spent years putting the information I learned together.

I have had a deep conflict for many years now about whether this information—which has been so carefully preserved and deliberately kept hidden down the ages—should be displayed at all. Yet I'm convinced now is the right time. The expansion of Western ideas and culture has had some negative consequences for the "rest" of the world, through a personal ethos that favors the aggrandizement of the individual over caring for and respecting our world and one another. I wish to avoid further desecration by sharing this transforming knowledge now. It is a strong responsibility, one that I tried to deny many times, but a multitude of dreams and signs showed me that I could not refuse. I realized that the information came to me—a young haole (white) girl with a Polynesian name—for a reason, and that reason is to help people use the ancient knowledge for good.

Huna provides many tools for our inner journey, the most important journey of all. That is the journey Mircea Eliade, anthropologist of the sacred, described as being toward the mind to God. As the physicist Paul Davies wrote, it is also the mind of God. Put simply, it's coming home to the power within us. I invite you to journey with me through these higher, brighter worlds of wonder, with this book as your guide.

Let us begin with two lines from a Hawaiian prayer for knowledge:

Ho mai ka loea, ka'ike, ka mana
I a'e ka honua lā

Bring cleverness, knowledge, great powers
So the earth may ascend.

1
Hidden Light

And see, no longer blinded by our eyes.

RUPERT BROOKE

Now, living at the sunrise of the new millennium, we are told that our earth has already been discovered. Land has been charted and mapped. Unlike Christopher Columbus, we know that when we sail on the ocean we won't fall off the edge of the world. But nothing could be less true. The world's edge is still there, although it is shifting. The greatest discovery of all awaits us, the last great unexplored continent of the mind.

That exploration can encompass an endless system of growth and discovery, which is known as Huna. Huna, some say, is the world's oldest spiritual tradition and has been in existence since time before time. Huna contains ways of traveling toward our own Higher Mind, ultimately linking to all other minds and the great light beyond. We journey by removing subconscious blocks, as well as by growing in consciousness and its use. Nothing is more important.

Many Hawaiians are aware of what scientists now tell us: we normally use only a tiny percentage of our mind power. By spending time in Hawai'i—whether in the islands themselves or in our greater mind that the power of Huna represents—we can get in touch with this source of all. In so doing, we'll learn to recover our own power, the power to do or be all things.

1

The islands of Hawai'i are islands of magic, but Hawai'i, like many blessings, is initially pretty difficult to grasp. The Hawaiian Islands comprise the most geographically isolated group of islands in the world, yet they form part of a far greater whole. They are part of an island group named Polynesia, which also includes Tahiti, Easter Island, New Zealand, Tonga, the Marquesas, Samoa, and many other islands. At the same time, each island appears very much a "world unto itself," especially when you are standing on it and looking at the biggest ocean in the world stretching away from the land in all directions!

We need to change our mind to "see, no longer blinded by our eyes," to take in the bigger picture. The Hawai'i this book reveals encourages us to relate the islands to our own mind, our own process. In so doing, we can find a bright new world, not a new world that will be with us as long as we are in the islands, but one that will stay with us and improve the quality of our life.

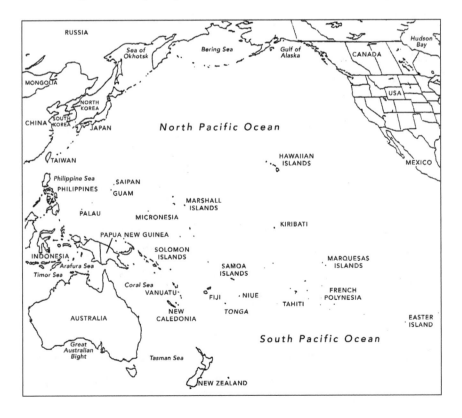

The key is always perception. I can still remember the first time I looked into a prism—in a boring school science class in north London—and the shock when I noticed the rainbow of refracted light. The familiar world split open, the way the prism had splintered the wave and revealed the blossoming colors of light. I was used to seeing light as clearly defined colors, such as the blue of the sky or the brown of the table. Never again! Seeing some of the previously invisible colors of light, all together, all at once, for the very first time, was like looking into a brave new world.

In all our looking we need to remember that, as Jonathan Swift said, "real vision is seeing into the invisible." The techniques to see into the invisible are so important because they are the very techniques to help us do well in our lives. Hawaiian is not just a pretty language full of beautiful rainbows and stories. It has many qualities that will help this earth ascend into a higher dimension, at this pivotal point in our consciousness. Its words teach us how to really see, how to be the architects of our own bright structure, the structure that will lead us into the light.

As in many cultures, light stands for knowledge in Hawai'i, but—unlike in many other countries—much of Hawaiian culture is hidden, like the rainbow unseen in pure light. Insight into how and why Hawaiian knowledge has been hidden can be gained first, by realizing that most of our ideas about Hawai'i *haven't come from the Hawaiians themselves* and second, by taking a brief look at the history of the islands as seen through a conventional lens.

Since first contact with the West, different groups—sailors, missionaries, soldiers, writers, artists—have visited the islands of Polynesia and recorded their impressions, which have generally fallen into two main categories. The first is artificially bright: "Hawai'i is a paradise." The other is dark and dank, as expressed by one missionary who said, "Hawaiians are creatures of the 'night's brown savagery.'" We'll look at both interpretations because, even if we don't believe them, they are so pervasive that they have a subconscious effect on us.

ISLANDS OF DELIGHT

*For me its balmy airs are always blowing, its summer
seas flashing in the sun, other things leave me, but it
abides; other things change, but it remains the same. In
my nostrils still lives the breath of flowers perished
more than twenty years ago.*

MARK TWAIN, ON HAWAI'I

Hawai'i. That name is famous all over the world. People everywhere think of fantasy islands of waving palm trees, well-balanced girls dancing on the beaches. Lands where the enchanted days are measured only by the beating waves of the purple Pacific. A paradise where the sun is always shining, the people are always smiling, and the flowers are always in bloom. Can't we picture it already? Hawai'i in our mind.

We get the bright picture-postcard image of Hawai'i from the writings and images of the last couple of centuries. Right from the beginning, the Polynesian islands were known as islands of delight. The French explorer De Bougainville wrote on arriving in Tahiti in 1768: "I thought I was transported to the garden of Eden." De Bougainville was the first of many explorers who described the islands as paradise: not only the nicest places they had ever been to, but also the culmination of everything they had ever dreamed of.

Captain James Cook was on his way back from Australia to England when he noticed some unexpected islands. One windy day in January 1778, his boats anchored off Waimea Bay, a wide golden beach on an island he later learned was Kaua'i. The Hawaiians spotted the ship and then—in the words of one of the crew—"some people of a brown color" who "though of the common size were stoutly made" scrambled on board and began to dance. The way they danced was the Westerners' introduction to the islanders' delight in sex and sexual gestures: "they moved their Legs . . . wriggled their backsides and used many lascivious Gestures."[1]

That, as they say, was the end of the beginning, for the islands were never the same again. The first explorers were rapidly followed by missionaries, writers, and artists, all with their own way of viewing and representing Hawai'i. In the twentieth century, Hawai'i spawned the "South Sea" genre of films, such as *Blue Hawaii*. The movie *Polynesian Odyssey* contains a reenactment of white men arriving at a Polynesian island for the first time. A young boy perched on top of the mast of their ship watches the native canoes of greeting approaching. As the boats move across the decreasing distance, he asks one experienced old sailor:

"Is that what it's always like?"
    "Aye lad, welcome to paradise. Paradise will change forever."
    "Change, sir?"
    "Yes lad, maybe for good, maybe for evil, it will never be the same. May God judge us kindly."[2]

"Paradise" did indeed change, and, although some Hawaiians judge Captain Cook harshly, his voyage was not itself responsible for the later widespread desecration of their land and culture. Many say the missionaries who set out to destroy the "sinful darkness" of the Hawaiian culture have more responsibility. Yet it is certainly true that the popularity of the explorers' reports led many visitors to the island group named Polynesia. The bright legend of Polynesia was born, a legend so powerful that one French aristocrat, sentenced to death in the French Revolution, died on the guillotine with the word "Tahiti" on his lips.

The multitudes who tuned in to the myth of the Polynesian islands as paradise were most famously exemplified by the artist Paul Gauguin, who left his family in France to find a new life in Polynesia. Gauguin resisted finding the Polynesians civilized. He wrote that he preferred to call the natives "savages" rather than "barbarians": "because it renders more precisely the active opposition to the civilized."[3] Gauguin tried to create his own Polynesia: his individual islands of desire. The playwright August Strindberg wrote of him: "Gauguin, the savage, who hates a whimpering civilization, a sort of Titan who, jealous of the Creator, makes in his leisure hours his own little creation . . ."[4] He carved into the wood of his final house on Tahiti the words: *Soyez amoureuses, vous serez heureuses*, "Be amorous and you will be happy."

Did Gauguin succeed in his desires? Perhaps he failed on a personal level. He probably did not intend to die of syphilis on a remote Polynesian island. And he never really understood much of the Polynesian culture. The missing link was emotion. Gauguin was not in tune enough with his emotions and the emotions of other people—he would take his daughter to watch executions in Paris—to know how to re-create the world in the image he wanted. But on a greater level he succeeded in representing Polynesia to many: the Polynesia that was in his mind. Even though it was a shadow of a deeper brightness, Gauguin's Polynesia is now known to millions and has influenced many journeys, both mythical and actual. For example, the English poet Rupert Brooke, who fell in love with Polynesia, wrote: "And you may figure me in the center of a Gauguin picture, nakedly riding a squat horse into white surf."[5]

ISLANDS OF DARKNESS

In the heart of the mussel shell lies the pearl of light.
POLYNESIAN CHANT

The other famous interpretation of Polynesia is that the islands are islands of darkness. This became popular at the time of Captain Cook, because the Hawaiians killed him. The captain—who had survived terrible ordeals—was killed by a few Hawaiians at the edge of the ocean on the morning of Valentine's Day 1779. When the world found out, there was an uproar, for Captain Cook was a very highly regarded and respected explorer. A newspaper of the day reported the reaction of the king of England: "His Majesty, who had always the highest opinion of Captain Cook, shed tears." Some of the world said: "What else can you expect from savages, living in darkness?"

This dim view of the Hawaiians was confirmed by the missionaries who came hot on the heels of the first explorers. They were expecting to find darkness and that is exactly what they found. Many missionaries longed to reach Hawai'i, thinking: "There lived a ripe people—ripe with sin." The legendary beauty of the islands merged with their beliefs, giving them a sense of mission. Mrs. Judd, the wife of an early missionary, described the scene from the ship's deck when they first approached Hawai'i: "It is land! The clouds suddenly opened and Hawaii lay itself out, blue and green and beautiful, like . . . a pilgrim's land." Then "some poured their hearts out in thanksgiving, others exclaimed in delight, and yet others sat alone on the deck in tears and silence." Yet they were to find darkness there, *because they expected to.* Just after her moving description of the glowing land of Hawai'i, Mrs. Judd wrote: "Can anything so fair be defiled by idol worship and deeds of cruelty?" Sadly, the answer, according to them, was a resounding "Yes."[6]

The missionaries have had, and continue to have, a huge influence on Hawai'i. They did their best to stamp out the "sinful darkness of the people" by forcing Hawaiians to cover their bodies and passing laws forbidding traditional practices. The "darkness" the missionaries found in these bright islands included surfing and other games, tattooing, the hula, and even sexual pleasure itself. The naming of the "missionary position" is no coincidence: it was introduced by the missionaries so a woman would be less in control in sexual intercourse and hence gain less pleasure. It cannot be assumed that the civilizing influence is a beneficial one.

One missionary viewed the hula, dance of mystery and magic, as "the Devil's nest, in which he looks about, rears himself up, and sniffs for the person he wishes to swallow." The missionaries were not wrong when they associated the hula with sexuality: it was, and remains, a vastly pleasurable dance. And the *hula 'ūlili* ceremony, for example, broke free of many taboos that normally governed sexual behavior. Nathaniel Emerson, writer and teacher, described it graphically:

Imagine an assembly of men and women in the picturesque illumination given by flaring *kukui* torches, the men on one side, the women on the other. Husbands and wives, smothering the jealousy instinctive to the human heart, are there by mutual consent—their daughters they leave at home—each one ready to play his part to the finish, with no thought of future recrimination. It was a game of love-forfeits. . . . Two men, armed with wands furnished with tufts of gay feathers, pass up and down the files of men and women, waving their decorated staffs, ever and anon indicating with a touch of the wand persons of the opposite sex, who under the rules must pay the forfeit demanded of them. . . . The wand-bearers as they move along troll an amorous ditty [reproduced here with Emerson's translation]:

Pili la, a pili i ka'u manu
O pili o ka Lā hiki ola.
Hana i ka mea he ipo.

The wand touches, heart-ease!
It touches my bird—
Touch of life from the sun!
Brings health to the million
Ho! Here comes the fun.[7]

Not only was sex encouraged—"Ho! Here comes the fun."—it was also thought to "bring health to the million." As we will see, both sex and the hula are integral to certain aspects of Hawaiian shamanism. Both were participated in from one's Higher Self—the part of a person that is linked to God—rather than as simple bodily pleasure. Hula is not just a dance; it contains many elements in the hidden meanings of the words that accompany the dance, ranging from advice on making love to stories of the gods.

Alas, the missionaries missed all that. Dancing your way to God did not fit with their belief system. They saw the delights of the body as sinful, and so tried to squash this dance of beauty and wonder along with the rest of traditional Hawaiian culture and spirituality. And they came to believe that their suppression had worked. As one missionary wrote: "They exchanged the violence and degradation of excessive sensuality for the order, strictness and sobriety of their new religion . . . and in exchange accepted the Bible, meeting house, schoolroom, and prayer circle and loyally sustained their chiefs in their inquisitorial spread of new ideas."

Luckily, this viewpoint represents only a small part of the whole. For example, as one academic of the hula wrote, "[A]way from the mission stations and the pious chiefs the hula continued to be taught and practiced."[8] Several *kumu* (ones with knowledge of the root) kept the traditions going in secret. Mary Pukui, the Hawaiian matriarch who is quoted extensively in this book, said: "I used to wake up at night and hear grandmother chanting. And so I memorized the chants."[9]

Contact with the Europeans and the Americans was, in the main, very difficult for the Hawaiians. It brought disease and the loss of much of the Hawaiian population, the destruction of the temples, and the questioning of everything they had ever believed in. New races were imported in an attempt to "flood out" the Hawaiians, and new ways of doing things introduced. Everything Hawaiian was portrayed as sinful by the missionaries and everything Christian (or their particular denomination of Christianity) right.

NEW VIEWPOINTS

He ʻonohi kū i ka moana
A fragment of rainbow stands over the ocean
HAWAIIAN CHANT

Neither of the former views is particularly true, but we often get stuck in such "islands" of viewpoints, as we can see in American Bill Sherman's sad reflections on his visit to Tahiti:

> I don't really want to return to the US mainland and back . . . Still homesick and have given up hopes of meeting a woman I dig who will travel with me. But then I left my heart in French Polynesia . . .

Well, I've thought and written that kind of thing before . . .
Everywhere I go it's the same and even when I'm lucky enough to be
with someone, it never lasts, and there's always pain. Psychotherapy,
analysis, poetry, straight jobs, nothing really turns it around.[10]

The islands were not enough for Sherman to change his patterns.
How could they be? Without the application of consciousness, Polynesia
remains painted islands, powerful enough to live on in memory, but
without any lasting effect. When the islands we visit or hear about consist of what other people have told us, or transmitted to us, those viewpoints largely influence our thoughts and experiences. David Lodge put
it beautifully in his novel *Paradise News,* in a conversation that took
place as the tourists were waiting to board a plane that would take
them on their first visit to Hawai'i:

"Look at this"—he whipped out of his briefcase a holiday
brochure and held it up in front of Bernard, concealing with his
hand the printed legend on the front cover. It featured a colored
photograph of a tropical beach—brilliantly blue sea and sky,
blindingly white sand, with a couple of listless human figures in the
middle distance reclining in the shade of a green palm tree. "What
does that image say to you?"
  "Your passport to paradise," said Bernard.
  Sheldrake looked disconcerted. "You've seen it before," he
said accusingly.[11]

In a sense we've all seen that Hawai'i before, and it does influence
what we expect to find there. It's said that most Americans get their
image of Hawai'i from films and video. That's why such incomplete
views of Hawai'i can last. To us, it's all we know, so it is *all there is.*

To see a brighter Hawai'i, we need to change our world. The beauty
is that we don't actually need to visit Hawai'i to learn about this new
way of being. We just need to be open to learning from the ancient wisdom of Huna, which is capable of bringing us greater love, compassion,

and understanding. Huna is a system that will help us with every aspect of our lives: love, busyness, prosperity, meaning. Huna joins rather than separates, helping us to know that we are connected to everything and everyone. Just like the islands of Hawai'i, we are each part of a much greater world, linked by systems of ritual and belief, which can help us "find our path." Huna reminds us that we most benefit from travel not by "getting away from it all," but by making sacred journeys, where places are visited in order to gain inspiration from them.

SEARCHING FOR PARADISE

The living beauty of Hawai'i physically represents the
living beauty within us that we can all map out and get
in touch with—a beauty of spirit.

PILA

Whether the preconceived images we have of Hawai'i are of paradise or of darkness, they are likely to be discolored and incomplete. In order to see a small slice of what we are missing, let's take a look at some extraordinary features of the islands themselves, for Hawaiian culture is integrally related to the land from which it has sprung. Starting from the south, the Hawaiian Islands are known as Hawai'i, Maui, Kaho'olawe, Lāna'i, Moloka'i, O'ahu, Kaua'i, and Ni'ihau. Each of

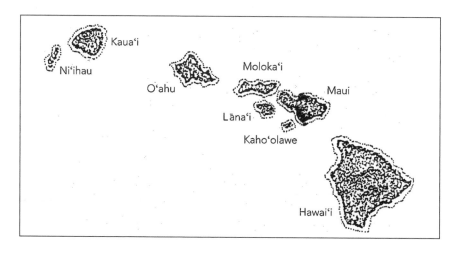

them is recognizably Hawaiian, in some indefinable bright essence, yet is also essentially itself. Everyone has his own favorite island, one he feels drawn to for some particular quality. A brief overview of some of the different qualities of the islands will enable you to see which one magnetizes you. Whether you visit it literally or metaphysically, following that call will enable the qualities of that particular island to reveal aspects of yourself to you.

The Hawaiian Islands are traditionally associated with the colors of the rainbow. Kaua'i's color is purple and its position at the northernmost end of the Hawaiian chain corresponds to the highest vibration of visible light. O'ahu's color is blue, Moloka'i's shade is green, Lāna'i's color is orange, Maui's color is pink, Kaho'olawe shines with a silvery light, and the Big Island's color is red. I am indebted to Pila for this insight.[12]

Each island is also associated with a flower that is the same color as the island. Kaua'i's flower is the fragrant *mokihana* that grows on a straggly, native citrus bush. O'ahu's flower is the *'ilima* tree. Moloka'i's flower is the *kukui* blossom, Hawai'i's official tree. Kaho'olawe's flower is the silver *hinahina,* a ground-hugging plant. Lāna'i's plant is the *kaunaoa,* a rusty orange vine. Maui's flower is the *lokelani,* "heavenly rose," one of an introduced pink species of rose. The flower of the Big Island is the crimson pompon blossoms of the *ohia lehua.*

The Big Island of Hawai'i—more than twice the size of all the other islands put together—has a spectacular, rocky beauty all its own. Surely only the moon could even come close. Not even the moon, however, has the Big Island's bubbling beaches of black, white, and green sands making love to dark blue seas, its constantly steaming rocks, its active volcano, Kīlauea, with its fountain jets of blazing lava. The weather changes every few miles along the road; indeed this particular island has twenty-two out of the twenty-three climates of the world! Two huge mountains—Mauna Loa and Mauna Kea—stand on this southernmost island of Hawai'i. Skies are bright where snows are high. The remote, snowy summit of Mauna Kea has a tremendous quality of brightness to it and is the head of the highest mountain in the world, when measured from the seabed. Not your usual sort of tourist island!

Nor is Maui, the next island to the north. Many ancient temples grace this island, dotted with rain forests and groves of wild ginger. While there are crowded condos and beaches on the west side, Maui is also home to the world's largest dormant volcano, the wild Haleakala. One meaning of *haleakala* is "house of the shadow of the sun," and on some days, those climbing the crater see their shadows projected onto the clouds *below* them. A circular rainbow, formed of glancing light droplets, shimmers around the crater like a halo. Interestingly, scientists on the Big Island study the moon, but here they study the sun, fitting with the Hawaiian meaning of Haleakala.

From Maui you can see the island of Kaho'olawe, appearing pink as the afternoon wind whirls its red dust around. This island was closed for decades because it was used as a target by the U.S. military in its bombing practice. In 1994 a very emotional ceremony to return the island to the Hawaiians was held on a Maui beach. Kaho'olawe is probably the most vivid symbol of the violated, yet surviving, sacredness of the Hawaiian Islands. It was raped and defiled (the bombs and mines are still being cleared by the Navy), but is now being lovingly restored by the Hawaiian people. Although the island is open once a month to visitors, permission first has to be obtained from the PKO, the Protect Kaho'olawe Ohana. As there is no docking space for boats, visitors must swim in, and wrap up their luggage in plastic bags to be passed, hand over hand, through the surf. Many Hawaiian ceremonies are being created and re-created on this quiet and growing island.

Neighboring Lāna'i is a flat, understated island, and its extinct crater is now covered with pineapples. It is famous for its pineapple exports, incidentally difficult to buy in the local shops. Almost all of the land is owned by the pineapple company and it has just begun to develop it by building a couple of hotels and a golf course. Lāna'i's population is only a couple of thousand and over half are Filipino in origin. On its beaches are lava shelves, swirls of lava rock cooled and caught into solid form. The strange rock shapes in the Garden of the Gods look as though they are about to move too.

The nearby island of Moloka'i is very special indeed. More than half the inhabitants of this island are Hawaiians. It was never invaded by the more physically powerful chiefs of the other islands; some people say the residents used magic to ensure it never would be. Many Hawaiians believe there is a lot of magic still being practiced there and Moloka'i's inhabitants choose not to say. The famous leper colony of Kalaupapa remains, dreaming below the highest sea cliffs in the world on the northern end of the island. Many people know Kalaupapa as the place of Father Damien, the saintly Belgian priest who cared for the sufferers for decades and then contracted the disease himself. Moloka'i still has its sacred aspect; there is no building higher than a coconut palm tree and hardly any resort life. As one Hawaiian told me, there is little to see on Moloka'i unless you see with the eyes of the spirit.

Such sacredness and saintliness is not usually associated with the next island of O'ahu, where lies Honolulu, the most fabled town in the Pacific. Hula girls are paid to dance outside the skyscraper hotels, tourists sip cocktails with names like mai tai and chi chi and traffic roars down the road behind Waikīkī Beach. The waves on the northern beaches are the biggest in the world and a popular haunt for surfers. The island's natural beauty is not obscured, however: tourists can hike to waterfalls with names like Sacred Falls; cars sometimes seem to crawl over the precipitous central hills, lit up by amber light from low, gold clouds; clouds of bright pink bougainvillea spill over walls and the air is redolent with their scent.

The next island, Kaua'i, is the oldest of the main Hawaiian Islands and the most rugged. It is an island of extremes and includes the wettest place in the world, Mt. Wai'ale'ale, whose very name sounds like rain. Heavy rains have eroded the island over eons and scored deep valleys into the rock, including the famous Nā Pali sea cliffs. Waimea canyon cuts through its middle and Kaua'i's "wild West" is a frozen rodeo of ocher rock and tawny gorges. Kaua'i is an eternally dramatic island, of constant "scenes," and it is quite fitting that it is the favorite island of visiting film stars. However, on September 11, 1992, Hurricane Iniki led to the island being declared a disaster area, and the natural beauty of Kaua'i has never quite recovered. Nor has tourism, which many people say is an advantage.

The eighth island is Ni'ihau. This forbidden isle can appear shrouded in a purple mist when viewed from the island of Kaua'i, and very few visitors to Hawai'i even realize it exists. The island was sold to a taciturn Scottish family, the Robinsons, in the middle of the nineteenth century. They still own it, and don't allow the few hundred Hawaiians who live there much contact with outsiders. Although helicopter tours to the island from Kaua'i have recently been introduced, visitors cannot go near the only village, where the islanders live. It is the only island where people grow up speaking only Hawaiian. Ancient traditions, from what can be gleaned, are still firmly in place, although we don't know much about what they are because, at the time of writing, no researchers have been allowed on Ni'ihau.

So there is a chain of islands and a chain of being, too. If we put the different "lights" of these seven islands together, we have the colors of the rainbow. If we put the strands of the different plants together, we have a skein of flowers known as a *lei*, the famous garland of Hawai'i. But there are eight main islands, and Ni'ihau, the northernmost, is white in color, its symbol a tiny white *pūpū* shell. This delicate shell produces a valuable lei and the white is a fitting container for those blossoming colors of the rainbow.

Whether we are consciously aware of it or not, we are all searching for our own personal paradise. The more I learned about Hawaiian wisdom, the more I came to realize that the island we all yearn for is the peace and harmony inside ourselves. That's the bright land of our Higher Self. But certain islands existing in "outer reality" can represent that, and I know of none better than the Hawaiian Islands. You will probably be drawn to one island more than another. Follow that call. Your magnetic connection consists of the combination of you in all your splendor and the island in all of its. Getting to know the Huna knowledge each island contains offers us invaluable guidance on our most important journey ever, the journey to our own Mind of Light.

HAWAIIAN LIGHT

The task of the anthropologist is to uncover
the hidden meanings.

VICTOR TURNER

Today, when you visit Hawai'i, it looks as though the native culture has been overtaken. As you walk along the boiling asphalt and crowded sands of Waikiki, lost in the sea of bodies, bare nipples, and minuscule swim trunks, it is easy to believe that "This is Hawai'i" and that the old Hawai'i exists only in the Polynesian Cultural Center and the museums. To visitors drifting through the streets of Honolulu—the capital of the fiftieth state of the American union—the street signs of Hawaiian chiefs pointing into the blue sky look like memories signaling into empty space. And for those looking for culture outside of the city, resort hotels seem to glow on every beach, replacing the groups of huts that used to cluster under the coconut trees. Almost every visitor I met has gone home with the impression that Hawaiian culture has been destroyed, and many islanders will say the same.

But appearances can be deceptive. Although much has been destroyed, much is left. The Hawaiians have had, and still have, good reasons for keeping their knowledge hidden, or their light invisible. The culture may be hidden, but it is nonetheless *there*. It is vibrant, living in the flower garlands bestowed on visitors at the airport, living in the names of places, living even in the bright shirts known all over the world as "Hawaiian shirts." And it is there in far more significant ways as well. More Hawaiians than ever are now fighting for the spirit of their culture. Nationalism is booming on a scale unimaginable a couple of decades ago, and is going from strength to strength. There are many different movements, which all have in common one thing: the desire to officially regain their land of Hawai'i. Native Hawaiians have arguably the strongest claim to sovereignty of any indigenous group within the United States, because Hawai'i was recognized by the world as a sovereign nation before America's takeover in 1893. Additionally—uniquely among the native peoples of the United States—there has never been a treaty giving the American government power to annex Hawaiian lands. In a recent historic statement, the government acknowledged that they were agents of an "illegal overthrow" and offered an apology to Native Hawaiians on behalf of the United States for the overthrow of the Kingdom of Hawai'i. That bill was made law in 1993. This puts the Hawaiians in a potentially very strong negotiating position.

The Hawaiian nationalists stress traditional Hawaiian values in support of their cause. Land is the mainstay of those values, and every nationalist group claims the right of the Hawaiians to fish and gather foods in the islands, since landownership was never a concept in Hawaiian thought. The land is a living and growing progenitor, and the Hawaiians have always seen themselves as intrinsically connected to it. Selling it would be as impossible as selling one's own spirit. One group claims communal possession of all the land of the archipelago, including the domains of Wākea (the heavens above), Papa (the earth below), and the seas around. This would be awkward for certain industries, but is absolutely valid in Polynesian thought.

There is a often conflict of interest between the Americans and the Hawaiians. Negotiations are hampered by each side having a different way of looking at the same issue. To the Western developer, land is a commodity like any other. If the land is in a prime position, overlooking the sea or in the rain forest near a major highway, then the developers may well want it. They don't care that the site stands on the ruins of a sacred temple. They don't want to lose their profit because "a few natives are making a fuss." There may be no acknowledgment, or even conception, of the singing sacredness of the land, a land that acts as a portal between dimensions. While this belief system prevails, Hawaiian sacred sites are being destroyed. However, common law is still valid in the islands. This leads to numerous court cases, particularly over landownership. As the court system itself is a product of the Western point of view, not the Hawaiian, it is not easy for the cases to go the Hawaiian way. To date, there has been little attempt, unlike in New Zealand–Aotearoa to try court cases according to Polynesian values.

So a situation continues in which some Hawaiians are not able to access their ancestral lands. They may be sleeping on beaches or living in their cars. They are still worshipping their gods, still praising their ancestors, but without the roots and resources they need to be truly effective. It is my humble hope that this book will help foster understanding about some aspects of Hawaiian belief and that it may inspire "landowners" in Hawai'i to consider allowing natives and ritual specialists to access their land and even to live on it. Eventually, I suspect, more and more people will choose to "give back" the land to its true keepers.

THE RAINBOW IS WITHIN

One must look with the heart.

ANTOINE DE SAINT-EXUPÉRY

In this book I will share with you some of what I have discovered about the rainbow of Hawaiian culture, including its language and myths, the shamanistic practices of hula and magic, sacred pilgrimage, and Huna's powerful teachings about brightening our consciousness for good.

Looking at Hawaiian culture through the imagery of light and the rainbow is not just a poetic viewpoint. It's clear from the vocabulary of Hawaiian words that color, light, and consciousness are considered vitally significant. In fact, one of the most important ways the culture is maintained is through the language itself, which is enjoying a renaissance. For example, *la'a kea,* the word meaning "sacred light," also means happiness and is often represented by a rainbow. That is because the sacred light brings happiness, and the rainbow is a sign of the connection to spirit that has been made.

Another example can be found in the word for consciousness, *'ike ho'omaopopo,* which contains *'ōma'o,* the word for the color green, the color of growth in nature. It also contains *'ike,* the word for "to see" or "to know," implying that we can grow *(hō)* from what we "see" or "know." But the word also contains *popo,* meaning "to decay," implying that there is always a choice involved. Do we grow or do we decay? It all depends on our 'ike, our perception. Our perception may have many different lights, but just as green is the middle color of the rainbow, so it is the medium for growth. Even one of the words for color, 'a'ai, has the light in it. 'A means "to burn," "to blaze," or "to glitter or sparkle as a gem."

In fact, every Hawaiian word holds different meanings inside it. The Hawaiian language is far more than just words; it is *a system of encoding ancient knowledge.* That is why it is so important that now, after years of suppression of the use and teaching of the Hawaiian language, both Hawaiian and English are official languages. In 1987, the State Department of Education allowed Hawaiian language experts to begin teaching two experimental Hawaiian language immersion programs. The new generation of Hawaiian children may begin their study of the Hawaiian language at Pūnana Leo, preschools where the pupils speak only Hawaiian, and they can continue it at the Kamēhamēha Schools. As we shall see, the knowledge gained from a study of the Hawaiian language provides some keys to unlocking ancient wisdom.

The words themselves hold power. For instance, places were always named and those place-names are Hawaiian. The streets around the international airport in Honolulu, for example, are named after clouds. They include *ao lewa,* "flying cloud," *ao wena,* "glowing cloud," and even *ao loko,* "inner cloud." Less romantically, Waikīkī means "spurting water" (*wai* meaning "water" and *kīkī* "to spurt"). However, *wai* also means "semen," resulting in a meaning perhaps not too inappropriate for modern Waikīkī's role in representing sexy Hawai'i! There is a beach on O'ahu called *ule hawa,* or "filthy penis." This island is not atypical; places on every island were named very carefully, for the hidden meanings of their names bring out certain qualities. Take Honolulu, for instance. Honolulu literally means "sheltered bay," but *honu* also means "bad-smelling" and *lūlū* "to scatter."

The power of these layers of meaning is also found in many unexpected aspects of Hawai'i, such as the words that accompany hula dances. The hula dance has long stood as the unofficial symbol of

Hawai'i, but less well known is its connection to ancient Hawaiian shamanism, a connection that we will explore in detail in chapter six. While it's fair—and undeniably tragic—to say that the traditional Hawaiian culture has been oppressed by Westerners since the time of first contact at the end of the eighteenth century, the good news is that the suppression did not work. As one Hawaiian put it: "The hula dance carried on, being taught in secret in the darkness of the villages." There are now hundreds of hula schools dotted throughout the islands. The hula is blossoming, just like the flowers worn in the dancers' hair, and these days many Hawaiian children learn to dance the hula.

Intimately connected to language and hula are the magical practices of Hawai'i—rainbow techniques of consciousness—and the myths and legends that link humans, animals, and gods. The magical practices have traditionally been handed down by kahuna, but anyone can practice them as long as their consciousness is sufficiently green, sufficiently grown. This is portrayed in the myth of Pele and Hi'iaka—which we shall look at in chapter nine—by the goddess Hi'iaka being accompanied on her spiritual journey by Wahine 'Ōma'o, "the lady in green." The presence of color indicates a spirit that is brightening, for ultimately, the myths are codes for ways to grow. That is why they have endured for so many millennia. And that is why it is so useful for us to understand them in all their different dimensions of light.

The most subtle sign of the Hawaiian culture or spirit is the most difficult to talk about, yet the most pervasive. It is the particular, very intense energy of Hawai'i and the meaning of places to the people who love and respect them. This is reflected by one meaning of the word Hawai'i: "agent of the spirit of life." Hawaiian energy may be particularly strong in sacred places, which often have a KAPU, or forbidden, sign outside. *Heiau,* or temples, usually consist of a certain arrangement of stones with a block of rock inside it: the ancient altar. Hawaiians must have known about the first law of thermodynamics, which states that "energy can never be created or destroyed," because they say the sacredness of a place can be defiled but never lost. On the island of Kaua'i, for example, there was one case of hotel toilets, built on a sacred spot, refusing to flush. Experts were called in, but they still would not work, and finally the pavilions had to be built elsewhere—where the same toilets worked at once!

The special energy even extends to the objects in the sacred places. Objects have power and they want to be in their proper place, something that has been experienced by many people, even those who are not expecting it. The volcano on the Big Island is considered sacred, and so are its rocks, expressed by the Hawaiian "myth" that the rocks belonging to the goddess Pele should not be removed from her home, the island of Hawai'i. In the local museum there are many letters from people stating that they are returning a volcanic rock after having experienced a catalog of disasters. These letters all ask that the rock be put back where it came from. And—echoing my own sacred experience in the mountain clearing—the director of the movie *North Shore* described a Hawaiian temple where they filmed as "an unprepossessing pile of rocks that had a deeply spiritual effect on cast and crew."[13]

Although Hawai'i is not a famous part of the planet's "sacred geography," with a reputation like that of Mecca, Benares, Lourdes, or Lhasa, the islands deserve to be, for the land is the land of the gods and goddesses, and traveling through these beautiful islands is traditionally a pilgrimage. The land is not just full of sacred paths, where every rock and every flower is significant; the land itself is sacred. The Hawaiian concept is similar to that of the Australian Aboriginal dreamtime, in which the mythic dimension of the land is brought alive each time it is activated—for example, by walking through it or chanting to it. According to Huna, when you make a journey, you chant to the place you are traveling to or, in a deep sense, creating, for no one else will ever have your experience there. Every meeting is a blend of your consciousness with the power of the particular place.

Everything is sacred and so everything needs to be acknowledged. That is why every kind of wind, every group of rocks, every clump of trees has its name in Hawai'i. The shapes of the clouds have their name; every little grove and dell is named. Each place also has its own chant, and particular associations with myths and gods. Every time a place-name is spoken, the meaning of that name is activated, revitalizing the connection between the speaker and the land itself. "These Rocks Remain," as Gavin Maxwell put it in his beautiful book about the Highlands of Scotland, and the original wisdom of the land, held in its bedrock, can never be destroyed. Meanwhile, indigenous cultures act as sacred calabashes of knowledge. It's good to know that today not only are the Polynesian traditions being revitalized, but so too are the Native American, the Inuit, the Aboriginal . . . you could say the rainbow of traditional knowledge is shining over the world again.

HAWAIIAN KNOWLEDGE

Hiolo ka pali kū, nahā ka pali pa'a.

The standing precipice falls, the solid cliff breaks.

HAWAIIAN PROVERB

The experience of the land coming alive around me in that forest temple marked a stage in my own journey toward the light. But I am no exception, and there are more and more people having similar experiences, for—as we shall see—rocks, like humans, are indeed composed of light and so can be transformed. But that can happen only if we are able to believe it's possible: nothing has validity save what we believe. That's why, in this proverb describing the gaining of knowledge, the "standing precipice" must fall, the "solid cliff" break. We must overturn our old assumptions in order to open to new ones.

But if such a wealth of Hawaiian culture remains on the islands, why don't more people know about it? Why have the Hawaiians, a people never afraid of standing up for themselves, let the false impressions remain? There are two main reasons. The first is to preserve the culture, the second is the nature of the traditional system of knowledge in Hawai'i, where someone is taught only when he or she is ready to learn.

Hawaiians will admit, when pressed, that the cultural features we have talked about are there, *but they will never be acknowledged as being there for a purpose*. Again and again inquiries will be brushed away with responses like: "People used to know about these things but they're all dead now" or "The meaning's been forgotten." For example, Hawaiian *kupuna* (one who knows how to grow) Leinani Melville learned a great deal of Huna from his grandmother, or *tutu*. But when a missionary wanted to know about the knowledge, it was different, shown by Melville's childhood memories of the missionary coming to visit:

> He was always received most amiably: Ah, but the tutus could tell him nothing. They knew absolutely nothing about the primitive concept of gods and goddesses. . . . "Our former deities departed nearly a century ago. That was before our time. We are Christians and worship the same God that you do," was more or less the stock reply. Invariably the testimonies of faith swerved the old missionary from his curiosity. He would beam at the gathering and bless them all, including me.[14]

Once the missionary made the statement that "it was impossible now to extract them from the pit of confusion." The old ladies agreed with him. Why? To preserve the culture and to preserve the missionary (he was not ready to learn). Defending themselves would not have been a loving thing to do, and they were kupuna who acted with love and strength—which never precludes humor. Melville wrote that after the missionary left, "one of the women chuckled, 'We are not confused, he is confused. We know what we are talking about, he doesn't.'" That's why the old ladies did not defend themselves.

Given the history of Hawai'i, the decision to keep the culture a secret may have helped to preserve it. There is a time for darkness as well as a time for light. The Hawaiians showed considerable common sense in downplaying the vibrancy of their culture, recognizing that *if people think there is nothing of value in a culture, then they do not try to destroy it.*

The Hawaiian system for passing knowledge on to future generations shows the same restraint. The ancient Hawaiian wisdom tradition of

Huna was passed on in a very interesting and unusual way. It was not taught according to a set program. Rather, knowledge was considered very sacred and valuable and to be shared very carefully, to the right person at the right time in his or her development. Right from the beginning, guidance was individual. Each child would train under a different kahuna, each of whom had his or her own field of expertise. The kahuna was selected according to the gifts of the child: a child good with his hands might be taught by a canoe-building kahuna; a very intuitive child might learn the art of divination with a specialist in divining. The child learned through participation. The kahunas answered only the individual questions each pupil asked. *They did not volunteer verbal knowledge.* And there was no idea at all that a child should learn as much as the kahuna knew. So not only did each child know slightly different information, the ones who knew less did not *know* that they knew less. They thought they knew as much as everyone else!

This system of passing down knowledge guards against people gaining unwelcome knowledge, recognizing that "a little knowledge is a dangerous thing." The validity of the idea that people abuse knowledge they are not ready for has been illustrated again and again on the world historical level. Albert Einstein—the greatest scientist and thinker of the twentieth century—gave the world the knowledge of the power released by atomic fission, but the world abused it by dropping bombs on Hiroshima and Nagasaki. Toward the end of his life, Einstein said: "If I had known, I would have been a shoemaker."

Knowledge, given in appropriate ways, to the appropriate people, is very, very important. Knowledge must be grown, like a much cared for plant. It must be planted in receptive soil, from which the wrong elements have been removed. The vulnerable plant must be nourished by the right amount of sun, wind, rain, and care. At the same time, the ancient Hawaiians had a safeguard against knowledge not being passed down when no one was ready to know: certain chants and other types of oral lore were always passed down. Although their interpretations would not be taught if no student was ready to receive them, the *kaona*, or hidden meanings, of the chants would remain dormant, ready to be activated when someone sufficiently aware came along, even if that was several generations later. Meanwhile, the "skeleton" of the chant was sufficient to preserve the hidden knowledge. This is why there was such an emphasis on the exact repetition of oral knowledge in Hawai'i. Genealogical chants were passed down in this way, as were myths, songs, star names, and many other types of knowledge. Encoded in these chants are messages, messages that ultimately explain the relationship among humanity, gods, and the whole cosmos. But to understand the messages one needs to be ready to hear.

When I began to study with one kahuna, it was she who gave me a valuable insight into the Hawaiian system when she said she would answer every question I asked but she would answer *only* the questions I asked. This system of passing on knowledge is still in play, impacting visitors who remain unaware of it. The word for truth in Hawaiian, *'oia 'i'o,* contains the syllable *'i'o,* which means "substance or muscle." The other letters represent the many layers that are inevitably wrapped around the truth. The whole word thus means "truth telling has many dimensions." If a person asks a question about something on the outer layer, that of appearance, and he believes the answer he is given, then that is just as "true" *for the questioner* as is something on the harder-to-reach inner layer.

Often tourists ask very few questions, and they are answered in clichés. So, "Yes, the hula dances with their gestures and undulation of the body are sexy." Their role as a system of religion, myth, and magic is not mentioned. In clichés, after all, there is a kernel of truth. And so the hula dances *become* sexy dances to attract the tourists, and in the process they are stopped from being anything else to them! The visitors do not know how little they know! That limited knowledge becomes "true" knowledge, the way a particular substance identifies itself by the absorption and reemission of one particular shade of light. The information visitors find out becomes their "shade." They radiate it and talk about their knowledge, and it becomes their "substance." That's what they believe and what they manifest.

Not knowing the questions to ask is a very real drawback. It is surprisingly difficult to let go of our own belief systems to learn about those of others. This is the case even if you are an anthropologist and supposed to do it professionally. As recently as the 1970s, an anthropologist named Valerio Valeri wrote: "Hawaiian religion is childlike and limited," an assumption that reflects his not having *asked the right questions*. Unfortunately, he then generalized his own experience to a derogatory assumption about the subject concerned, keeping the prejudice of his own "standing precipice."

It is certainly necessary to jump out of one's categories to ask questions about the Hawaiian religion—it isn't exactly obvious. For example, it took me many weeks on Kaua'i to discover that the hula was the system of ritual shamanism I had been searching for. Talk about missing what was right under my nose! And many people never discover that the hula is a very sophisticated part of the Hawaiian religion and shamanism because their belief systems have not prepared them to think of dancing as part of religion. But the deeper I have looked into Huna, the more dimensions I have seen. I'm constantly amazed and astounded by the levels of understanding I continue to discover, and those are just the ones I'm able to see!

Although this book may appear simple, it has many layers of meaning. Different readers will take it on various levels, and the same reader may take new meanings from it at different times, like a crystal that reflects the different colors of light when viewed from different angles or viewpoints. Throughout it all we must be prepared to let the solid cliffs of our received knowledge crumble. And the reader can find meaning in every color he or she sees. The next chapter will introduce the code to do so: the Hawaiian language.

2
Contrasting Lights

'A 'ohe pau ka 'ike i ka hālau ho'okāhi.

All knowledge is not taught in the same school.

HAWAIIAN PROVERB

Even though English has only one word for knowledge, our exploration of Huna will be benefited by differentiating between two kinds of knowledge: *sacred* knowledge and *cultural* knowledge. The Chatham Islanders—living at the opposite end of Polynesia from the Hawaiians— poetically expressed the difference between these two kinds of knowledge in their division of their history into two periods, known as "The Wind Clouds" and the "Hearing of the Ears." As the mythologist Katherine Luomala wrote: "The legends about the people and the events of the earlier period, The Wind Clouds, were wafted to them, the islanders say, from Hawaiki, the ancestral home. In The Hearing of the Ears period, the traditions tell of life after the settlement in the Chathams, and these legends have been heard more recently and distinctly than those borne anciently from afar, from Hawaiki, like misty wind-swept clouds."[1]

The Wind Clouds represent *sacred* knowledge, which usually originates further back in time and is based on the ancient way of growing back toward God. Sacred knowledge is found in every religious tradition and always states similar principles. Qualities such as compassion and goodwill are stressed, as is the person's being part of a greater whole. The Hearing of the Ears represents *cultural* knowledge, which is more recent and varies around the world according to the qualities each culture holds to be important.

In Hawai'i, the old and sacred knowledge is usually considered more important than cultural knowledge, although cultural knowledge can be a way to it. The key lies in differentiating between the two. In Polynesia, for example, high cultural value is placed on hospitality, and Polynesian hospitality is legendary: guests are to be taken in, fed, and offered a place to stay. This should be done with great goodwill, even if in a different form from traditional Polynesian hospitality, where mates were often provided for the night: one Tahitian thought a missionary's offended look meant that he wanted two women, rather than one!

Hospitality is also linked to the sacred taro plant from which humanity originated. According to missionary Henry Lyman, the first child of Papa, the earth goddess, was born without any arms or legs and was buried at night. The next morning the stalk and leaves of a taro plant appeared, and her mate, Wākea, the sky god, named it Hāloa. Papa's next child, a human, was named after this plant.[2] The Hawaiian race is said to have descended from the second Hāloa, while the first Hāloa, the taro plant, is still a staple food for Hawaiians, being cultivated on many *lo'i* (terraces) around the islands, and is a prime ingredient in hospitality. These days, visitors are shown their welcome by being fed, and fed as much as possible! One Hawaiian writer said: "Eating was pleasant. Man felt closer to his fellow man when his *'ōpū* [belly] was being filled."

While such cultural knowledge cannot in itself lead one to the happiness signified by *la'a kea,* which, as we have seen earlier, also means "sacred light" or "sacred knowledge," it can be an entry to it. One never turns away a friend—or even a stranger—who shows up at the door. It's important to share what you have, for how can you ever really know who anyone is? For instance, the goddess Pele is said to sometimes appear as a lady who needs help. If you do not help her, your visitor, and deny the goddess, you will fail an important spiritual test. The principle of Hawaiian hospitality thus is to treat everyone like you're acknowledging the god or goddess within. When you have passed such a spiritual test and shown that you are worthy, the quality of the knowledge you are privy to increases. It descends on you from a higher and brighter place, sometimes in such a shower of light that you don't know what to do with it all!

In contrast, Western cultural knowledge—which has become the dominant tradition in the world—does not act as a doorway to sacred knowledge. In fact, it claims that sacred knowledge is not important. For example, when I studied Pythagorean geometry in school, Pythagoras came across as a shady figure who did something strange with triangles. We did not learn of the sacred principles he lived by and taught; it was merely boring numbers. The same happened in religious education, where I learned about different beliefs, but I was never taught about the importance of having faith. The consequences of this are very serious. Because there is no idea of the necessity for us to experience the sacred for ourselves, we often don't know how. Hence we often make decisions with our heads, rather than our hearts. That's how rivers get polluted, how wars begin.

As we shall see, some of the aspects of Western cultural knowledge—such as the high value placed on judging right and wrong and on knowing "the facts"—actually *get in the way of* our sacred knowledge. In order to free ourselves from such blinders, it's important for us to understand the roots of our knowledge, so we can realize it is cultural, not natural. (When I say "us" or "our," I am referring to mainstream Western experience and cultural assumptions.) Comparing our knowledge to that of traditional Hawai'i— where there isn't the same split between cultural and sacred knowledge—provides a good way to do that. So let's see how each culture weaves its individual rainbow of light.

First let's look at the world from the point of view of a traditional Hawaiian figure still found in Hawai'i today: the kahuna, or shaman, who has consciously clung to the "old ways." The kahuna is in the center of a magical universe in which *everything is connected.* He *is* magic, connected to the force running through everything and thus capable of cracking open the cosmos with his knowledge and making it brighter. The kahuna's experience testifies to several of the many meanings of the word *ao*, which means both "world" and "light" or "enlightenment." All the manifestations of light he experiences are signs of his *mana*, or power. The kahuna is a free and flexible creature who knows he can incorporate new circumstances and ideas, so does not insist on having things his way.

To the kahuna, all of nature is her family and everything that happens in her environment is related to her. If she is thinking a certain thought and an animal crosses her path, it has a message for her. The gods come in many different forms and everything is a sign of God. She chooses which gods she manifests and when.

Everything is significant. The kahuna's own name has a message; other people's names hold a message; place-names hold a message; dreams are signs. Each type of weather provides a signal: when it rains it is a sign that the kahuna—or someone close to him—is feeling emotion; if it's a certain kind of rain—a fine, light mist—it means his prayer has been heard and answered.

By comparison, the average person from the West certainly doesn't feel at the center of the universe, which is a huge place. There are galaxies beyond galaxies, the solar system is part of one of them, the earth only one planet in it, and on this planet many countries. There he is, in one of those countries, maybe in a city, one person among many. He's living in a huge and complicated world over which he doesn't have much control.

Everything is differentiated and disconnected. That means things are separate from each other, in different categories. They hold themselves apart from him too: nature, other people, even God. Even if he does believe in God—and he sort of does—the Christian God is separate, a figure apart, sitting in another realm. When an event happens to him it doesn't usually have any deep significance. He needs to work at a job he probably does not enjoy in order to get money to pay his bills and his taxes. He could be like Joe Banks in the movie *Joe Versus the*

Volcano. Before he sets off for an unknown world (and floats around the Pacific with the woman of his dreams), he symbolically loses the sole of his shoe. He's stuck in an office, without his sole or "soul." Perhaps because of this, he needs to feel in control of his life, and isn't flexible or open to giving time to new things or new people.

The kahuna and Joe Banks represent two cultural systems that result in completely different experiences of the world. They are so different that if you've always had one kind of experience, and so has everyone you know, you could live your whole life (and many do) without ever knowing there could be another way of looking at and experiencing the universe.

To foster the expansion of our cultural vision, we can look more closely at some of the elements that combine to create cultural knowledge. These include the fundamental assumptions encoded in language and the belief systems expressed by cultural myths and creation stories. By contrasting our assumptions with those of a different culture, we will be able to see our own views much more clearly. Only then can we decide whether or not we want to keep them!

HAWAIIAN: LANGUAGE OF LIGHT

Words, they take you home.

A HAWAIIAN

We tend to take our own language for granted, since we learned its vocabulary and grammar when we learned to speak. Because our own language thus feels so "natural," most human beings are rarely aware of how deeply our language and its implied concepts color our perceptions of reality. However, a quick comparison of European languages and the Hawaiian language will show that the Western concepts are not natural, but rather just one way of apprehending the world. Indeed, Western concepts can be quite damaging, because the way words are parceled out encourages us to think of the world as something separate and apart from our consciousness.

Every European language is divided into nouns, verbs, and objects. Words like *tree* and *cat* are used to label anything we can see or touch that we believe has a separate existence from us. In the sentence "I touched the tree," *I* is the subject, *touch* the verb, and *tree* the object. European languages also have verbs that are "doing" words, like *making* a quilt. Without our being aware of it, our action words or verbs reinforce the existence of nouns, things *that are separate from us.* Words shut us off from the universe. We are not usually in contact with things, only the words which stand for them. The result is an emphasis on the material at the expense of the human spirit. "Having refers to things and things are fixed and discernible. Being refers to experience and is in principle not discernible."[3]

That perception of separation has had some quite catastrophic consequences. For instance, it led to the invention of the little word *I,* which marks us off distinct and separate. The mystic Alan Watts wrote: "Is it not obvious that what may start out as a small and unnoticed mistake may turn into a catastrophe as one rolling pebble may start an avalanche? Who could have known that the mistake of regarding men as separate egos would have had such disastrous consequences?" *I* is now the most common word in the English language.

We tend to take our own language for granted, but anyone who has tried to learn another European language will remember the need to sit down and learn grammatical complexities such as long lists of irregular verbs. Russian, for example, has a particularly complicated grammatical structure, where you really have to think before you can say a simple sentence correctly. There are twenty-eight verbs for *to go,* for instance, according to whether you're going and returning, going by foot, and so on.

In Hawaiian, the principles of language are completely different, and learning Hawaiian requires *a shift in perception,* as well as the normal requirements of language learning. Nouns and verbs as we know them do not exist in traditional Hawaiian. This does not mean that the ancient Hawaiians were undiscriminating. It means quite the opposite, as their language arose from their understanding that *nothing exists that is separate from us.* Traditionally there could be no nouns, verbs, subjects, or objects because the ancient Hawaiians had an infinite apprehension of the way creation happens, and represented that in the very form of their language.

Benjamin Wharf's analysis of the Hopi language of Arizona could be used to describe the Hawaiian language too. He notes that the distinction between nouns and verbs is irrelevant in a worldview that believes that the uttering of a word is sufficient to bring the thing it describes into being. First something exists in a thought, then the word to describe it is spoken, and in due course it exists in the visible world. The speaker, like the kahuna, is the active center of the universe. A similar idea is expressed by a popular Hawaiian proverb, *Hua ʻōlelo,* which means "words bear fruit": the world is constantly being created through words (even in English the words *word* and *world* are close).

Every traditional culture has a similar holistic view of the universe, in which seemingly disparate things and spheres have an underlying connection, and pulling on one thing will invoke another. A separating grammar would not be appropriate to describe that world; indeed, none of the languages of Polynesia has a grammar anything like that of the European languages. Unfortunately, though, the Hawaiian language is now being taught using Western grammatical structures, and many metaphorical attributes of the ancient language are being lost.

What many Hawaiians believe, put in a coconut shell, is that *everything is constantly changing.* The world *cannot* be fixed into nouns, verbs, and objects. This awareness of constant change relates to many, many aspects of the culture, including the sound of the language itself, which is very musical. Even when words are spoken, they sound like they're being sung. Hawaiian is so melodic because every word in Hawaiian, every syllable even, ends in a vowel, which has a kind of fluid, open-mouthed quality.

There is a much greater ratio of vowels to consonants in Hawaiian than in English. Hawaiʻi's Western visitors were the first to transcribe what had traditionally been a spoken language. When the early scribes wrote Hawaiian phonetically—each sound represented by a letter in the English alphabet—they could find the equivalent to our five vowels *(a, e, i, o,* and *u)* but could only find seven consonants *(h, k, l, m, n, p,* and *w)* to our twenty-one. A quick perusal of the Hawaiian dictionary shows that in Hawaiian, a vowel acts like a verb, denoting change, and each vowel represents a different kind of desired change (a topic I will explore in detail in my next book, *Star-Seeding Hawai'i).* Every word and syllable ends in a vowel because everything *has the seeds of its change within it.*

Perhaps this is why—unlike in Western languages, where every verb has a tense—the Hawaiian language does not indicate past, present, or future. In Hawaiian you cannot say the world *was created;* rather the sense is that the world is *constantly* being created. An artist carving an "object of art," for example, is re-creating the creation of the earth through his actions. So it is not just an object, "a thing in itself," but energy-made material, whose seeming solidity is actually vibrating. When the Hawaiians carve a god onto a bowl or cover a coconut with sharkskin (more likely goatskin today) for a *pūniu,* or "thigh drum," they may not be just making something, they may be *worshipping.* They are making something defined out of something amorphous, "carving the angel out of stone." The act of *creating* the object is more important than the object itself.

In Hawaiian, words create the thing they describe, and taking apart words shows us how they do that. The word *honua,* meaning "earth," provides an example. *Hō* means "to give" or "transfer" and *nū* "to make a noise," such as coughing, grunting like a pig, cooing like a dove, or pattering like rain. By giving away a little of ourselves and making a noise, we establish land, *honua.* But those noises such as cooing and grunting are inarticulate *(they are not words)* and that is why *honua* means "the land of the chiefs before it has anything growing on it." We need the focus of words to plant; they are necessary for the creation of fertile land. As we will see, this process of taking words apart also provides a clue to decoding the magic of Hawaiian words, finding their *kaona,* or "hidden meanings." One of the hidden meanings of the word *kaona* itself is "to attract." The more meanings we attract, the more we brighten the word. In doing so, we expose the Huna in the kahuna, the hidden qualities of the shaman, and discover that—however buried— they are part of each of us. That's how words take us home.

THE CREATION OF THE WORLDS

Stretch out the seven heavens
let ignorance cease
Create the heavens
let darkness cease!

POLYNESIAN CHANT

Belief systems don't just happen; they come from somewhere. And recognizing "where we come from" can aid us in deciding the relevance of our beliefs. A good place to begin is at the beginning: Let's compare the Hawaiian and Western stories of the creation of the world. (In this discussion, my references to the Western belief system are to the dominant Judeo-Christian one, as its beliefs are generally understood. My apologies to members of other traditions, including the "mystery" and "inner traditions" of the West. I do not attempt to discuss the words, concepts, and parables of the West on a deeper level, where they have more sacred meanings, closer to the Hawaiian. For those who would like to know more, that kind of comparison has been explored in depth by the scholar and teacher Max Freedom Long in his book *The Huna Code in Religions,* the best book I know of on the topic.)

The first words of the Bible are: "In the beginning was God and God created the heaven and the earth." From the very first line of Genesis ("the origin"), we are told that we are separate from God; God is apart from earth, and so is heaven. The idea of the earth as a difficult, imperfect place, where we are striving for an ideal we cannot reach, is introduced at the very beginning of the Bible—the most popular and influential book the world has ever seen. The concept of separation is strengthened a few lines later when we are told: "darkness was upon the face of the waters." Then God, in a sudden revelatory sentence, said: "Let there be light" and "there was light." Then, and here's the crux: "God saw the light, that it was good; and God divided the light from the darkness."

Here we have the first reference to *judgment* and the seed of the concept of good and evil: the light is good and the darkness is different, so it must be bad. On this divided planet two conflicting forces are believed to exist: light represents the good and darkness the evil. This idea of good and evil has a huge effect on us. We tend to think in terms of black and white, not the shades in between. Concepts are separated out, and so are people: some things—and people—are judged to be good and others evil. Some countries are good and others are evil, as seen in the reference made by an American president to the "Axis of Evil," inscribing countries not his own—a definition that may have been one of the factors that led to war against one of those countries. The idea that some others are evil is the basis for retribution, such as in state-ordered executions; it is responsible for a lot of our fears of the "bad" people who wish to harm us. The separation of good and evil is responsible for a lot of our guilt, too, because we cannot be only "good" or have only good impulses—we merely think we should.

A closer look at this line—"God saw the light, that it was good; and God divided the light from the darkness"—also reveals the roots of the concept that evil is *unchangeable*. God's division of the darkness from the light is a pretty final act. The idea that something evil is *irredeemably* evil has an absolutely huge effect on our society and thought. We think things are "meant" to be a certain way and from that we get the concept of "right or wrong." If things are the way we think they're meant to be, then they are right; if not, they are wrong. Moving from "wrong" to "right" is considered to be a very difficult thing to do. We question whether it is *really* possible for a person to change and our lack of faith makes the struggle much harder. This lack of faith can be seen in many aspects of society: from the debate regarding the correction or execution of criminals, to our doubts as to whether our diet will *really* work, to a thriving industry for mental health professionals.

Therapy often continues for many years, as in endless Woody Allen movies, with few discernible results in the end!

The traditional Hawaiian approach was very different, starting with the creation chants passed down in Hawai'i from time immemorial. My reading of the *Kumulipo*, the best-known Hawaiian creation chant, confirms this viewpoint. *Kumulipo* is usually translated as "out of the source," but it also means "the pattern of the unseen" (*kumu*, "the pattern," and *lipo*, "a deep blue-black color, as of a sea-cave or a thick forest"). The first line of the *Kumulipo*—'Ō *ke au i kāhuli wela ka honua*—can be translated as: "The thrust of the flow of the foundation transformed to a heat that burns." No one being necessarily created the world. The earth began moving *of its own volition*.

A few lines later "intense darkness, deep darkness" is described and soon afterward: "the night gave birth." The *pō*, the night, gave birth to life in various wild and wonderful forms such as the coral, the starfish, and the conch shell. The various forms are listed, then suddenly the line *He pō uhe'e i ka wawa*, or "Darkness slips into light," appears. The ease of darkness "slipping" into light implies that the veil between light and darkness is thin and misty. Instead of God making the world and delineating the darkness and the light, there is a gradual and inevitable progress toward light.

The existence of many different creatures in the seemingly irrelevant long list that precedes the statement that "darkness slips into light" tells us that *the variety of life brings light*. Things may be one particular way, but there are many alternative ways and no single way that is "right" or "wrong." This insight can also be seen at the fundamental level of the formation of words. *Hala* is usually translated as "sin," but that concept didn't exist in old Hawai'i, and *hala* really means "to pass by." Interestingly, this is similar to the original Greek meaning of *sin*, which meant "to miss the mark." *'Ino* is the closest word to "evil" in Hawaiian and it means to "injure," "hurt," or "harm." *Maika'i*, the word usually translated as "good," has connotations of going in a certain direction. *Mai* is a directional prefix and *ka'i* has different meanings including "lead," "direct," and "to come dancing out before an audience"! The notion of movement implied in every meaning emphasizes the idea that in Hawai'i good and evil are not poised at opposite sides of a gulf, but are part of a spectrum of possibilities.

As in every belief system, ideas about the cosmos are re-created at the individual level. The sense of there being only a thin veil between light and dark has important implications in Hawaiian belief and its relevance to us today. It implies that the movement of a person from darkness to light is a journey that is always possible; the only question is how easy or difficult a person makes it.

The line "Darkness slips into light" is very different from the Bible's "And God saw the light, that it was good; and God divided the light from the darkness." Perhaps it explains why, unlike Christians, Hawaiians do not judge *their* belief system to be intrinsically better than any other belief system; they recognize that all things are relative, *including* what they believe! Hawaiian belief is the only religion I have ever found that says that its own belief is not necessarily the only true one.

THE IS.LAND

Hanging Clowds and a thick horizon are certainly no
known Signs of a Continent . . .

CAPTAIN JAMES COOK

Certain beliefs have created for Westerners a separated reality where there are great gulfs between Creator and created, between right and wrong, between countries and people, and even between aspects of one's own self. I call this fragmented reality our "is.land" because it eventually becomes land, the foundation of life in the West, our sense of *how things really are*. It is built on certain concepts such as "facts" and "scientific laws." In contrast, Hawaiian cultural knowledge is like land without the "is": land that initially is so unfamiliar that it conforms to "no known Signs," and yet offers us a gateway into sacred knowledge, the key to growing back to God. As we compare the two, the very ground on which we are standing may shift.

Facts are the bedrock of the Western systems of science, justice, and morality. We learn long lists of facts in school and hear about facts every day on television, in the newspapers, in the books we read. We believe that facts show "what actually happened" and are *outside* our systems of belief. They are the "facts," after all, and facts are "the truth."

But "in fact" (see how pernicious it is), facts are very much *inside* our belief systems, in terms of both the facts we select and the way we use them. History professor E. H. Carr wrote in his famous little book, *What Is History?* that there is no such thing as a "fact," and many scientists now agree with him. What did he mean? *Only certain facts are selected for us to learn,* not because they are "true," but because they suit the mood of an era.

In the university course I taught, part of the curriculum was teaching students to be wary of believing something is valid just because it is a "fact," for a fact is only a fact to someone who believes it is. Certain items out of many possible pieces of information have been chosen to illustrate a particular point the speaker or writer wants you to agree with. We can see this for ourselves by questioning the "facts" in the media and gathering the evidence to argue for a different point of view. And we need to remember that the particular paradigm it supports will certainly be overturned—like all the others.

Modern science, for example, is presented as being a system of knowledge about "natural laws," such as those of Newtonian physics. This is the physics we all learned in school, and it taught us to think of matter as solid, worked on by cause and effect: drop a brick and it falls. One thing inextricably leads to another, and you have no control once you have set the forces in motion. That's the way it is, and it is unchangeable.

Now, however, scientists have discovered something beyond those laws. The new science is known as quantum mechanics, or the new physics. Quantum physicists disproved what had been thought of as "laws" of nature. Heisenberg's Principle of Uncertainty showed that scientists cannot predict where a particle will move next. They can only predict where it is *likely* to move, based on past experience, not where it *will* move. The average person, however, does not know about the new physics and its implications. Schoolchildren aren't taught these principles. They are still taught the old Newtonian science, more than half a century out of date.

Only people who decide to specialize in science discover that what they have learned *works only on a very limited level*. When I studied at Cambridge University in England, I went out with a scientist who said that in their very first university lecture, hard scientists are told that what they have learned *is not true in the higher dimensions they will now be studying*. Imagine being told that what you have learned no longer works on certain levels, in the most famous scientific university in the world!

This overturning of Newtonian science by quantum physics is not just an isolated example. Scientific knowledge has always progressed this way, one "closed system" being followed by another "closed system," each one represented as the ultimate system, complete and sufficient unto itself. In his book *Scientific Revolutions,* Thomas Kuhn notes that scientific progress happens as a series of revolutions, "paradigm shifts" whereby old theories give way to new ones. Then the old theories are seen in a particular sociohistorical or even technological context. The advent of the telescope, for instance, meant that new planets were discovered and our solar system "changed shape." But it had not changed; only our perception of it changed. "Scientific research" is less valid than we might think, for research works only if a certain paradigm or belief is in place.

Until our perception changes, we continue to think that the current paradigm of scientific knowledge is "the one and only truth." In medicine, for example, theories from contexts other than the last few hundred years in the West are discredited. This blanket denial extends from the Chinese tradition of acupuncture to the "granny remedies" of herbal medicine. The people who miss out are the patients who do not have access to the knowledge that has been gained across the world, as well as the physicians, who may not have their belief systems stretched.

Hawai'i provides a contrasting example. Knowledge opens like a flower, *pohala,* one layer gently unfolding onto the one that goes before. When the dancers learn a hula chant, for example, each one understands it on a slightly different level. The teacher does not teach a generalized interpretation that is "one size fits all." This is possible only because of the many meanings within the Hawaiian language.

What are considered to be facts in the West can be manipulated in many different ways. Some "facts" may be *culturally induced,* such as men being better at science than women in the West, because men are *expected* to be: "Men are better at science than women, so it is not surprising that you find science harder than your brother does."

Other "facts" are *culturally emphasized.* Historical events and perspectives are passed down, not according to what actually happened, but *according to the morals of the society that is remembering them.* When Stalin was in power in the Soviet Union, Stalinists rewrote the Russian revolution to ignore the hated Trotsky. They even blacked him out of photos, and Stalin's role was always emphasized. This is not surprising from a society everyone knows did not live up to its ideals, but *every society does the same.* Harvard, one of the most famous universities in the United States, is a case in point. Harvard's Great Hall is dedicated to the veterans lost in the American Civil War. Carved into its venerable stones are the names of those who fought for the North and died. The people who fought for the South—"the other side"—have been left out, as if they never existed.

Every society reinterprets or ignores facts according to its beliefs, and as individuals, we do the same. We "lose" people in our personal history, for instance. A mother might tell her young daughter that she should not see her father. When the child gets older and asks "Why not?" she will be told "Because of such and such a reason . . ." The bad things about her father will be emphasized and the good things, or the "fact" that he may really want to see her, are left out. Our histories are also not solid; they change as we do. If we go out with a lovely guy for a couple of years, and then he goes off with our best friend and doesn't want to be our friend anymore, we are likely to remember those years as less happy than if the relationship had ended a nicer way.

One of the main differences between Western and Hawaiian societies is that the Hawaiians *know* they're seeing things only from their own perspective. Pali Lee and Koko Willis explain it beautifully in their book *Tales from the Night Rainbow*:

> History, as anything else, is seen and understood by where a person stands on the mountain. All people climb the same mountain. The mountain, however, has many pathways and every pathway has a different view. A person knows and understands only what he sees from his own pathway. And as he moves his view will change. Only when he reaches the top of the mountain will he see and understand all the views of mankind, but who among us has reached the top of the mountain? Tomorrow we too shall see a different view. We have not finished growing.[4]

These Hawaiians believe we see from "where we stand on the mountain," but many Westerners believe we only see "what is actually there" and forget that what we see depends on our cultural reference grid. As we explore Hawaiian wisdom, we need to be aware of the concepts, lodged deep in our subconscious, that constitute the Western view of reality as something separate from us and truth as something immovable and eternal, as Parmenides defined it in the fifth century B.C. These are tough concepts to let go of, because they provide our terms of reference. Even if we don't consciously believe them, they are still our foundation, our land, our cultural system.

Changing our belief system means we change our world. When I learned in Hawai'i that magic actually works, I was devastated. My first encounters with it undermined my existing belief system, and I didn't have another to replace it with. However, I gradually learned that when we let go of our "is.lands" of facts and isolation, we are able to see that we are all part of a glittering continent underneath the ocean, surrounded by the sea of universal connection. That sea contains different dimensions of experience, from the *koholā*, whales of the deep, to the *'anae*, mullet of the surface. Yet those different dimensions can all happily coexist, and we can all move among them.

DIMENSIONAL THOUGHTS

I almost wish I hadn't gone down that rabbit-hole—and yet—and yet—it's rather curious, you know, this sort of life! I do wonder what can have happened to me!

FROM *ALICE IN WONDERLAND*, BY LEWIS CARROLL

One of the first cultural differences I became aware of in Hawai'i was a different way of looking at the body. There the body is seen as an extension of the soul, without the great divide between the mind and the body the way there is in the West. There is more of the body on show in Hawai'i, and shorts and T-shirts are considered appropriate attire in most places—including the university conferences I gave papers in, for example. Somehow sex and sex play seem like a more natural part of life, rather than a big deal and a "should I, shouldn't I?" question. There is no conflict at all between religion and sex; indeed sex, infused with love, is seen as a wonderful way to sacredness, as we will explore in chapter seven.

In the West, we believe we need our body to live, yet there is inherent conflict within our belief system, which was expressed by Plato when he wrote that truth is the product of the mind alone and the needs and desires of the body and senses "lead men astray":

The body is a source of endless trouble to us by reason of the requirement of food, and is liable also to diseases which overtake and impede us in the search after true being: it fills us full of loves, and lusts and fears of all kinds, and endless foolery, and in fact, as men say, takes away from us all power of thinking at all.[5]

As a result of this kind of cultural foundation, we deny our own senses and physical being and try to suppress them. The mind/body split that the French philosopher Réné Descartes represents with his statement "I think therefore I am" encapsulates this conflict. Many people do believe that their own body is indeed a "source of endless trouble" and that it has nothing to do with their own consciousness. Separating our body from the rest of our being contributes to our sense of ourselves as victims of forces we can do nothing about.

This can be seen very clearly in our beliefs about illness. Generally we grow up with the idea that illness is "bad luck." If a child goes to the school swimming pool and catches a cold, a mother will say it's because he's been exposed to "all those germs." And when we get a disease, as Larry Dossey, M.D., wrote, then we *have* the disease. We *have* chicken pox, we are not *chickenpoxing*. The verb has become a noun: the disease is not seen as a collection of particles interacting with our atoms, but is instead regarded as existing separately on its own. Its semantic existence as something separate from us translates into the physical realm, leading to our thinking that we have no influence over it. As we are helpless to do anything about it, we must rely on external factors—such as doctors, specialists, medicine, diet—all of which aim to restore the body from outside.

This is the case even though the idea that the body is a separate entity at the mercy of random forces is *scientifically out of date.* In the nineteenth century, many people believed in the "atomistic" model of the universe. In that model, all matter is made up of tiny discrete entities, moving around at random, at the mercy of hostile forces. According to that view, we "catch" a disease "by accident": a germ invades us and takes over our system. So we need to expel it by attacking it with drugs or "zapping" it with X-rays. Western medicine, for some reason, is still based on this model.

In Hawai'i, it is very different. One Hawaiian proverb goes:

He hale ke kino no ka mana'o.

The body is a house for the thoughts.

In other words, our unmanifest thoughts become our manifest body. As a result of the Hawaiian understanding of the interrelationship between mind and body, illnesses are often regarded not as simply "happening," but as products of our thoughts. Changing our thoughts means we can change our illness. Since our deepest, and often most destructive, thoughts have to do with family relationships, these are especially looked at, often in the form of *hoʻoponopono,* family conferences, where relationships are set to rights through prayer, discussion, confession, repentance, and mutual forgiveness. The traditional practice of *hoʻoponopono,* which means to "align" or "balance," is used by Hawaiians in a variety of ways. One master told me this practice involves "clearing" to find our way to the original light, or as he simply put it, "home." He does *hoʻoponopono* a couple of times a day and says the ability to forgive helps him to get rid of his ego and realign and rebalance with the higher source.

This point of view is based on the premise that the body is constantly changing and *we create it.* "Scientific research" confirms that the body is changing: our hair is growing, our cells multiplying, our skin renewing itself, and in seven years' time, no cell in our bodies will be the same. Our ability to flourish, even our ability to survive, depends on our ability to incorporate change into our belief system, for change is part of the human condition. As the song *Puff the Magic Dragon* says: "a dragon lives forever, but not so little boys." All little boys grow into the pictures they project. Change sings and rings and we ring in the changes. We must then adjust the rest of our consciousness to the image we have created with only part of our minds.

The famous "stress doctor" Hans Selye defined stress as "the nonspecific response of the body to any demand made upon it." He went on to say: "*It is immaterial* [my italics] whether the intensity of the situation we face is pleasant or unpleasant, all that counts is the intensity of the demand for readjustment or readaptation."[6] If the intensity of the demand is too hard for us to adapt to, then we have what is known as a *crisis.* A crisis forces us to take action, and we make things easier for ourselves if we follow a path of change. Do we see crises as problems or as opportunities? When they're over, do we blame ourselves for the time we've wasted or do we look at what we *have* learned, and *can* learn, from them? Some of it may depend on our attitude to time, and our consciousness.

One of the crises most of us face is illness. The determining factor in whether we recover from a serious illness at all seems to be the will to live. Dr. Hütschnecker, the author of an excellent book of that title, described many instances of patients expected to die, living; and patients expected to live, dying. The "will to live" is an intangible quality, but perhaps one of the ways it can be expressed is a "knowing," a knowing that you have a purpose to complete on this earth. A crisis brings out your will. The doctor said that in his experience, people who were seriously ill when they were young ended up living longer. He speculated that this was because the prospect of infirmity galvanized their will to live and led to their taking better care of themselves and conserving their energy for things they really wanted to accomplish. We can all learn from that. Virginia Woolf described her illness this way:

> How tremendous the spiritual change that it brings, how astonishing when the lights of health go down, the undiscovered countries that are then disclosed.[7]

A person who has the ability to learn from crises, to learn the "undiscovered countries" of the inner self, is an enormously creative person. Her vibration has increased and she never will be—never *can* be—as she was before her discoveries. That brings us back to "the last great unexplored continent," the mind. When our perception lengthens and broadens, the moment seems to expand, yet at the same time we are aware of just how quickly the world is vibrating. This is because we are living on a much faster wavelength of light than normally found on earth. What we think of as "space" contains this much-faster vibration. Many of us will never be able to physically get out there and check it out, but an astronaut who could had this to say about the view of the earth from that far point:

The clouds were always different, the light was different. Snow would fall, rain would fall—you could never depend on freezing any image in your mind.[8]

We need to accept that the world is in flux. When we stand back from our life, we gain perspective. With more distance, we see that all of the things we thought of as solid, permanent, and unchanging—our family, the table in front of us, the town where we grew up—are really changing all the time. They may be changing so slowly that we are normally unaware of it, but they are changing nonetheless. This continual change has huge implications. Just because something used to be a certain way doesn't mean that it still is—unless we think it is. Our expectations are self-fulfilling. Dr. Irving Oyle wrote:

> As humans we create our reality from second to second. Just because you were ill a month or a year ago doesn't mean you're ill right now. You need to free yourself from a belief in present reality so firmly connected to past reality. Only then can you create a future in the shape you desire.[9]

We need to change our expectations, and look beyond them. Huna understands that change follows our thoughts. In fact, the Hawaiian word for body, *kino,* is defined by Serge King as "a sacred plant consisting of aimed thought."[10] Perhaps the so-called miraculous stories of healing aren't so miraculous after all, but rather a product of a change in our thoughts and thus a change in our "house."

Interestingly, modern science has "discovered" the validity of the transformative way of looking at the world. Now any scientist will tell you particles are constantly vibrating, even in so-called solid objects. To see it, *all we need is a change of perspective.* I remember when I first realized this, traveling in Greece when I had just started university. I was reading *The Tao of Physics,* by Fritjof Capra, late one afternoon on a remote part of Crete, perching on a rock by Homer's "wine-dark sea." Suddenly the rocks seemed to buzz with life, interacting with the essence of the tides, and the whole glittering world began to dance. It was the first time I had any conscious idea that I could "meet and merge" with the world around me. I discovered that the world is full of far more potential and far fewer certainties than I had ever thought. This was my first experience of my own reality as part of a world of wonder, accessed by seeing differently. That is the world I rediscovered in Hawai'i, a world well worth the disorientation of falling down a rabbit hole.

My studies of Hawaiian cultural knowledge, its language, and its myths ushered me into the world of Hawaiian sacred knowledge. That is a world where anything can happen—and frequently does—where concepts of "logic" hold little force. It is a world where the learning is furious and intense and the rewards are unimaginable. It is a faster, lighter dimension. In the next chapter, we explore the wonderland of Hawaiian magic.

3
The Power of Mana

*There is one set of natural laws for the physical world
and another for the other world. And—try to believe this
if you can: the laws of the other side are so much the
stronger they can be used to neutralize and reverse
the laws of the physical.*

DR. WILLIAM TUFTS BRIGHAM,
FORMER CURATOR OF THE BISHOP MUSEUM, HONOLULU

Although Dr. Brigham was inspired to make these comments by his
study of Hawaiian magic, you can tell this description was not spoken
by a Hawaiian, for the notion of another world, "the other side," was
inconceivable to traditional Hawaiians. For them, everything was
linked together in one resounding universe, full of connections. The
connections were activated by a force that they took for granted but
which we call "magic," for we do not normally know how to use it.
Magic is an active example of the power the Hawaiians call *mana*, the
force running through and moving everything in the universe, from
flowers, cats, and starfish, to plants and planets.

Mana, like *taboo* and *tattoo*, is one of the few Polynesian words to
have found a home in English. But there is no exact translation, partly
because English is so imprecise in this subject area: the concepts behind

mana, as we shall see in the next chapter, are simply not acknowledged in the West. Mana is usually translated as "power" or "divine power." *Power,* according to the Oxford English Dictionary, has several meanings: "control," "strength," "the capability of doing something," and "energy." The OED also defines power as "deity." All of these definitions are relevant for understanding the common view of mana, but one that is simply not true in the Hawaiian context.

Pukui and Elbert's Hawaiian dictionary translates mana as "divine or supernatural power, miraculous power," a definition that is commonly used by many texts on Hawai'i, and by many Hawaiians. This viewpoint fits in with Western—particularly Christian—concepts, which place power outside of us, in God, the deity, which is perhaps why it is so popular. However, when I first visited Hawai'i, I asked the kahuna I studied with if mana really meant "divine power." We were on the island of Kaua'i, driving past some rather unromantic supermarkets, if I remember rightly, when she looked at me and smiled, her face glowing as she said, "No, that's what people think it means. It means creative power."

That immediately clicked with me: While "divine power" implies that the source of power is *somewhere else,* "creative power" means a force going out into the world from *within you.* It means that we are each responsible for our own power. We each create our own reality, *whether we believe it or not.* The force itself is neither good nor evil: it just *is.* As we have seen, good and evil are culturally specific concepts. How we feel about mana depends on what we do about it. That is entirely our decision: we can consciously incorporate it into our lives, for the greater benefit of all, or we can resist and re-cyst. How we translate the word makes a huge difference in what we feel we are able to do with it. We all eventually need to take on the definition of mana as meaning creative power. That will prepare us for learning how to apply it and make magic. Then we will be skilled and knowledgeable, just like the kahuna of ancient Hawai'i.

MAGIC IN ANCIENT HAWAI'I

An island is linked only to the harmony that predates it.

MICHEL TOURNIER

According to my sources, ancient Hawaiians believed that magic was the very stuff of life: every action was magic and so every action had its appropriate ritual to be followed. There was a constant awareness of mana: every thought and action was taken with awareness, as it could either increase or decrease one's personal mana. That is why ancient Hawaiians would not pluck a blossom or enter a valley without the appropriate chant or sit down to eat without a blessing.

There were many taboos related to the preservation of mana in what is usually understood as ancient Hawai'i. A person's mana was so sacred that mouth-to-mouth kissing traditionally was not permitted. Kissing was done nose to nose instead. The breath of one's mouth, one's *hā,* was so sacred and powerful that it was shared only when a person was dying. Then, with one's last breath, one's mana was passed directly to one's successor. Men and women could not eat together; commoners could not get too close to a chief. A chief's mana was so great that he was said to shine like the midday sun, and even the stars in the sky were named after him. Commoners were forbidden to walk in a chief's shadow or laugh in his presence, because that could take away his mana. Sometimes a chief was so sacred that the only person permitted to mate with him was his own sister. Hawaiians and Egyptians had the only royal families we know of practice brother-sister mating for the purposes of procreation, to ensure the mana of the blood was not diluted.

Ancient Hawai'i has been heavily criticized by anthropologists, missionaries, and others because of the famous excesses that grew out of the system of "divine kingship." There were constant wars, as they were needed by the kings to increase their mana. The wars also required at the temples ritual sacrifices, which were often human, what the Tahitians called "long bananas." The chiefs had such power that a transgression of their rules could bring instant death, no questions asked:

I ka 'ōlelo no ke ola, I ka 'ōlelo no ka make.

Life is in speech, death is in speech.

I was puzzled: such a rigid system of taboos seemed to support the definition of mana as divine power, power outside of a person. It didn't fit in with the understanding of mana as creative power. But further research revealed that the system of divine kingship and related taboos was not the indigenous Hawaiian system. It was an *imposed* system, brought over by Samoan invaders, led by Pā'ao, around the fourteenth century. As Hawaiian writer Moke Kupihea described it, the system of kings and taboos was a corrupt form of a more true and ancient system of power:

> The ancient kahuna, in the light of the procreators of their race, were taught from birth that their connection to spirit lay in their ancestral links to it. Thus, as the light of the procreators began to distance itself, the three priestly lines—Kāne, Kū, and Lono— developed to preserve the origins of the *akua 'aumākua*. In time these priesthoods became corrupt and secretive, and during the period we call the *na 'aumākua o ke ao* (within the time of our ancestors of the recent past), they replaced the eternal and immortal spirits of our people with the living spirit of man. When the priests elevated the *ali'i,* "ruling class," to the status of living gods, our true origin became dormant, and misdirected *'uhane* [conscious mind] and *'unihipili* [subconscious mind] replaced our original *'aumākua* chain.[1]

It's important to bear in mind Kupihea's point if driven to compare "the West" and "Hawai'i" as unitary systems, as many academics and others do. The Hawai'i most people see as being Hawaiian was not the true and ancient Hawai'i. This begs a question about some of the foundations on which racism rests.

Although King Kamēhamēha, of the Big Island, following on from Pā'ao of Samoa, used war and sacrifice to conquer the other islands of Hawai'i in the eighteenth century, the system of sacrifice does not, and cannot, fit in with the understanding of mana as creative power. In "truth" there was more than one system of power coexisting in Hawai'i, but that usually isn't realized; the system of taboo and "divine kingship" is often thought to be the *only* system of power. For example, there are few representations of a more ancient culture in the Bishop Museum, so many tourists think that what they see is "all there is." Yet this would be misguided, for there were several islands this system of force could not conquer, such as Kaua'i and Moloka'i, several parts of the mind it could not influence. Even on the islands where this system was strong, the *kahuna nui,* the main kahuna, was often considered to be more powerful than the king.

In modern Hawai'i, the old kingly orders have disappeared, and the ideas contained in the alternative system of the kahuna are taught as the way to gain power. Many kahuna believe in the definition of mana as creative power, and believe the answer to problems is not to fight them, but to *increase* your own internal power. Central to that teaching are the concepts that one must not conquer by force but integrate through love and that true power is found only in internal sovereignty. In a sense we are all islands, growing our own power from the buried continent of mind. Eventually we will link up to the continent of love and light above, the continent that, some say, once existed on earth. There are remnants of magic in Polynesia today, which just have to be looked for.

THE LONG SEARCH FOR MAGIC

They (the kahuna) use something that we have still to discover, this is something inestimably important. We simply must find it. It will revolutionize the world if we can find it. It will change the entire concept of science. It would bring order into conflicting religious beliefs.

DR. WILLIAM TUFTS BRIGHAM,
FORMER CURATOR OF THE BISHOP MUSEUM, HONOLULU

The Bishop Museum is one of the most popular tourist attractions in Honolulu, and the most highly respected museum for Polynesian culture in the world. William Tufts Brigham was its curator at the beginning of the twentieth century. Brigham was a highly respected scientist who spent many years in Hawai'i. During this time he saw many examples of magic, all of which flabbergasted him. He saw kahuna who were capable of using magic to heal, to walk across fiery lava overflows barely cooled enough to carry the weight of a man, to look into the future and change it for their clients, and even to kill. They caused him to search extensively for an explanation that fit his understanding of reality. However, he came reluctantly to the conclusion that the *only* explanation for those phenomena was magic.

For the rest of his life, Dr. Brigham's burning desire was to find out how magic worked. However, he realized his time was running out and he almost certainly wouldn't succeed. Then, one day, when he was in his early eighties, a special visitor arrived at his office in the Bishop Museum. Max Freedom Long, a young teacher in the Hawaiian Islands, started to ask him questions about kahuna and their magic, questions Brigham had been waiting for someone to ask. Long became the disciple of the doctor, and until his death, four years later, Dr. Brigham shared his accumulated years of research into the kahuna with him. He told Long humbly: "I've hardly made a beginning. Just because I'll never know the answer is no reason why you will not."[2]

Long *did* succeed in discovering some secrets behind magic and went on to write many books about Hawaiian magic, until his death in California in the 1970s. Long's most popular book, *The Secret Science Behind Miracles,* documents his search and offers a variety of different examples of magic, a few of which we will explore: fire walking, praying someone to death, the magic of rocks, and stories of "the little people."

THE POWER OF WALKING ON FIRE

Hoā ke ahi, kō ʻala ke ola.

Light the fire, for there is life-giving substance.

HAWAIIAN PROVERB

The first example we'll look at is Dr. Brigham's report of his own experience of fire walking. It occurred because the good doctor found it difficult to believe that the kahunā he had watched "walk on fire" with his own eyes had really done so. In true scientific tradition he wanted to test the theory for himself.

There were several stages to his experiment. First the doctor had to wait for a lava flow from a volcano on the Big Island that promised to be a long one. The next step was to call the three kahunā he had already seen run barefoot over burning coals. After waiting a week for them to arrive round the coast by canoe, and then waiting for a celebratory lū'au, or feast, in their honor to be finished, Dr. Brigham and the kahunā set off across the lava to the flow of fire.

Many hours of walking across a strange land of cinders and ashes brought the small party to the source of the flow. In Dr. Brigham's own words:

> It was a grand sight. The side of the mountain had broken open just above the timber line and the lava was spouting out of several vents—shooting with a roar as high as two hundred feet, and falling to make a great bubbling pool. The pool drained off at the lower end into the flow . . .[3]

Through the red light filtering through the smoke, Brigham could see the flow "had built itself up enclosing walls of clinker. These walls were up to a thousand yards in width and the hot lava ran between them." The small party bedded down on the rocks and the next day found what they were looking for—a suitable place to walk on fire.

> The flow crossed a more level strip perhaps a half-mile wide. Here the enclosing walls ran in flat terraces with sharp drops from one level to the next. Now and again a floating boulder or mass of clinker would plug the flow just where a drop commenced, and then the lava would back up and spread into a large pool. Soon the plug would be forced out and the lava would

drain away, leaving behind a fine, flat surface to walk on when sufficiently hardened.[4]

The kahuna were ready for action as soon as the lava would bear their weight. The scene inspired awe and terror from the doctor:

> When the rocks we threw on the lava surface showed that it had hardened enough to bear our weight, the kahuna arose and clambered down the side of the wall. It was far worse than a bake oven when we got to the bottom. The lava was blackening on the surface, but all across it ran heat discolorations that came and went as they do on cooling iron before a blacksmith plunges it into his tub for tempering. I heartily wished that I had not been so curious. The very thought of running over that flat inferno to the other side made me tremble—and remember that I had seen all three of the kahuna scamper over hot lava at Kīlauea.[5]

First the kahuna wrapped their feet with tī leaves—probably the most sacred leaves in Hawai'i—which are universally used for fire walking in Polynesia. As he watched the kahuna tie three tī leaves over each bare foot, the doctor decided to keep his strong, leather, hobnailed boots on. At this time he still believed that there was a physical explanation for the magic and thought he'd be safer that way. The kahuna merely grinned at him and told him the boots would be a sacrifice to the gods. Then they left him to tie the tī leaves over his boots while they began their chants:

> The chants were in archaic Hawaiian which I could not follow. It was the usual "God-talk" handed down word for word for countless generations. All I could make of it was that it consisted of simple little mentions of legendary history and was peppered with praise of some God or gods.
>
> I almost roasted alive before the kahuna had finished their chanting, although it could not have taken more than a few min-

utes. Suddenly the time was at hand. One of the kahuna beat at the shimmering surface of the lava with a bunch of tī leaves and then offered me the honor of crossing first. Instantly I remembered my manners; I was all for age before beauty.

The matter was settled at once by deciding that the oldest kahuna should go first, I second and the others side by side. Without a moment of hesitation the oldest man trotted out on that terrifically hot surface. I was watching him with my mouth open and he was nearly across—a distance of about a hundred and fifty yards—when someone gave me a shove that resulted in my having a choice of falling on my face on the lava or catching a running stride.

I still do not know what madness seized me, but I ran. The heat was unbelievable. I held my breath and my mind seemed to stop functioning. I was young then and could do my hundred-yard dash with the best. Did I run! I flew![6]

As he ran, the doctor's boots started to curl, almost tripping him up, until finally the seams went and his socks caught fire. Finally he was able to leap off to safety:

I looked down at my feet and found my socks burning at the edges of the curled leather uppers of my boots. I beat out the smoldering fire in the cotton fabric and looked up to find my three kahuna rocking with laughter as they pointed to the heel and sole of my left boot which lay smoking and burned to a crisp on the lava. I laughed too. I was never so relieved in my life as I was to find that I was safe and that there was not a blister on my feet—not even where I had beaten out the fire in the socks.

There is little more that I can tell of this experience. I had a sensation of intense heat on my face and body, but almost no sensation in my feet. When I touched them with my hands they were hot on the bottoms, but they did not feel so except to my hands. None of the kahuna had a blister, although the tī leaves which they had tied on their feet had burned away long since.[7]

The doctor tried to figure out reasons for his ability to "walk on fire" without burning. One theory he tested was that lava forms an insulating surface when it cools—it doesn't. Finally, his various experiences and investigations led him to tell Long: "It's magic . . . part of the bulk of magic done by the kahuna and by other primitive peoples. It took me years to come to that understanding, but it is my final decision after long study and observation."[8]

It's funny, but magic has never seemed particularly strange to me. Maybe it's the comic books and programs full of characters with supernatural powers kids grow up with today. Maybe it's some memories that lie deeper than that. But it always seemed to me magic was something it was possible to do, like flying or reading people's thoughts. Of course it is possible to walk on fire when you can control your consciousness and it becomes stronger than the beliefs of the world around you. That's why magic works. I have walked on fire, in the unexpected environs of the very north of London. It's a great test. Famous magicians, such as David Blaine, simply believe in themselves, and know how to utilize their own power. Now for a more sinister example of magic, one, sadly, still used in the Hawaiian Islands.

THE DEATH PRAYER

Na waimaka o ka lani

The tears of heaven.

HAWAIIAN PROVERB

Although mana itself is neutral, it can be used in different ways. Like any power, magic can be abused, and the "death prayer," *'anā'anā,* is an example. A kahuna who can cause someone's death, *only by praying,* is often featured in stories and films about Hawai'i. Long found several case histories from sources such as the doctors at Queen's Hospital in Honolulu. He found that "not a year passed but one or more victims of the potent magic died, despite all that the hospital could offer in the way of aid. And the old time doctors had recognized the familiar symptoms year after year."[9]

One example is the case of a "rough-and-ready" Irishman, a taxi driver in Honolulu. He dallied with a young Hawaiian girl, who fell so in love with him she broke off her engagement to a Hawaiian boy. Not a religious man, he ignored veiled threats from the girl's grandmother that "heaven would punish him" unless he left well enough alone. Then, one day, his feet "went to sleep" and the numbness crept slowly up his body until, after about fifty hours, it reached his waist. By this time he was in the Honolulu hospital, and the doctors could do nothing to stop the spreading numbness. Then an old-time doctor identified the symptoms as those of ʻanāʻanā. Careful questioning of the scornful Irishman drew out the story of the Hawaiian girl and her grandmother. The doctor knew the correct procedure for such matters and went to visit the girl's grandmother. The ensuing conversation went like this:

"I know you're not a kahuna and have had nothing to do with this case, Grandma," said the doctor. "But just as a friend will you tell me if you think anything could be done to save this man?"

"Well," said Grandma, "I know nothing about the matter, and I am no kahuna—as you know. But I think that if the man would promise to take the next ship for America and never return or even write back, he might recover."

"I will guarantee that he will do just those things," said the doctor.

"All right," said Grandma imperturbably.

The next step was to explain the situation over and over again to the disbelieving Irishman, but when he finally understood, he was terrified and willing to do anything to remove the curse. "That was in the early afternoon. That night he was on his feet again and able to catch a Japanese ship for the Coast."[10] Needless to say, he never returned to the islands.

Examples of ʻanāʻanā can still be found in Hawaiʻi today, and they illustrate the closest word to evil in Hawaiian, ʻino, meaning "to harm *with intent*." I know of at least one eminent writer about Hawaiʻi who wrongly generalized about Hawaiian beliefs and was "prayed to death." In general the "death prayer" is a force to be aware of but never to use.

Misusing one's power on such a massive scale may result in certain spiritual powers being taken away, for the sender is forcefully controlling the future from his or her subconscious mind. In addition, using the prayer shows that the person has not yet learned the power of compassion. That is why heaven weeps, for the one sending the death prayer does not. Such a person does not have the faith and courage to feel—even in cases where an obvious wrong has been done—that the wrongdoer's own karma will take care of it: the effects will strike the sender in this dimension or in other dimensions, for that is the law of turn and return.

In Hawai'i, skilled practitioners, such as the kahuna known as *kahuna 'anā'anā kuni,* can easily send the prayer back to harm the originator, even more powerfully. Hawaiian historian Samuel Kamakau wrote that in one instance, the force of the "sending-back" was so great that "solid rocks were melted away by the mana of the prayers, and thunder and lightning vibrated like a rattling piece of *tapa* at the fireplace of the *kahuna kuni.* Any large tree that stood close was withered as though it had been scorched by fire. That was through the mana of the prayer."[11]

Despite such practices, Huna fundamentally teaches that true power is found in inner sovereignty, not in blaming an outside force for our problems. As Leonardo da Vinci said: "Man has no greater or lesser dominion than the dominion over himself." The answer to problems is not to fight them or attack others, but to *increase* our own creative power, our own mana. That teaching is based on the understanding that, although we all seem to be separate, our power comes from our inherent connection to all, which we are reminded of by stones.

THE SINGING STONES

Stones, like all things in the universe, had an element of being, of power and life beyond the obvious . . .

JUNE GUTMANIS

It is no coincidence that the section on the death prayer is followed by this section on stones, for they have many things in common. I do not approve of the death prayer, but like every creation on earth, it has the seed of light growing within it. So do rocks and stones. On a deep level, rocks represent continuity, underpinning everything on earth. Imagine what rocks have been party to in their millions of decades: the forming and dissolving of continents; new oceans appearing and disappearing; the rise and fall of islands; societies passing in what must seem like an endless procession; creatures being born, living, and dying. And all the while, there are always the rocks.

This is why so many sacred points on earth are represented by stones. The holiest shrine for Muslims at Mecca contains the sacred stone Qaba. A stone covered in blue dye near Calcutta is a goddess. There are sacred arrangements of stones all over the British Isles, from the Ring of Brodgar in the Orkney Islands in the north to the tip of Cornwall in the south, and there are such examples on every continent. One old Hawaiian said to me, "Stone, that's old," and he meant a great deal by it.

My experience at the mountaintop temple taught me never to underestimate the importance of rocks and stones in Hawai'i. Not only do they form the "bedrock" or the foundation of the islands themselves, but temples are made of stone, an upright stone is often found on household altars, and special stones mark the directions, the passage of the solstices, certain sky activity, and other important events. A stone was also traditionally given when knowledge was achieved, such as upon graduation from the "star schools" of ancient New Zealand, which taught knowledge of fertility.

Samuel Kamakau refers to the type of rock found on a family altar—which can represent the spirit of a particular family—as a *pōhaku pu'uhonua*, a "gate to heaven."[12] It is usually a single stone, standing upright like a phallus. The upright stance represents generation, and indeed, it's passed down in a family from generation to generation. It will be prayed to and decorated, for instance, by a shell necklace or a garland of leaves. The care and love involved in doing this infuses the stone with mana and this in turn helps the stone act as a guardian to the household. The name for such a stone—*pōhaku o Kāne*, or "rock of Kāne"—is very significant. The word *pōhaku* means "stone" or "rock," but also means "the movement of potential, *pō*, through the breath, *ha*, of the subconscious, Kū." The God-mind or Higher Self is called Kāne. The "stone of Kāne" brings these two meanings together, teaching that one way to align the subconscious with the God-mind or Higher Self is through the prayer and care for the stone. Similarly, the arrangement of rocks in the temple I visited, where a smooth horizontal rock covered vertical ones, is a formation full of meaning: it is an altar known as a *kuahu, ahu* being "a cairn of stones" that—when used for worship—gives a way to go through Kū, the subconscious mind, to the Higher Self.

Stones are here to help us. Some examples are the "wizard stones" of that popular tourist destination Waikīkī Beach. They are said to contain the spirit of four great wizards and priestesses. Harry Potter fans might be interested to know that these stones—Kapaemahu and his partner Kahaloa, Kapuniʻi and his consort Kinohi—commemorate their great healing powers. It is worth visiting them when at Waikīkī, touching them and gently asking for healing for oneself and the earth, for stones, like stories, are not stuck in the world they represent, but are symbols of other worlds on earth. Sharing their vibration can help bring "higher knowledge" to earth.

Individual stones are regarded as having the power to attract particular people they wish to help, as reflected in the Hawaiian saying "Your stone finds you." One pungent legend of old Hawaiʻi is of a stone called Kāneikokala, which is on display in the Bishop Museum:

In recent years two children lived with an old man called Wahinenui near a fish pond on the island of Hawaiʻi. One night the old man woke them in the middle of the night, prepared fish and coconuts, led them outside and bade them to dig in a particular spot. They dug and dug until they found something hard—the stone. When the rock was out of the ground the old man poured some liquid into its "mouth." Then he took three mullet and placed them in front of the stone and a bunch of coconuts which he hung around the stone's neck. Wahinenui told the children the stone's name was *Kāneikokala* and that he himself would die in three days' time. He did and the stone *Kāneikokala* (the one with a crooked mouth) was later donated by one of the children to the Bishop Museum.[13]

The stone "spoke" and the old man was able to hear. This story is an illustration of the mana that runs through and connects everything, even such seemingly separate entities as a human and a stone. Mana is the force that powers the universe, the motor for "the sacred power of Huna," which leads us to eventually align with the great god Kāne. The name of the stone, Kāneikokala, also provides us with a clue about the quality of compassion we need to practice in order to be similar to Kāne: *iko* means "to imitate, copy" and *kala* "to forgive."

Many Polynesians are drawn to a particular stone for its capacity to connect them to earth's mana, and they find it helpful to carry their stone with them at all times. The New Zealand Maori writer Keri Hulme told me she would not feel right without the greenstone that always lives on her chest. She wrote:

I have a stone that once swam
strange warm ancient seas.[14]

Today stones are becoming more and more popular, as the proliferation of crystal shops attests. Each person may have his or her particular crystal, key ring, or necklace of stone. Each stone, just like each person, has its own vibration. That vibration helps people tune in to the old knowledge contained in the stone. Perhaps we are all, as one sculptor said, "trapped angels in a block of stone," and caring for stones helps us get closer to our true core.

Stones that are well looked after are so powerful that they are said to even have the ability to give birth. On the Big Island, there is a very special black sand beach, fringed by palm trees and a lagoon, within sight of volcanic mountains. There, big green turtles like to swim in the gleaming ocean. One proverb calls the place Punalu'u, *i ke kai kau ha'a a ka malihini:* "Punalu'u, where the sea dances for the visitors."

In Punalu'u live some special rocks known as the "birthing stones of Punalu'u." There are male and female stones. "Male" ones are phallic and closely grained, "female" ones more oval and porous. It is said that if you put these stones close together and look after them properly—oiling them, dressing them, and keeping them near water—then "by and by the female pebbles give birth" and another smaller stone will appear, a "bebi stone." The stone itself gives life. In Huna there are many such examples of stone indeed having an element of "being, of power and life beyond the obvious." In "Gods Sliding Down Rainbows" we shall learn more about how the care of stones is associated with the birth of light. Stones indeed contain wizardry.

And now for a Hawaiian group of small wizards who are said to know how to look after rocks.

THE MENEHUNE

Not all storytellers give the same account.

KATHERINE LUOMALA

The Hawaiians tell stories of "little people," legends whose origins reach back to the ancient period referred to as The Wind Clouds by the Chatham Islanders. According to the mythologist Katherine Luomala, the little people reputed to live in Hawai'i are of three kinds: the Menehune, who are the most well known; the Mū, "the people of the silence," who are said to be rough and hairy and love bananas; and the E'epa, creatures of strange forms, such as a boy who was born as a piece of rope. Often the terms Menehune and Mū are used interchangeably.

Many Hawaiians today say they are descended from the Menehune, or Mū, who lived on a lost continent known as Lemuria (or Mū), described by Leinani Melville in *Children of the Rainbow:*

Havai'i originally referred to the enormous continent that existed in prehistoric times in the Pacific Ocean, and not to the beautiful strand of emerald isles which are now known as the Hawaiian Islands. It was on this lost continent that the now extinct *Mū* once lived. The present islands are former mountain peaks of that submerged continent . . . Tradition has handed down the knowledge that a few of the *Mū* survived the cataclysm which pulverized their ancient civilization. These few preserved the traditions of their forefathers and handed them down to the next generation.[15]

When this fabled and fabulous continent of light was flourishing, it was a time of balance among the mental, emotional, physical, and spiritual natures, when all people knew their power and all were capable of what we now call magic. Although much was lost in the great deluge, the legacy of Mū is kept alive by the kahuna, and by the Menehune themselves, who are also known as the Manahuna or "the power of Huna." Perhaps the Menehune are some of the few creatures remaining from that time. Some stories say the "wee folk" still live on the floating islands of beauty that come in and out of sight if you glance a particular way across the ocean.

The Menehune—often represented by small, brown, goblinlike figures—symbolically appear everywhere in Hawai'i, from Menehune bottled water with the picture of the dancing elf on the label to the mascot of the University of Hawai'i football team. They are usually described as being two or three feet tall and very muscular, while "their clothes are so unimportant they have never been described." Ruth Park has a wonderful account, very true to the Hawaiian traditions, of a child with a Menehune friend in her novel *My Sister Sif*. Many Hawaiians believe in them, just as the Irish and Scottish believe in their little people: leprechauns, gremlins, goblins, pixies, fairies, and elves. In fact, stories about "the wee folk" are found throughout the world.

There are many tales about the Menehune in Hawai'i that tell of how they love having fun, playing games like spinning tops, shooting arrows, and sliding down a cliff and splashing in the ocean at the bottom. Their musical instruments include the nose flute, the tī leaf trumpet, and the sharkskin drum. According to one legend, the Menehune or Mū live on *Kāne huna moku,* "the hidden island of Kāne"—a paradise island of the gods Kāne and Kanaloa—and sometimes sidle out to the islands of Hawai'i, always returning home before daybreak is marked by the cry of the 'elepaio bird. According to other stories, they are always present but come out only at night to interact secretly with the human world. Apparently their leaders advise them not to marry humans, but it is said that not all Menehune obey the commands!

The most visible evidence of the Menehune is their stonework. It is said that they moved rocks to build nine or ten temples around Honolulu, for example, and two fishponds. Marks resembling tiny fingerprints on a boulder by the O'ahu Country Club are seen as evidence of the fighting of Menehune tribes over a particularly desirable rock.

They work silently and only at night, with great concentration, but also with great ease. Unlike humans, they do not need to work particularly hard. Perhaps that's because they have direct access to their Higher Selves, the place where the phrase *hard work* is meaningless. Tasks do get accomplished from the Higher Self, but they are infinitely easier, for they are filled with light. This may be why the Menehune make "light work" of moving the rocks. As we might expect from beings living in paradise, they are filled with light, and have the power to make the rocks light too. The Menehune bring things out of the night mind and into daylight. Some Hawaiian proverbs say of them: "No task is difficult. It is the work of one hand" and "In one night, and by dawn it is finished."

Menehune may be blamed when workmen find stonework they left intact at dusk mysteriously undone overnight. In 1951, men moving rocks in Diamond Head Crater quit their job because they said disgruntled Menehune tampered each night with the work they had done during the day. But it is also said that if the Menehune are happy with work being done, they'll help out, standing in lines during the night and passing the rocks from one to another. Then the workmen will arrive the next day and find their work mysteriously accomplished.

The Menehune are particularly associated with the island of Kaua'i, where there is hardly a group of rocks that does not have its attached Menehune story. There is a particular kind of stonework, unique in Polynesia, scattered throughout the Hawaiian Islands, of which the best-known example is the Menehune Ditch, near the small town of Waimea on Kaua'i. The stone-wall ditch forms the left side of the modern road that leads out of town. When Captain Cook saw the ditch, he estimated that the walls were about twenty-four feet high. Although they now are only about two feet high, they still do their job of diverting water from the Waimea River to irrigate the taro patches below. The special thing about this particular wall is that the stones have been hewn into each other, so the top of the wall is level. The structure is so alien to Hawaiian culture that anthropologists have suggested Tahitians built the wall, or even the first Europeans! Many Hawaiians, however, continue to say that it was the Menehune.[16]

Who knows? The many stories of magic in Hawai'i certainly make no "sense" within the belief system of Newtonian science, but that has been disproved anyway by quantum physics. These stories are reminders that reality is more than "what we see." In the next chapter we will look more closely at the unseen factors that, for me, provided the "missing link" that explained just how magic can work and got me "believing in magic." Aspiring Harry Potters, read on!

4
Making Magic

Nothing was born
Nothing will die
All things will change.

ALFRED LORD TENNYSON

What is magic, if not the process of influencing change, the process of growing our consciousness and using it to forge our world anew? So is it really *magic?* Yes and no. It depends on our perspective. From the perspective of Newtonian science, yes, it's magic; from the perspective of Huna, it's commonplace. This is because, on a deep level, magic makes sense. Dr. Brigham explained to Max Freedom Long how magic *could* work:

> Always keep watch for three things in the study of this magic. There must be some form of consciousness back of, and directing, the processes of magic. Controlling the heat in fire walking, for example. There must also be some form of force used in exerting this control, if we can but recognize it. And last, there must be some form of substance, visible or invisible, through which the force can act. Watch always for these, and if you can find any one, it may lead to the other.[1]

Although Dr. Brigham did not himself discover how magic worked, he gave Max Freedom Long—and us—a valuable framework for revealing the hidden knowledge of Huna by describing three qualities that are necessary to *make magic happen:* focused consciousness, a controlling force, and the substance through which the force acts.

Let's begin our investigation with the final factor, the "form of substance, visible or invisible, through which the force can act," which in Huna is called *aka,* meaning "matter" or "essence." Aka is the essence of everything we see and don't see. It is in everything natural and everything man-made too. Aka is amorphous, an undefined substance in which everything is constantly evolving.

There are some interesting parallels between the concept of aka and recent scientific research, which has undermined previous depictions of the world as being made up of separate, independent atoms zinging around in emptiness. Biologist Rupert Sheldrake in *The Rebirth of Nature* reflects the discoveries being made in many fields of science when he says that there can be no such thing as a "vacuum" of empty space. He quotes the famous physicist, an old friend of mine, Paul Davies, who wrote: "A vacuum is not inert and featureless, but alive with throbbing energy and vitality."[2] This is because the phenomena we are used to thinking of as clearly defined atoms (a nucleus, surrounded by electrons) are actually "quanta of vibration," which are undergoing continual spontaneous change, part of a dynamic sea of energy.

Aka also implies energy, being composed of *ka,* "to hit or smite," and *a,* "with direction." Here's what Long had to say about this concept:

> The root *ka* in *aka* also means a vine whose branches run and divide, linking the meaning of the word directly to the idea that the mana flows along the shadowy substance masses or threads. *Ka* also means to radiate out like rays of the sun, symbolizing the radiation in all directions of the numberless threads which connect every individual with the people and things he has touched.[3]

As we have already seen, the second factor, the controlling force, is mana. In his investigations, Long discovered that the kahunā "knew the force as a thing which had to do with all thought processes and bodily activity. It was the essence of life itself. The kahuna symbol for this force was water. Water flows, so does the vital force. Water fills things. So does the vital force. Water may leak away—and so may the vital force."[4]

He observed that the kahunā could infuse various objects with more mana. In times of battle, kahunā would hold wooden sticks in their hands and charge them with their vital force, using an effort of mind. The power of this force was so great that such a stick thrown at an enemy by a kahuna could knock even the strongest warrior unconscious.

In addition to meaning "power," *mana* also means "branch," and a branch is an excellent symbol of connection. It is mana that connects previously unrelated things, such as the wooden stick and the life force of the kahuna.

Although we are examining mana and aka in the context of magic, these concepts are not confined to that realm. Both are descriptions of reality, albeit reality that is not visible. Whereas aka is the potential for consciousness, mana means that the potential for consciousness *has been activated*. This can be seen by looking at the connotations of the two words. I find *aka* refers to potentialities: it is the embryo at the moment of conception, a newly hatched fish in the stage where its body is still transparent; it is the faint glimmering preceding the rising of the moon; it is the potential for light that lies within all substance. Mana is the stage in the growth of a fish "in which colors appear" and the stage of a fetus in which limbs begin to develop. It means that consciousness has been injected and is coming into being.

This brings us to the most important ingredient of magic, the first quality identified by Dr. Brigham: some form of directed consciousness. *Directed consciousness* is the focusing of the potential (aka) through power (mana). In Hawaiian, directed consciousness is known as *mākia*, which means "aim" or "purpose." Thought is the vine that turns the aka into a long cord, the color of moonlight, stickily connecting one with the focus of one's consciousness. Directed consciousness is the focusing of all the potentialities of a person's consciousness onto a certain objective or objectives.

Great focus brings great power: sunlight focused by a magnifying glass has the power to burn. When it is strong enough, directed consciousness—even if held by only one individual—can change the course of nations. Remember Mohandas Gandhi, who by overturning the rule of the British in India overthrew the greatest empire in the world? Not only that, but the Mahatma, "the Great Soul," managed this through the principle of *ahimsa,* or nonviolence.

Directed consciousness is the power that makes magic happen. It is that focus which saved the feet of the kahuna from being burned when they walked over hot lava. Their focus was also strong enough to preserve Dr. Brigham's feet. But how did they direct their consciousness? It took Long years to find the answer to this question, but he finally succeeded. He describes the excitement of his discovery when it finally came:

In California I continued half-heartedly to watch for any new psychological discovery that might again open up the problem. None came. Then, in 1935, quite unexpectedly, I awakened in the middle of the night with an idea that led directly to the clue which was eventually to give the answer. If Dr. Brigham had been alive he certainly would have joined me in a scarlet flush of embarrassment. Both of us had overlooked a clue so simple and so obvious that it had continually passed unnoticed. It was the pair of spectacles pushed up on the forehead while we hunted for hours unable to find them.

The idea that had struck me in the middle of the night was that the kahunas must have had names for the elements in their magic. Without such names they could not have handed down their lore from one generation to the next . . .[5]

Long had broken the code to understanding Hawaiian magic: the chants done by the kahuna before they and Dr. Brigham began fire walking would no longer be seen as just the "usual God-talk," handed down word for word for countless generations. Hawaiian words have a multitude of purposes. One of them is to act as a container for sacred knowledge; another is to focus consciousness. Words are a particularly powerful focus of consciousness when they are chanted in repetition, like a prayer. This was the way ancient Hawaiians knew words, not as something written down, but as something actively spoken, heard, or remembered. Words put all three aspects of Brigham's search for magic together: they direct consciousness, incorporate mana, and work through aka. Let's take a deeper look at how words act as a sparkling rope that unites different spheres.

THE WORD ROPE

He koʻe ka pule a kahuna, he moe no a ʻoni mai.

*The prayer of a kahuna is like a worm, it may lie
dormant but it will wriggle along—give it time.*

HAWAIIAN PROVERB

In any human society, words are very important: indeed, they are often seen as the distinguishing characteristic of being human. Words are a very strong agent of change for humanity. The enormous success of books on subjects like the power of prayer and affirmations shows that word power is a growth industry now in the new millennium. Words focus the different syllables of speech and foster the force of directed consciousness. This force can be incredibly powerful, such as depicted by the biblical creation story in which words make light happen: "God said let there be light and there was light." Every society on earth prays, and what else is prayer but directed consciousness? The idea is that words in some way "contact God" and set up a link with the sacred. In other words, directed consciousness sets a person's mana moving toward God, and the link is made possible because of aka, the substance through which it moves.

Words have such power that they can bring life or they can bring death, as is shown by this Hawaiian saying that refers to the word of a chief who had the power to decide whether his captive in war would live or die:

Aia ke ola i ka waha, aia ka make i ka waha.

Life is in the mouth, death is in the mouth.

Words are extremely powerful in our society too. They can marry us, as when each person in a couple says "I do" in a wedding service, or they can kill us. In a notorious case in England in the 1950s, a nineteen-year-old youth named Derek Bentley was convicted of murder and hanged. The man who died was a policeman, and there was never any question that Derek Bentley killed him. He did not. Derek Bentley's crime was to say "Let him have it" before his accomplice fired the gun. The accomplice could not hang, as he was under age (he is still alive today, running a market stall in London), and Derek died instead. *He died because of his words.* Derek's sister Iris passed away relatively recently. She never gave up her fight for a full pardon from the Home Office. But the Home Office said that it could not give him one because he *did* say those words. He finally received a pardon in 1998.

Ancient Hawaiians were very experienced in using words to direct consciousness: they prayed for whatever they wanted. Here, from the collection of June Gutmanis, is a prayer to a mulberry tree, the tree from which the famous tapa cloth of the Polynesian islands is made.

O kokolo ke a'a i ka pō loa,
O puka ka maka i ke ao loa,
O 'oukou i ka pō,
Owau nei lā ke ao,
E ulu e, e ulu . . .

That its roots will grow during the night,
So that its eyes may be seen during the long days,
You during the night,
I during the day,
Shall cause it to grow, grow . . . [6]

The prayer is addressed directly to the gods, asking them to foster the mulberry's growth during the *pō,* the night. The human world takes responsibility for the growth during the *ao,* the daytime. Through the "double whammy" of gods and humans, the mulberry plant will grow and grow. The prayer ends, as does every prayer, with a word for "letting go," such as *'āmama,* which has a kaona of "let the words fly free."

Here is a prayer against impotency, which, unlike Viagra, aims to remedy the cause of the dysfunction:

> *Ia Waiwai'ole*
> *Pale ka pō*
> *Puka i ke ao*
> *Owau nei, o Kanohoaloha.*[7]

> *To Worthless,*
> *Ward off the period of night*
> *Bring forth day*
> *It is I here, the dweller-with-love.*

This prayer is addressed directly to the penis (Worthless) and, through it, the gods. The person tells the gods that he is the dweller-with-love. This helps him actually become the dweller with love. It's not the only route—we will explore later in the book other things that help a person to make love consciously—but it's certainly an important one. Obviously the one-with-the-penis should not be doing or saying things to his lover that contradict dwelling-with-love. Then the penis will wriggle like a worm to its goal.

A canoe chant from the collection of Kamakau (116, 117) shows how focused consciousness can help the paddler of the canoe (a traveler through the seas of life, just like you and me) reach the desired destination.

Kū mai, kū maki, kū mai	*Arise, arise*
Ka nalu nui mai Kahiki ea	*Great waves from Kahiki*

I Wawau e, i Uapou e	*From Wawau, from Uapou*
I Helani e, i Keku'ina e	*From Helani, from Keku'ina*
I Ulunui e, i Melemele e	*From Ulunui, from Melemele*
I Uliuli, i Hakalau'ai e	*From Uliuli, from Hakalau'ai*
I Borabora e, i Nu'uhiwa e	*From Borabora, from Nu'uhiwa*
I Hoanekapua e	*From Hoanekapua*
Hoehoe pae; pae au lā	*I will paddle until I reach shore;*
	I have landed[8]

The words help the paddler to concentrate on the sacred through all the waves of the sea. Kahiki refers to a faraway paradise and the other names refer to sacred islands and stars, which guide the traveler to a safe landing. Saying "I have landed" at the end helps the landing to actually happen.

But the *Kumulipo,* the Hawaiian song of creation, is perhaps the best example of the way words invoke the sacred. The stanza below is *Ta Wa Ewaru,* stanza eight, which refers to the arrival of the humans on earth. The Hawaiian is the Kalakaua text; the translation is my own.

O tama auri, auri anei
O tama i te au o ta pō tinitini
O tama i te au o ta pō he'enalu mamao
'Oroherohe tāne hānau i te ao
'Oroherohe ta wāhine hānau i te au
Noho mai rā ia tāne
Hānau Tapōpō he wahine
Hānau Po'ere'i, hānau Po'ere'a
To raua hope mai o Wehiroa
Na rakou nei i hānau mai
Ta tititi, ta matatata
Tu nu'u muiona ta muimui ana
O tanata rere ware, o tanata nei rā
Ua a –o[9]

The foundation sends down a beloved one of difference,
    a different one is here
The children of the flow of the foundation of the night
The children of the flow of the foundation of the night come
    down surfing the highest of waves
The male principle giving birth to the light from above
The female principle giving birth to the flowing and the filling
Dwelling in the north, the direction of the sun, the spar of a
    celestial canoe, the male principle
Giving birth to the striking out of the invisible darkness in the
    south, the female principle
The dark spring of the night flows into a gourdlike bowl and
    gives birth, the dark spring of the night is charged with
    energy and gives birth
So follows the progression of the long, dark decoration of the
    cosmos
The forms are rumbling away in the distance, coming ever
    closer to being born
The tiny fish, the fresh buds blooming on the corm of the taro
    plant, are constantly in communication
The standing assembled small worms, the measurement of the
    high and silent design
The bodies of the flying foundation of slime, which has
    reached out of the sky, the murmuring human bodies of the
    day
A prayer has been replied to, consciousness is charged and
    answered, it is light!

This verse shows the difference a prayer makes: "consciousness is charged and answered, it is light!" Words are associated with the charging of consciousness, the answering appearance of myriad life-forms, and with the revelation of light.

There is another crucial point to make about words, which Long did not talk about. Another essential ingredient of magic is the ability to let go of outcome. That is how to avoid becoming a dark magician, bent on domination, a trap certain "New Age" gurus fall into. We need to surf our wave, sow our seeds, sew our weave, and let go.

Now we'll see how changing our perception helps the whole green earth and the blue beyond.

THE LIGHT OF NATURE

Nature is God's Greatest Teacher.

LEINANI MELVILLE

One of the reasons we, like Dr. Brigham, may find magic hard to believe in—even when it has been demonstrated to us—is that we have lost our connection to nature. The words of Alexander Pope, written at the end of the eighteenth century—"Unchanging Nature, still divinely bright, / One clear unchang'd and universal light"—would be unlikely to hold true for most people today, for the way humans think of nature has changed throughout the ages.

Today most people think of nature as something outside and separate from us. And we don't see nature as divine. This hasn't always been the case, as shown by phenomena defined as the "nature-worship" of the Celts and Druids, the "nature-consciousness" of the Native Americans, and the "pantheism" of the ancient Greeks. But the rise of industrialization has led to a separation from nature. Now many of us live and work in controlled environments and nature may no longer play a daily role in our lives. Even farming has been transformed from a relationship with the land and the creatures on it to a mechanized, chemical-filled industry. Utilization has even spread so far that many kill living creatures for profit, something that could never have been conceived of in ancient Hawai'i!

These practices are not conducive to understanding the greater consciousness in oneself, nor in anything else! To be able to do this, we need to expand our perceptions. If we could hear the sad song of the earth, as the chemicals spot and poison her soft surface, or feel the fear of the harmless animals as they are herded together to have their lives taken away, we would find other ways to grow. But, alas, our present separation from nature makes it far more difficult to believe that everything is made of aka and has the potential for consciousness. Hence it is more difficult for us to feel.

One of the reasons it's hard for us to experience our connection with nature is that we regard it as fundamentally different from ourselves. Adventurers such as Captain Robert Falcon Scott and Sir Ranulph Fiennes succeeded in some fabulous achievements at the most extreme edge of nature—the poles. But how about the way they did it? Their life's work has been a process of "pitting themselves against nature." They are typical of the Western plight: we are not taught how to be in tune with nature nor told that we can't control certain aspects of it, so we subconsciously fear nature and each endeavor becomes a battle. We can even become so estranged that we are unable to believe it is possible to be connected. Sir Ranulph Fiennes, for example, described a time when his expedition was going to a certain bay and he ignored a warning from the local Iñupiat people that the weather was about to change. He decided to press on anyway and suffered greatly from cold as a result. It didn't really make sense to him that they could be that aware of nature, so he ignored their warnings—to his peril.

Yet there are far more ways of seeing nature. The first need is to consciously reconnect. We can go out for a walk and really look at the world we see. Or grow a plant and marvel over the appearance of the blossom. Backpacking—where we travel directly on the earth and sleep on her warm surface—enables us to become more in tune with the light of our original spirit. I always regretted something about growing up in the "big city" but never knew what. When I first made a connection with nature, at the age of nineteen or so, and knew the exertion of climbing a mountain and the feeling of sunlight running all the way through me, then I knew what I had been missing.

Perhaps that is why we talk about "going back to nature," something that was never necessary in the past. This is worth doing, for as we travel directly on the earth and sleep on her warm surface, we become more in tune with the light of our original spirit. All over the world there are movements and groups to help us reconnect with nature, such as the Sierra Club. Even so, in the vast majority of cases, people are still "making an effort" to regain a sense of connection. *It may not happen naturally.* This can be shown by the equipment many people take when they "go out into nature," some seeing tents, sleeping bags, medicine, insurance, and cooking facilities as essential.

It is very different in Hawai'i, where nature is considered part of one's family. Every Hawaiian family, although they don't talk about it to strangers, has its 'aumakua, or "guiding spirit," which often appears as an animal such as a *manō* (shark), *mo'o* (reptile), or *pueo* (owl). These 'aumakua are part of the family, because when a family member passes away, his spirit may inhabit an 'aumakua. Death was considered to be a loss of consciousness (*make,* the word for death, means "to faint") but not a loss of the spirit, which remains "out there," beyond the body, and can appear in other forms, such as the 'aumakua particular to that family.

The 'aumakua are a way of expressing the web of connection: If a family's 'aumakua is the shark, for instance, it is of the 'aumakua manō and is thus also spiritually related to all the others who share the shark 'aumakua. Whenever the family 'aumakua appears to a person, it is a sign from his lost relative that he is nearby. The creatures often show themselves when people are in a crisis to let them know that they are being protected. And in return, the family looks after the creatures. I know one Hawaiian family who used to dive down to a cave where their 'aumakua—a shark—lived. They brought it tasty pieces of breadfruit every day. It is said that a shark will never attack one of this family—and there are no known shark attacks on members of the 'aumakua manō. Instead there are several stories of rescues by sharks!

In her book *The Polynesian Family System in Ka'u, Hawai'i,* Mary Kawena Pukui—the matriarch of contemporary Hawaiian scholarship and one of its most respected authors—includes an extensive section on nature, because the Polynesian family cannot be understood without it. She writes: "without understanding the quality of spontaneous *being-one-with-natural-phenomena which are persons not things,* it is impossible for an alien to understand Hawaiian values."[10] The sense of connection is not limited to one's family 'aumakua. Seen from the perspective in which everything in the universe is made up of aka and everything has the potential for consciousness within it, there can be no inherent difference between humans and nature.

As everything is made up of the same substance, it is possible for one type of consciousness to influence another. Humans can influence nature, such as in the prayers we looked at, and Hawaiians believe this is because we influence the gods, who always lie hidden within the forms of nature. Here is one hula chant that describes the shelters they may choose to dwell in:

Noho ana i ke akua i ka nahalehele
I alai 'ia e ke ki-ohu-ohu, e ka ua koko
O na kino malu i ka lani
Malu e hoe . . .

The gods dwell in the woodlands
Hidden away in the mist, in the low-hanging rainbow
O beings sheltered by the skies
Clear our path of all hindrance . . . [11]

There are a whole flock of gods and goddesses in Hawai'i who are constantly creating the world, together with humans and the rest of creation-in-motion. These gods and goddesses have recognizably human qualities: one god can be vain, another can be jealous, and a particular goddess loves dancing. This is very different from the concept of an all-powerful God who knows everything and is responsible for having created everything. In Hawai'i the qualities of the gods are seen as being reflected in the world that humans and gods co-create. According to Pukui, "A rosy dawn is not merely a lovely Natural Phenomenon: it is that beloved Person named The-rosy-glow-of-the-Heavens, who is Hi'iaka-in-the-bosom-of-Pele."[12] The pink glow in the sky is one of the forms of Hiʻiaka, the beloved young sister of the volcano goddess Pele.

Nature in Hawaiʻi is bright with the lights of many different gods and goddesses. Perhaps this is why it is said that a person can know whether her prayer has worked by a change in the nature around her. The weather, for instance, is the intermediary between the realms of the humans and the realms of the gods, showing both the changing human consciousness and the feelings of the gods and the goddesses. This may be why the state of the weather is part of almost every Hawaiian chant: the gods themselves can be found there, such as in the forms of the great god Kāne:

E Kāne i-ke puahiohio
E Kāne i-ke anuenue

O Kāne of the whirlwind
O Kāne of the rainbow.[13]

The more aware we are of the spirit of the world around us, the greater our capacity for magic will be. If we are able to see the forms of the gods and goddesses in the clouds, tune in to the spirit of our computer, and smile at the fairies in the garden, then the world will clearly sing—at least for us. Our connection to nature can be fostered by purification rituals, such as the one I participated in as preparation for a temple ceremony on the island of Kahoʻolawe. It was November, the time of the Makahiki festival, the opening of the gates of Lono, the god of consciousness. The night before the ceremony we each performed the *hiuwai,* or cleansing ritual, naked and alone for an hour, which seemed like eternity, out of our depth in the Pacific Ocean. Then we were called out of the dark waters of the night by the blowing of the *pū,* or conch shell, and the cry I'll always remember: *Lono i ka Makahiki,* or "Lono of the Makahiki!"

Rituals like this are not a compulsory part of Huna, however. Beware of any teacher who insists that a ritual is necessary, for the greatest link to power is always within, and it is possible to make the link and forgo the ritual. For example, it is possible to go into an altered state simply by asking for it. The rewards of such instant connection are great. I now am always aware of the spirit within nature, and treasure the amazing holographic resource that is open to me. Nature is truly God's greatest teacher. My awareness of beauty has exponentially increased. And if it can happen to me, it can happen to anyone!

FOCUSING THE LIGHT

May the force be with you!

FROM THE FILM *STAR WARS*

The practice of magic is certainly not confined to Hawai'i and not even to the kahuna of Hawai'i, although they are famous for their mastery. As we have seen, the keys to being able to "make magic" are to be aware of our interconnectedness with the substance of all and to generate power by focusing the great light of our being. The free-floating, silvery pieces of aka, the stuff of which the universe is made, do not possess mana in themselves. All they possess is the potential for mana, which must be activated. They are like a circuit whose electrical current hasn't been switched on; in fact, the lines of the circuit first have to be connected by the practitioner. When consciousness is directed, aka can be visualized as turning into a long cord that connects the practitioner and the person or object being focused upon.

The gods—known as *akua*—are also made of aka, but aka with a difference. Akua is separated from aka by one small letter: *u*. That letter means "quality of." The quality that separates aka from akua can be known as the quality of light. The word *aka* also means "a dim reflection of the moonlight." Akua is a bright shining light like the midday sun blaze. The light of the akua has changed and grown and become effulgent, affecting all around it. The word *akua* also means "a fully-formed-idea-in-action," as King pointed out. In other words, a god is a god because it has reached its full manifestation of consciousness.

It is possible for all of us to transform our aka into akua if we learn how to activate our consciousness. We each have the power to put out our branches of mana for ourselves and thus to change our own structure. All matter in the universe has a tendency to take of the form of the lowest energy possible. That is why a lump of coal not forced to become a diamond by the application of heat and pressure will remain a lump of coal. Exactly the same is true for us. Unless we transcend our habitual states of mind and increase our mana, we stay the way we are.

That's why creativity is so important. Being creative doesn't necessarily mean having a "creative" career, like being an artist or a writer; we can also be creative working in a bank. It *does* involve dancing between the structures of the ordinary. Creativity is how we liberate ourselves from our habitual structures and familiar choices.

Creativity means doing something different every day: going to work a different way or trying that apple pancake for tea even though we usually have toast. It means trying on an item of clothing we wouldn't normally wear. Creativity means buying a magazine on a subject we know nothing about (and are thus not interested in) and being surprised by just how interesting it is. Creativity means talking to people we would not normally talk to and really listening to their replies. The ability to be open increases our vibrational frequency and makes us far more "attractive" people. We will appear more alive—glowing, in fact. It helps us to become much more aware of the *kaona,* or hidden meanings, in the vibrant life all around us. Instead of "cutting off" bits of ourselves, like most of the population, we will have the ability to be much more "present," for ourselves and for others.

Huna offers us ways to become far more creative—indeed to transform ourselves into magnetizing diamonds—through the sacred teachings about the dimensions of the mind. In the next chapter, we shall explore that wisdom and the guidance it offers for the journey into the brightness within.

5

Journey to the Mind of Light

For the soul is all light and fire
And its joy is to expand to the universal.

KRISTIN ZAMBUCKA

In this chapter we shall look at the Huna concept of the "three minds," and at the possibilities offered by ancient Hawaiian wisdom to expand the dimensions of our mind into greater brightness until our soul-shine is "all light and fire." Although this discussion refers to three minds— in common with some other writers about Huna, such as Max Freedom Long, Serge King, and Anne Brewer—this is simply one way of conceptualizing a huge area of knowledge, and many other ways could be equally valid. Many Hawaiians speak of several dimensions of mind. While there could be twenty minds or twelve hundred, we can use the concepts of the three minds to guide our further exploration of Huna.

As we shall see, Long and others make reference to the different minds as though they represent different levels, such as low, middle, and high. However, the word *dimension* is more representative of Hawaiian ideas in which opening to all the aspects of the human mind increases understanding and opens the world.

The three minds referred to by Huna are: the subconscious, known as *'unihipili;* the conscious, known as *'uhane;* and the superconscious, known as the 'aumakua. Huna teaches that in most of us, the three minds are separate entities that work independently of each other. For instance, as Long pointed out, "ghosts" are the hauntings of the subconscious mind experienced by the conscious mind. In fact, each mind is conceived of as having a shadowy body. The one of the superconscious is gauzy and golden, the one of the conscious mind a little thicker and less light, and the one of the subconscious thick, dark, and dense. This idea of an aspect of the mind having a "body," or separate sphere of influence, may sound pretty strange to us, but modern science is not too far behind. The concept of "spheres of influence" was first "discovered" by scientists in the 1840s. Then Faraday and Maxwell found out that electricity and magnetism are not "things in themselves" but instead spheres of influence, which they called "fields." Rupert Sheldrake described the regions of influence that surround every biological organism in this way: "These fields were like the known fields of physics in that they were invisible regions of influence with inherently holistic properties; but they were a new kind of field unknown to physics. They existed within and around organisms."[1]

When the three minds are separated, their properties often work against one another, a dynamic well known in the field of mainstream education—where the disruptive role of the subconscious is well recognized—and reflected by many books on how to change oneself, which include ideas on how to link the subconscious and conscious minds. Much less is known in the West of the capacity of the three minds to work together to make significant transformation possible. However, the ancient Hawaiian system of knowledge not only explains the separate activity of the three minds but also offers ways to join them. It is not easy to gain a clear understanding of that knowledge and how to consciously apply it but—as we have seen before—Huna can be accessed through the medium of the Hawaiian language.

When Max Freedom Long analyzed the root meanings of the words used to describe these minds (which he called selves), he uncovered not only the theory behind Hawaiian magic, but also a very sophisticated system of psychology that offers great insights to anyone wishing to make the internal journey of expansion into the possibilities of the superconscious mind. The journey through our minds is a passage toward greater light, in which the subconscious and conscious minds are connected more clearly to one another and both are "opened up" to the blazing light of the superconscious. When we "clear" our subconscious, then we can let in a little more light from our conscious mind, and only when we "open up" both those minds are we able to operate in the blazing light of our Higher Self. The Hawaiian blessing for food is a metaphor for that transition:

> *Auhea oe, e ke kanaka o ke akua, eia kaua wahi ʻai, ua loaʻa*
> *maila mai ka pō mai, no laila nau e ʻaumakua mai i ka ʻai*
> *a kāua.*

> *O man who serves the god, here is food for you, received*
> *from the night, so bless our food in the name of the*
> *ʻaumakua.*

The food is received out of the pō, the darkness of the realm of the gods, and the humans are asking for blessing, asking for help to transform the food in the name of the ʻaumakua, the Higher Self.

Let's now look at the qualities of each mind in turn. In doing so, we'll see how the *kaona,* or "hidden meanings," contained in each ancient name can help us transform.

THE SUBCONSCIOUS MIND

> *For only subconscious forces behaved badly*
> *in your name.*
>
> KRISTIN ZAMBUCKA

Each mind is a separate entity, with thoughts, wishes, and desires of its own. Nowhere is this more clear than with the subconscious mind, the source of our most personal urges. When we are infants, we operate according to the subconscious mind ("I want," "me, me, me"). The rest of the world doesn't exist except insomuch as it can be of service to the youngster. In adults, the wish of the subconscious to control others in order to satisfy its urges can often still be seen operating. The subconscious also contains a hidden record of everything we've ever thought and felt.

The subconscious mind corresponds roughly to the Western concept of the unconscious, whose best-known exponent is the Austrian psychoanalyst Sigmund Freud. I understand Freud's thesis of the unconscious as being essentially that in us which is judged as being "bad," hence repressed and incompatible with our culture and our higher self. Whether or not we have studied psychology, we all have a sense of an aspect of ourselves that is "below the surface" of our conscious mind. However, our ideas about it are shadowy, as shadowy as the subconscious itself. It seems that our parents have had a huge influence over it and that our dreams and fears come out of it. But basically it is a vast, unknown territory, one that lives inside our heads. In Huna, however, the subconscious mind has been known, studied, and worked with since ancient times.

One word for the subconscious mind in Hawaiian is 'unihipili. Long's analysis of 'unihipili is particularly fascinating. He begins with an exploration of the root meanings of *u* and continues through the rest of the syllables:

> *U:* (1) to project, indicative of the projection of threads of the shadowy body and flows of vital force along them (2) to impregnate or tincture or intermingle with something else, which tells the story of how the low self and middle self are intermingled in the physical body as well as in their shadowy bodies; (3) to drip, leak or drizzle a slow drip of water, this meaning symbolizing the manufacture of vital force or mana by the low self, and its slow use in the work of living and of supplying the middle and, at prayer times, the High Self.
>
> *Nihi:* This root means to be thin and weak so as to appear almost broken. It embodies the symbolic description of the shadowy

threads when they are not filled with vital force or activated—when they are as nothing.

Pili: "cling to" This root has the meaning of sticking to a thing, as the shadowy body of the low self sticks to whatever it touches. Upon drawing away after the touch, the threads of shadowy substance are pulled out much as one touches the sticky balsam on flypaper. There is also the meaning of attaching oneself to another as a servant, companion, or close associate. This is a very definite and direct statement of the relationship of the low to the middle self.

Long also analyzed the syllables separately:

Hi: Here we have the symbol of the flowing of vital force. This root means to flow away, as water. Doubled to make *hihi,* the meaning becomes a vine, and points directly to the other meanings (mana) held in the vine and water symbols.

Pi: "To sprinkle, as water with the fingers." Water refers to emotion, and here emotion has the attribute of being let go slowly.[2]

Thus the subconscious can be seen as consisting of shadowy threads that have the ability to cling, such as in the experience of unwelcome thoughts going around and around. In addition to meaning "vine," hihi also means "web" or "snare." If we remain ruled by our emotions, we make snares for ourselves. For example, a smell or a piece of music can have an association that triggers a feeling from the past. *Pīpī, pī* doubled, is the Hawaiian pearl oyster, which—at one stage in its development—is the embodiment of clinginess. As a result of its clinging nature, the subconscious is a creature of habit, and expects the future to be like the past, such as when someone who has been treated badly in past relationships subconsciously expects to be treated badly in future ones.

Hidden in the very meaning of its name is the teaching that the subconscious needs to learn to flow, rather than cling. Letting our emotions flow is an essential part of this. We should not cling to our feelings, cut them off, or bury them. Rather, we should express them appropriately. Our "water of life" should not be held in a dam, for the water of our subconscious is the source of mana for our middle and high selves. Without it we simply cannot create appropriately. My doctoral dissertation concerning the kaona of Hawaiian words gives further clues as to how we can move through the subconscious.

Each of the three minds can be associated with one of the primary Hawaiian gods. The subconscious mind is associated with the god Kū. After the imposition of the system of war and of human sacrifice upon the Hawaiians, Kū came to be associated with those violent acts. But violence is simply one possible manifestation of the power of the subconscious. There are many other possibilities too. The meanings of Kū's name give us a clue. They include "to stand" and to "have an erection." Kū represents the beginnings of power, when you are beginning to stand on your own, ready for a pleasurable journey perhaps. Kū also represents the power of the physical on earth. There are many epithets for Kū, each of which has its form on earth and represents a slightly different quality. They are known as his *kinolau,* or "bodies." According to Pukui, breadfruit is a body of Kū, as is the coconut tree. The young child is also a form of Kū. Finally, Kū is now associated with fishing as an organized enterprise, and the fruits of that fishing: the captured fish.

All these qualities are the qualities of the subconscious, which is our repository of memories, the cache from which we draw to make sense of each new encounter of life. The roots of the subconscious are deep, consisting of our primary relationship with the physical world, and give us access to power. However, it has limited awareness, so we often experience obstructions in understanding our intimate relationship with the world. We also need to learn to channel the energy creatively instead of destructively. That is why it is important for us to expand our dimensions to include the capacities of both the conscious and superconscious minds.

THE CONSCIOUS MIND

Kāholo i ka lani!

A voice reverberating in the heavens!
LINE FROM LIFE-GIVING PRAYER DEDICATED TO THE 'AUMĀKUA

According to Huna the next mind, the conscious mind, is associated with the ability to talk and listen and thus to process information and reason. We usually access it after the age of eight or so, and the function of formal schooling is to teach us how to operate according to our conscious mind. The conscious mind has many wonderful attributes. It has the ability to talk and reason. It's also the sensible mind, capable of discriminating.

The Western ideas most prevalent in the world are associated with this mind. They include the gods of "education," "development," "ownership," "medicine," "progress," and "research." Some associated buzzwords are *rational, inferior, terminal, viable,* and *nonviable.* The use of the conscious mind without the involvement of the Higher Self is responsible for a great deal of the ills of this world, such as colonization (associated with "development" and the gathering of others' resources for "ownership"), pollution (associated with "progress" and the misuse of "resources"), and the mind-body separation, shown by the word *rational.*

Ultimately, the conscious mind needs to be a channel for the Higher Self, which the Hawaiian root meanings show us. The Hawaiian word for the conscious mind is *'uhane,* about which Long commented: "From the shortness of the word and the little descriptive matter carried in its roots it is to be seen that the kahuna of old did not believe that the middle self had much native ability other than that of using inductive reason."[3]

Long notes that in uhane, the letter *u* carries the connotation of separation. Like the subconscious, the conscious mind is a separate and independent unit of consciousness. It is important to understand that the separate existence of the conscious mind is not eternal; as Moke Kupihea wrote: "The 'uhane, as the life spirit, has evolved solely to serve one's current existence. Unlike the 'aumakua, it has never lived a prior life, and once this life is done, its consciousness will cease to exist."[4]

To continue Long's translation, the *hā* is a "pipe or channel for water," and indicates the ability of the middle self to take and convey the vital force made by the low self. *Nē* means "to talk or whisper." Thus, the conscious mind can take force from the subconscious and talk or whisper weakly on its own. It needs to convey the water of our emotions appropriately—by talking or whispering.

The conscious mind can be conceived of as "the mind in the middle," between the subconscious and the superconscious. How well it works is determined by the energy it receives from the subconscious and the inspiration it receives from the superconscious. If our subconscious energy is going in a different direction from our conscious focus, it will not support the learning capacity of the conscious mind. And if the conscious mind closes itself off from the influence of the Higher Self, then all it can do is repeat information. Unfortunately, many revered academics, even at the most famous universities where I have studied, seem to repeat the same thing over and again. This is because they're not in touch with their unacknowledged Higher Self.

The ability to repeat information is reflected in the interpretation of the conscious mind as the god Lono, who is particularly associated with the sense of hearing. The dictionary meanings of Lono include "news, report, tidings." Another meaning of Lono is "to resound." One must listen to "the voice reverberating in the heavens." Then one must respond. He is also associated with the rain, *ua*. Linguistically, ua is a sign that "an action has been completed," and the falling of gentle rain is said to be a sign that a prayer to Lono has been answered. It is also a sign that the humans calling on him are growing in wisdom. One proverb is:

No'eau ka hana a ka ua; akamai ka 'imina o ka no'ono'o

Clever are the deeds of the rain; wise in seeking knowledge.

The interaction between gods and humans is ongoing, as exemplified by the five-day ritual I participated in on the island of Kahoʻolawe. It was part of the celebration of the Makahiki festival, which welcomes Lono back to Hawaiʻi each year, chiming with the reappearance of the Pleiades. The dedication ceremony was held at the simple stone temples in the valley of Hakiowa. The day dawned cool, and the clouds were hanging low over the island. After dressing in white *kīkepa* (unbleached muslin cloth) and preparing our offerings, we lined up barefoot. The women left their offerings, wrapped in ti leaves, at the Hale o Papa, or "women's temple," and the men left theirs at the Hale Mua, or "men's temple." Many of us could feel Lono's presence, especially when a light rain began to fall and the face of a gentle and bearded man appeared in the shining clouds above the Hale Mua. No one seemed particularly surprised, for it is understood that when rituals are done properly, Lono may appear. I believe Lono's presence was a sign of affirmation of the way the land is being reinvigorated and cared for again.

Lono is also often seen as the god of agriculture and growth, appearing in many forms, from the gourd plant to the pig to the sweet potato. Learning about the ways of Lono is akin to growing in wisdom and tenderness; thus, a way to describe someone who is very knowledgeable is *he ipu ka ʻeo,* or "a gourd full of knowledge." That person has grown, like the gourd plant. In the growing the person has opened to the knowledge of the third mind, the superconscious.

THE SUPERCONSCIOUS

The superconscious Mind of Light.

MAX FREEDOM LONG

The superconscious is the source of all: stretching over everything like a great sky of light, holding everything like a great eye of night, containing everything like a great sigh of delight. The "Sky Mind," as the Tibetans call it, is our eternal soul, encompassing the realms of the angels, the gods and goddesses, and the source of all. It is the higher mind that contains all knowledge. It is the source of our intuition and our transcendent "knowing." Tuning in to it enables us to bring qualities of harmony, bliss, and unconditional love into our lives.

An exploration of the root words composing the Hawaiian word for the superconscious mind—*'aumakua*—can help us to understand the nature of this Mind of Light. As we have seen, the 'aumākua are the spirits of one's ancestors that sometimes appear in totemic form to offer guidance. According to Long, *makua* gives "the meaning of parent," conveying the sense of the superconscious as being like an "older, entirely trustworthy parental self."[5] However, when all the root meanings are looked into, this word also has a broader interpretation, as Long pointed out:

> *Au*, a self, also a period of time, a flow of water, an action of mind, and a condition in which one is entirely engaged in a certain course of action or in a course of conduct.
>
> *Mā* is to entwine as a vine.
>
> *Kua* is the high point of a land, as a mountain, giving the symbol of the High Self as higher or more evolved than the middle or low selves.[6]

Long gave the further elaboration that "the word *akua* has been translated 'God,' but it has more nearly the meaning of a higher being."[7]

I learned about 'aumakua through my first experience of traveling to Hawai'i. I began my journey by engaging my mind in *au*: making the decision to travel to Polynesia, and so allowing the universe to combine the necessary circumstances and make it possible. Enough money for my flight duly arrived. Just before I left for Hawai'i, I was given a statue of an owl at The Mystical Society at Cambridge University. It was the first sign of owl being my 'aumakua.

The next participle, *mā*, "to entwine as a vine," brought in more of my Higher Self. For instance, I traveled very cheaply, hitchhiking and not even having fifty dollars in emergency money for a night in a motel. I had to camp outside and couldn't even afford a tent. I was rather exposed, and more worried about men than weather! One night, a couple of Polynesian men came up when I was asleep in my sleeping bag by the ocean and shone a flashlight in my face. I thought, "Whoops, now they will have discovered I'm a girl; I just have to trust." One of them told me roughly to go with him. I got up, picking up my sleeping bag and bringing my backpack with me. I joined him in his beach camp, where he gave me his hammock, strung against some coconut trees. I never had any hassle from him; indeed, he offered me food and I "hung out" with him and his girlfriend. Luck or trust? I have had many such experiences and I am convinced they have to do with letting the superconscious flow. In other words, they have to do with trust. Indeed, if I had not traveled around Hawai'i so poor and so vulnerable, I would not have gained half the information I did. The vine of consciousness was being woven around my Higher Self.

The last element of the word is *kua*, "a high point of land." One day, I was sitting right on the edge of a cliff, where it jutted out over precipitous rocky valleys falling far, far away. Suspended in the bright afternoon, I felt like I was at the point where this world meets the next. The splendor of nature was helping to soothe my pain at being in love with a man who was busy denying his love for me as well as his own Higher Self. Then a *pueo,* or owl, flew alongside, pausing next to me when he was close enough to touch. For a moment our consciousness hovered over chasms and canyons as we stared into the depths of each other's eyes. Now the shivers the owl gave me remain together with the shivers the guy gave me. And they make me feel better. The owl was part of the hope, light, height, and perception of the Higher Self.

But I had no idea what was going at the time. I did not go through each syllable of 'aumakua, thinking "this-and-this-should happen." I had hardly even heard of the word! Rather, "I" got out of the way and allowed the universe to work its magic, enabling me to understand firsthand how 'aumakua can mean a spirit being appearing in the form of a creature. Animals, like all of us, are from the superconscious Mind of Light, and the gift of an owl on an island a long way away had begun the journey that was to help me access my Higher Self.

When we understand that our true nature is not a separated is.land but a flow in which we participate with all of creation, then our actions are integrated, gently entwined with the beingness of all. That naturally guides our evolution to more light-filled perspectives. *Makua* also means "the main stalk of a plant." The superconscious mind is the "main stalk" around which the other minds are entwined. It is the blueprint on which the other minds are based.

While the subconscious roughly conforms to Freud's idea of the unconscious, the Huna concept of the superconscious is similar to Carl Jung's idea of the collective unconscious; he saw it as a source of revelation, a symbol for God. Despite Jung's interest in it and many interesting scientific experiments that would appear to indicate its existence, there is still little general understanding of the superconscious mind in the West. Some people have experienced it in "near-death experiences," where they talk about a radiant light and an experience of utter bliss and peace and being enveloped by absolute love. And, in fact, most of us have experienced its presence at one time or another: the superconscious is the source of our "knowing" things we can have no conscious way of knowing. There have been many, many documented instances of this kind of enhanced perception.

Although nothing is more important than the knowledge of the superconscious mind, we normally access it only occasionally and often inadvertently, such as in times of crisis or danger or when a great discovery comes as the result of a "dream" or a "vision." Albert Einstein, for instance, had a dream of sliding down a sunbeam, then becoming the light itself, which led to his formulation of the theory of relativity. But we can develop our relationship with the superconscious. One way is to heighten our awareness of when it is "speaking" to us: the superconscious mind, unlike the much denser subconscious, is recognized by its lightness and clarity. Messages from the superconscious mind flow *(au)* quickly and easily, come naturally. When we do feel our superconscious, then "Ah!" There is power, there is beauty, there is magic, there is light.

It is even possible for us to learn to access the superconscious on demand and find ourselves capable of "extraordinary" capacities *on a regular basis.* Communication with the wider fabric of aka—which we call the universe—will no longer be in snippets. We will have learned, without doubt, that the action of consciousness and force upon matter makes up the universe and that we are co-creators of that universe. One who has learned to do that may truly be called a kahuna, one who is more *conscious* than most: one who bursts with the inner sunrise, one who is living in the light. Kāne, the great god of peace, is the Hawaiian god most associated with that clear mind. Interestingly, Kāne was never represented by an image, only by a stone standing upright, the *Pōhaku o Kāne.* The "undressed stone" that points to the heavens is a wonderful symbol for the power of our superconscious to link disparate spheres.

UNITING THE MINDS

And although self-awareness leads you to greater
freedom and power
It will also bring you pain
For the dawning of a higher consciousness will destroy
the only reality you have known
And as you become more conscious, your shadow will
loom larger than before
For when you step into the light, you may not see
its radiance . . .

KRISTIN ZAMBUCKA

In the ideal state, the three minds function as one and are then represented by another god, Kanaloa. Kanaloa is the god of the oceans, another wonderful symbol of expansiveness. Kanaloa is also associated with bananas, ocean life, and the island of Kahoʻolawe. It could be said that the ritual of Lono related earlier is a way to reach the integrated state of Kanaloa. But first the reunion between the minds must be made, and the degree of connection to the superconscious depends on how well the conscious and subconscious minds are united. There is another way of putting it: The journey through the three minds is a journey into the light.

Just as any bright light creates deep shadows, a lot of "shadows" will appear when we try to join our subconscious and conscious minds to the "radiance" of the superconscious mind. They can be from both our subconscious and our conscious minds and can initially be so strong that they provoke doubts about why we are on such a path, and why we can't be more "normal." That is all quite natural.

Our conscious mind can often block our passage into the light with its judgments such as "that doesn't make sense," which rise up whenever we have a spiritual experience. Indeed, society encourages us to follow those rationalizations, so it's easy for us to do. For instance, we often are encouraged to put material values first, and to study something "useful" at university. Then we need to get married, get a mortgage, get the children educated . . . and, lo and behold, we're being sensible, even though we may feel "stuck."

Animals provide us with a good example of an alternative approach, for they simply do not have these particular problems. They know a direct link between their subconscious and superconscious, without needing to go through their conscious mind. For example, if a monkey by the side of a road on a mountainside in Nepal feels like picking another monkey's fleas, then that is exactly what he is going to do. He is not worried about judgment, by either himself, the other monkey, or anything watching! One of the things we humans need to learn to do is go beyond our conscious mind. That is why so many religions and teachers talk about the necessity of "stopping judgments": they get in the way of manifesting our greater light.

The other main way we block ourselves is through the emotions of our subconscious mind. Our *subconscious* wishes can be so strong that we may be able to persuade ourselves that a wish such as "I know so-and-so is the right person for me, I just feel it" is an insight coming from the superconscious. Many things are hidden in the subconscious mind, which works "secretly" and "furtively" and does not like change. We saw that another word for the subconscious mind is Kū, and the meanings of Kū include "standing." Unless an idea is deliberately brought out of the subconscious mind into the light of the two brighter minds, it will stay there indefinitely, like a rock obstructing the flow of light.

The subconscious *doesn't want to change;* it loves repeating patterns. Repeating patterns are not bad in themselves; in fact, the world around us constantly displays them. New flowers on trees blossom in the same way as old ones; each new offshoot follows the same pattern as previous leaves. In temperate climates the colors change with the seasons: the greens of spring give way to the golds of summer, to the oranges of autumn, to the whites of winter, and then the green shoots poke through the snow again. This cycle repeats itself year after year, giving us feelings of constancy in the midst of change. But when our patterns are *unwanted* (when our perspective has changed, but our patterns haven't), that is when we want to get rid of them.

This is one of the places we encounter the difficulties of our minds wanting to work independently. Our conscious mind may tell us one thing, but our subconscious is in the same old rut. Affirmations such as "I am good enough" don't work if our subconscious sabotages them by saying: "I'm not good enough, really." Likewise, if a person wants more money but feels unworthy, he either won't make it or will make it and lose it.

To make matters worse, we don't really know how to listen to our superconscious mind. The lack of alignment between the minds leads to a lessening of mana, because focus is lost. It can also mean that our subconscious complexes and fears become much stronger. This exposes us not only to our own negative energies but also to those of others. For example, the death prayer, 'anā'anā, works only if it tunes in to someone's complexes. If there is nothing to "stick to" in the shadowy body of the subconscious, then the prayer cannot work. So in the case of the Irishman being "prayed to death," the kahuna had to have tuned in to one of his complexes, perhaps a Catholic sense that sex without marriage is a sin, leading him to *subconsciously* regard his alliance with the girl as morally wrong.

When we feel discouraged by how we are stuck in subconscious patterns, it helps to look from the perspective of Huna, which sees the world, composed of aka, as inherently moving. An additional meaning of *ka* is "to send out a vine." *A* means "acquired by" and there you have *aka!* However, as we have seen, Huna also teaches that there is more involved than simply releasing the subconscious and using that as an excuse for doing whatever we want, whomever we may hurt in the process. The subconscious needs to flow with *direction* or directed consciousness. In other words, we need to carefully decide what we want.

The dim silvery aka can be properly brightened only by applying directed consciousness, a vital component of mana. And not just once, but again and again. Consistency is vital. Another implied meaning of mana is that of steadiness: *ma* indicates "place" and *na* means "belonging to." The way an idea is drilled into the subconscious mind is through repetition. If we flit back and forth among many thoughts, the mana will attach itself to each fleeting one. The result will be that only insignificant ideas will be able to manifest, or a major idea will manifest only for a short time before the mind becomes distracted. When the direction from the conscious mind is *constant,* the unconscious mind will work with the conscious mind to "glue" mana to the sticky aka of the idea and bring it into being.

Each of us, whether we know it or not, is symbolically standing in the middle of the glowing aka, on the pulse of a luminous world, tugging on the sticky threads we create, responsible for everything we see. Nothing is important or unimportant in itself; everything has the significance we attach to it. By attaching significance and meaning we are attracting mana. Where there is mana, the energy is so great that more mana will come. In this way, the particular world we create for ourselves out of the luminous egglike substance of the fetal aka—which could have developed in any of a million ways—is reinforced until finally, and inevitably, we come to believe: "That is the way the world is!"

Once we've created a "skeleton of belief," of meaning, to link our conscious and subconscious minds, everything that fits into it is significant. Of course we then encounter things that don't fit, and there is a natural tendency to label such things as "wrong." But Huna reminds us that structures are not rigid: that the world, and everything in it, is always moving and expanding. Things that don't fit are there for a reason: we can learn from them and so grow the branches of our structure. Everything has a message to bring, to be understood according to our level of awareness. Ultimately this perspective results in our finding that we live in a dense, many textured world of significance. Along with that, we learn from experience that a negative is a negative only from a certain perspective. Viewed from a *Kua*, or higher perspective, *everything is perfect.*

Not only that: When we realize that everything is connected by the action of our mana-collecting thoughts in the aka, we don't just see a thing, *we are it!* The glowing aka is in our image, our likeness. Then we will be well on the way to manifesting the power of akua, or the fullness of completion.

THE GRACE OF SYNCHRONICITY

Ye blessed creatures, I have heard the call!
WILLIAM WORDSWORTH

The superconscious works in synchrony with other people, other minds of grace. That's why we often know the same thing at the same time. I was on the South Island of New Zealand with my then boyfriend. We shared an old green Ford van we were very fond of and had named it Rasputin. Despite his advanced years, Rasputin would perform incredible feats such as going up snowy mountains and through bubbling mountain streams *when our emotions were clear.* When they weren't, and our subconscious feelings shadowed our conscious minds, Rasputin would conk out, often literally on a harsh word in a fight. When we made up, the van would duly start.

I had the feeling I should break up with that boyfriend: I loved him, he was a wonderful guy, but he simply didn't feel like he was "the one for me." However, I thought to myself, "I'll leave it a few weeks longer." But not acting on your intuition can be dangerous! We had decided to travel to Fox, a glacier on New Zealand's west coast. However, I wasn't feeling comfortable and our emotions were running high. As we stopped driving to fill our water bottle in a mountain stream, I said to him suddenly, not knowing where the words came from: "If we carry on driving today, we're going to have a crash." He replied, "I know." *Our intuition was coming from the same place.* And then we looked at each other and said: "Should we carry on driving?" and we decided we would, regardless, as we didn't want to "waste time." As we were getting back into Rasputin I thought, "Should I do up my seat belt?" My whole life flashed before me in sequence and I thought, as though I was someone else, "I've been through too much to die now," and did it up.

The crash itself was utterly painless. I just remember my boyfriend saying: "We're slipping." Apparently Rasputin turned over several times on the mountain pass and landed upright, having not fallen over the edge or smashed into the rock wall or caught fire! Officials later told us that there had been several accidents on that bend, but we were the only nonfatal one. Without a seat belt, my head would have been smashed to a pulp, the way the cans of food traveling with us were. But we were pretty much fine.

The accident didn't shake me up as much as it might otherwise have done because *I had known about it before it happened.* I had been warned and the warning came from something far bigger than myself. Soon after I arrived in hospital, I had the feeling I should ring my mother in England to let her know. Normally I would have waited to tell her until I saw her again and she could see for herself that I was all right. But this time I *knew* I should ring her. She picked up the telephone immediately because she was sitting right next to it, researching the prices of flights to New Zealand. She told me that she had been out in her garden in the English summer when "something told her" I'd been in an accident "with that bloody van." She had "picked up" on what had happened to me through the medium of the superconscious, where distance means nothing.

Sheldrake called the shared access to the superconscious "morphic resonance." He explains how morphic fields "link together members of social groups and can continue to connect them even when they are far apart. These invisible bonds act as channels for telepathic communication between animals, people and animals, and people and people."[8]

This concept is far more important than it might first seem, because—unlike every traditional society in the world—people of the West are used to looking at events as "things in themselves." We don't see how they are connected to the pattern running through everything. When we *do* see it, our entire consciousness changes. As the physicist Buryl Payne wrote:

> If we look at events as something more like fields, focal points of energy, or informational flow patterns [patterns of energy change], and if we attend more to the wholeness of the field rather than the individual points within the field we will find our lives—and our consciousness—expanding enormously.
>
> From the field point of view, we are not separate from the universe which spawned us, but are instead multidimensional beings consisting of complex knots of organic fields, patterned structures of proteins, fats, carbohydrates, and minerals connected to the vegetable and animal kingdoms . . . our living and choosing form parts of fields . . . that transcend space-time, extending to all the realities that were, are, might have been, or will be. We extend in all directions, into all dimensions and are all interconnected. The We-Field comprises the entire universe in one whole.[9]

Although this may seem a bizarre or "far-out" notion, it carries more validity than the viewpoint held by most people. We cannot separate ourselves from our world or from each other any more than time, space, matter, energy, form, and consciousness can be split asunder. Mind and universe are as inseparable as front and back.

A striking example of this concept has been observed in the animal kingdom. In what has become known as the Hundredth Monkey Theory, scientists on an island off Japan managed to teach a group of monkeys to wash their sweet potatoes in the sea before eating them. *At the same time* another group of scientists on another island reported "their" monkeys suddenly began doing the same thing.

This could be similar to the power of "coincidence" Jung named "synchronicity." Jung found many examples of this in his life, which he backed up with scientific experiments; indeed his work has achieved general credence and respectability. His life ended with a striking example of synchronicity: When he died, the favorite tree in his garden in Switzerland was struck by lightning and killed *at the same time*.

A similar thing took place when the young Derek Bentley was executed: His family members were all sitting in their living room, suffering with him as he was put to death, when the clock in the room stopped (and it has not worked since). It was a spooky echo of W. H. Auden's *Funeral Blues*:

Stop all the clocks, cut off the telephone,
Prevent the dog from barking with a juicy bone,
Silence the pianos and with muffled drum,
Bring out the coffin, let the mourners come.[10]

The family found out later that the clock stopped at the exact moment of Derek's death, through the force of the young Derek's dying consciousness. This shows the principle of synchronicity at work through the resonance of the superconscious mind. Still, conventional Western medicine has tended to work with just two minds, the conscious and the subconscious. Most doctors are as yet unaware of the mind that can help us heal—or even stop us from having "accidents" at all—the High Self, or the superconscious. Although the influence of the mind on the vital forces of the body is becoming more accepted in the West, it is usually in the context of how we can prevent disease, rather than how we can become really healthy. Perhaps that is because the way the superconscious works isn't understood yet. It works on what Long aptly calls *mana loa*, "long power," miracle power, strong enough to reverse the things we are used to. One kahuna said of it, "Here is the trustworthy one! The one who gathers and directs and projects the light to fruit."

USING OUR POWER

E lawe i ke aʻo a mālama, a e ʻoi mau ka noʻeau

*He who takes his teachings and applies them
increases his knowledge.*

HAWAIIAN PROVERB

When we begin to open up to things we were previously closed to, our world changes. It literally becomes lighter. We have created more mana, so colors seem much brighter and bodies much lighter. It is almost as if things previously separate—such as people on a street—seem to flow into each other. Having left judgment behind, we gain a sense that everything is in its proper place.

Along with this comes a greater faith in the wider pattern, even in times of trouble. And there can be many "times of trouble" if we become aware of our newly generated power before learning *what to do with it.* When we have not consciously chosen our course, there can be so much free-floating energy around that chaos may seem to blast us along in our tracks. This is a time when people become particularly vulnerable to the allure of dope or harder drugs, "to open up even more," but such things do not direct with consciousness. Only our Higher Self can do that. It is also a time when others become involved in religious cults that take over the body, mind, and emerging spirit, giving up thinking for themselves because of their fear of their own potential power. Erich Fromm wrote a highly regarded essay, *The Fear of Freedom,* analyzing the appeal of dictators from this point of view. Indeed there is one ex-Yugoslav who loves living under dictators so much that he moves from country to country to find one.

In order to avoid these dangers, we need to *learn* how to use our newfound power. The mana we build with must have structure in order to last. For this we need principles, which form the basis of our "skeleton of power." Without principles we will still be able to create things, if our mana is strong, but they will not endure. By "principles" I mean consistently held beliefs with the strong roots of a moral basis that is appropriate for us.

A close look at word meanings once again is very helpful to guide our use of power: *mana* means "branch" as well as "root." One way to determine whether a principle is truly our root is to see whether or not it is limited to the area of life it directly affects. It should branch, stretch across into other areas. The principle of honesty, for instance, shouldn't work only in the arena of personal relationships, but also needs to be lived in the financial arena. Without principles, our lives are based on shifting castles of sand: we worry about getting "found out," so of course we subconsciously attract that and cause it to happen! On the other hand, when we integrate our three minds and direct our mana according to our principles, we grow in confidence.

True confidence is something that is gained, not granted, which was reflected by the rigorous programs of testing adopted by intending practitioners of Hawaiian magic. The final test for followers of one kahuna (and sometimes it was final in more ways than one) consisted of a demonstration of the power of thoughts even over "natural laws." Initiates were given a very strong poison to drink and left on the beach overnight, a test based on the Huna teaching that the body is made up of *aka,* held together by mana. Some died, some lived. It is likely the missing ingredient in those who died was *confidence* that their magic was stronger than the "natural laws" of poison. If there was any doubt at all, leakage would occur in the mana that holds the body together. The initiate who lived, on the other hand, had truly learned how to use the *mana loa,* the miracle power, the greatest power of all.

As we shall see in our exploration of the techniques of ancient Hawaiian wisdom in the next few chapters, Huna includes effective techniques for removing the shadows and blocks generated by both the conscious and the subconscious minds. In the next chapter we look at the hula dance—a system of directing consciousness that is practiced throughout Hawai'i—as a guide for anyone desiring to brighten his or her light.

6

Opening the Colors of Light: The Hula Dance

O white light,
broken into the many hues of the rainbow,
lighten our path,
that we may see into the invisible.

POLYNESIAN CHANT

One of the most famous aspects of Hawaiian culture is its traditional dance, the hula. Have a cocktail at any expensive hotel in Hawai'i and there will usually be a hula performance. Hula dances are so prevalent at tourist venues that the hula is usually viewed as "something for the tourists," capturing the essence of balmy tropical nights, the scent of frangipani in the warm air, and the sound of 'ukulele. Girls wear grass skirts and wiggle their hips, coconut shells poised precariously over thrusting breasts. Men wear loincloths and may thrust their spears. It seems that eroticism can be more of a focus than the dance, conveying the sense that something sexy can't have any meaning apart from the obvious.

What is not well known is that—unlike the *hula 'auana,* the "tourist hula"—the traditional hula dance is a system of shamanism, a ritualistic way of "opening up," of focusing the consciousness of the dancer. In

this chapter, we will explore some of the factors that reveal the shamanistic role of the hula, including its ritualistic properties, the hidden
meanings of the words that always accompany the dance, and the fact
that each technique of the dance is named for a color, which is associated with an emotion.

A hula dancer must learn to master each "color of emotion," and in
the process of doing so make his or her own journey toward the light.
The dancers' lessons in light can help us to increase our consciousness
and "see into the invisible." However, as we explore the deeper meanings of the hula, we must always remember that the dance holds all the
colors of light. Just as we can see only a small part of the spectrum of
light, we can see only a small part of the dimensions of the dance.

THE TRADITIONAL HULA

*In a ritual, the world as lived, and the world as imag-
ined, fused under the agency of a single set of symbolic
forms, turn out to be the same world.*

CLIFFORD GEERTZ

The use of ritual to transform one's world into a desired world, by fus-
ing together "symbolic forms," can be seen in the form, and agency, of
the traditional hula. Although many anthropologists have not seen the
traditional hula as a ritual, it was, and still may be, a religious ritual in
the fullest sense of the word. It demonstrates all the characteristics of one:
being performed at certain places, in certain specific ways, under certain
conditions, to produce certain effects—namely, to contact the sacred.

Dances were performed at night, lit by kukui nut flares, symbols of
enlightenment. The nights of the full moon (another symbol of enlightenment) were particularly popular! The dances were accompanied at
every stage by chanting and offerings to the gods. Pukui described the traditional gathering of greenery for the altar: the dancer "started at dawn
when silence ruled, uttering his prayers on the way and as he reached
forth his hand to gather each necessary plant he should have no fear."[1]

Dances were performed in certain places: primarily at the *hālau hula,* or "houses of the hula," where the dancers would live, learn, and perform. The hālau hula were mainly self-supporting, being dependent on the gifts that the audience would give them in return for their enjoyment of the dance. The hālau were often attached to the courts of the *aliʻi,* or kings and chiefs, where the dancers might compose and perform dances to mark special occasions in the life of the court.

Each dance troupe had a leader, called the *kumu hula,* who introduced the dance and beat the time. Some dances were named after the accompanying instruments. The *hula ʻohe ihu* was "the dance of the nose flute"; the *hula uliuli,* "the dance of the feathered gourds"; and the *hula pūniu,* "the dance of the thigh drum." In Hawaiʻi, the same dances were performed by both sexes. This contrasts with many other parts of Polynesia, such as New Zealand, where men and women usually do separate dances: the men do the resounding war dance, known as the *haka,* and the women must perform more graceful dances, with lots of wrist movements. But in Hawaiʻi, both dance the same dance. That is because differences lie in the *interpretation* of the dance, not in the gender of the dancer. The dances of Hawaiʻi were open to men and women of any age or appearance. Mary Pukui wrote that there were "dances for everyone, standing dances for those whose limbs were young and spry and sitting dances for those who preferred to sit like the aged and over-plump."[2]

The dancers chanted in time, and wore similar garb. Originally women were bare-breasted, and their breasts rose above a wraparound skirt made of beaten tapa that shone like the moon. They adorned themselves with a circlet of flowers around their hair, and had anklets and wrist bands made of feathers and flowers. Men were fringed with necklets, anklets, and bracelets of shark or dog teeth and wore loincloths that flapped with their vigorous movements.

Control of the thoughts and emotions—another characteristic of ritual—was an important aspect of a dancer's training. The dancer would usually be apprenticed at the age of seven, and during the first stage of training, which took over a decade, every aspect of the dancer's life was totally controlled. Often the budding "little flowers" were not allowed to speak and they were even told what to think, a level of control that would be unthinkable in dance schools of the West. There was great emphasis on growing consciousness, like a sacred plant, in the hula. My favorite description of the process of learning hula is this one:

I kupu ke a'a i ke kumu
I lau a puka ka mu'o.

That the root may grow from the source
That the shoot may put forth and leaf.[3]

The *kumu,* "root," is the hula teacher; the shoot is the pupil, building up his or her green consciousness through exposure to light.

Great care was taken with every detail, even down to the facial expressions of the dancers. An early diplomat, Théodore-Adolphe Barrot, wrote that it was as if the dancers "were moved by the same impulse of thought and will."[4] When they performed for a chief or king, the singing dancers, appearing all of a piece, were seen as increasing the mana of the ali'i. Yet the impression of uniformity and the resulting mana could be—and often was—undermined by a particular dancer's interpretation of the hidden meanings of the words he or she was singing, perhaps the most important of the shamanistic qualities of the hula dance.

All hula dances need to have words to them. These vowel-laden words sound chanted when sung to the rhythm of the accompaniment. The chants themselves were known as *mele,* which means "yellow" as well as "song." Both these qualities have the ability to take flight and reach the sacred. The voice is an important connector, and so is color, particularly a bright color like yellow. As we will see, there are hidden meanings in all the words of the chants, which, as we have noted earlier, have been passed down through the generations with great attention to their accuracy.

Today, the appearance of the dance has certainly altered. The dances are usually lit by artificial lighting and the dancers wear imported grass skirts or brightly printed cotton ones. Yet the substance of the dance has not changed. The dancers still dance the same dances and chant the same chants—though for the tourists, not for the ali'i. Every troupe has its kumu and the hālau still exist (although part-time), as do the musical instruments. In hula competitions and for particular rituals, dancers are encouraged to make their own costumes, which they do while chanting in Hawaiian. Each dancer learns the same "skeleton of knowledge," and the dancers creatively understand and use that knowledge in different ways. Many use it to help them toward enlightenment. Whether understood and actualized by all practitioners or not, the potent shamanistic properties of the hula have been preserved and are being taught to the few who are ready to learn.

As in the past, understanding is differentiated through the hidden meanings of the words chanted along with the dance and its preparations, so the first aspect of the hula we will look into is the accompanying chants: great examples of poetry in motion.

SEXUAL MEANINGS OF THE HULA

The oral literature is pregnant with kaona, *"hidden meanings," frequently erotic. It is a game all Hawaiians play, often more deftly than Western psychoanalysts . . .*
MARSHALL SAHLINS

Perhaps because Hawaiian is an oral tradition, being passed on through chants, it often hasn't been thought worthy of serious study. Yet Hawaiian remains a wonderfully expressive and evocative language, and the poetry of the wonderful hula chants deserves to be ranked with the great literary traditions of the world. It has been said that one of the reasons Shakespeare was such a great writer was because the words he used are "polysemous": they can be interpreted in different ways. In the same way, the Hawaiian "unwritten literature" is indeed great, as will be revealed by the illumination of even a tiny part of the intricate mosaic of Hawaiian verse.

Sexual meanings are a famous way of interpreting the "hidden meanings" of the chants. A sexual meaning can be found in every Hawaiian song by someone who knows what to look for. And—as we will explore in the next chapter—sexuality can also be a shamanic way of opening up consciousness. However, I want to stress that this is only *one* of the ways of understanding the hidden meanings of the hula.

The chants often begin by an appreciation of beauty, just as happens with one's desired lover. The songs of the hula all refer to the natural beauties of the islands, which are a metaphor for other things. Here is the chant for the *hula pā ipu*, or "dance of the gourd drum," performed by kneeling and playing the gourds:

> *Lau lehua pūnoni ula ke kai o Kona,*
> *Ke kai pūnoni 'ula i 'ōweo 'ia,*
> *wewena 'ula ke kai lā, he kō Kona . . .*

> *Leaf of lehua and noni tint the Kona sea,*
> *iridescent saffron and red,*
> *changeable watered red, peculiar to Kona . . .*[5]

This seems to be an innocent comparison of the sea to certain trees, the red-blossomed *lehua*, symbol of the Big Island, and the famous *noni*, the Indian mulberry tree, which bears pale yellow fruits. Notice is taken of the way the sea is always certain shades of red, peculiar to the area around Kona on the Big Island. However, colors always have sexual meanings, and the Hawaiians associate red, just as we do, with blazing passion. The next few lines are:

> *'Ula ia kini i ke uka o 'Alaea*
> *I hili ahi 'ula i ke kapa a ka wahine,*
> *I hō'eu ia e ka ni'a, e ke hana.*

> *Red are the uplands, 'Alaea,*
> *Ah, 'tis the flame red, stained robes of women*
> *Much tossed by caress or desire.*

'Alaea is the name of a place, but is also the red of the rainbow and the "flesh-like redness, especially the dark red meat close to the spine of some fish." So although *ahi* and *'ula* are the words that actually mean "flame red," we can see how the theme stretches. The reddened robes of women "much tossed by caress or desire" take up the theme of the changeable sea peculiar to Kona.

The chant goes on and the hidden sexual meanings become overt:

E ke 'auwai lino mai la a kēhau
He hau ho'omoe ka lau o ka niu
Ke oho o ka lā'au, lauoho loloa.

The weed tangled waterway shines like a rope of pearls,
Dew-pearls that droop like the coconut leaf,
The hair of the trees, their long locks.

Here, the "hair of the trees" is a woman's pubic hair and the "weed tangled waterway" marks the access to her hidden part. She is sexually excited and shining like "a rope of pearls." According to Nathaniel Emerson, researcher into Hawaiian traditions, this chant is ostensibly about "the period of intercourse between the North and South Pacific." The man is usually of the north and the woman of the south. The chant goes on to say the fisher "drops hook" and invades "the holy of holies," the woman's private sanctuary. In the next verse the storms come and the "birds" seek cover, and then they are "cooled and appeased by the rain mist" and rest quietly.

Another example of the sexual meanings hidden in the chants can be seen in just one line, traditionally sung by a weary traveler as he stands at the door of a hālau hula, requesting to be let in:

He pua 'oni ke kanaka.

A fickle flower is man.[6]

He means "a," as in "a tree," and also "the dividing line between lands," not inappropriate for a song of admission. In another sense it means "a grave to be buried in." *Pua* is a "flower" or "blossom," which particularly refers to the sweet-tasting and tempting sugarcane, used in love magic. *Pua* also means "to come forth," a pun, perhaps, on the part of the body a man is fickle with, as '*oni,* the word for "fickle," in the form of *oni,* also means "to jut out" and "to squirm or wriggle." *Ke* means "the" and "to criticize," especially a hula master to his pupils. *Kanaka* means "a man" as well as "clitoris"! So there we have what may seem like unrelated meanings, but they all tune in to each other and help illuminate the general meaning of the fickle nature of man and his position in trying to gain admission to the hālau hula—or a woman.

These are but a few examples of the sexual meanings to be found in every chant and in virtually every word—when they are looked for—but sexual innuendos are not the only hidden meanings. Let's look further at some other shamanic meanings of the hula.

DANCING THE DREAM AWAKE

The erotic dancing of the tropical islands of Polynesia . . .
was designed to stimulate and bring into action the mana
of the gods, who were believed to be motivated by the
same emotions as men . . .

DOUGLAS OLIVER

The "erotic dancing" of Polynesia may indeed help wake up the gods and goddesses. It also helps wake up the dancers and ourselves. Shakespeare's famous observation that "life is but a dream, and men and women merely players" reflects the starting point of the consciousness of a hula dancer—and of all who share the goal of waking up consciousness to life. What I am about to write concerning the hula has never been written about before. It is something the Hawaiians have kept secret, even in their teaching, because that way only those ready to learn would learn. *The hula contains specific techniques to widen consciousness.* The dance is a passage from pō, the world of darkness, to ao, the world of light. The aim of the dancers is to open up their consciousness and dance toward the much more powerful consciousness of the gods and goddesses: to transform their aka into akua.

The first aspect of the hula used to do this is the most apparently obvious: movement. The movement of the dance is significant, as it mirrors the movement of the creation of the earth. When the darkness, the pō, forms, then the earth begins to move. The hula dramatizes the process of creation expressed by the *Kumulipo*'s "darkness slips into light" through its use of the imagery of the moon, particularly the crescent moon. The movement of the dance begins with *hoaka,* which means "to open the mouth." Hoaka—formed from *ho* (the causative prefix that makes things happen) and *aka* (which, as we have seen, means "glimmer" as well as "essence")—also means "to glitter" and "the crescent moon." Hoaka, then, is a stronger light than aka, which is "the glimmer that *precedes* the rising of the moon." It is a signal of growing consciousness: *the opening itself creates light.*

Then the dancers consciously re-create the shape of the crescent moon, knotting their skirts in the "horn-of-the-moon" position and moving their pelvises in elliptic circles like the moon. The dancers must grow their light through the moon. The crescent moon motif is seen throughout Hawai'i, carved onto drums and woven into feathered cloaks. The symbol helps bring mana: one's light grows like the light of the waxing moon. The association between light and enlightenment is also expressed by Dr. Jacob Liberman, a physician on Maui who does light therapy:

> I see the human organism as a net. When the net is clear, the water flows unimpeded. I believe enlightenment is the ability to allow life's experiences to literally come through our organism without getting stuck—without us having any opinions, for, or against, a particular situation. The life experience is an energy experience, and what happens is that most of the energy we experience as

humans is in the portion of the electromagnetic spectrum which we call the visible portion. While it's the part we can appreciate as colors—the part we can see—it's not the only part we're sensitive to, but it's the part to which most of us are limited. To me the process of enlightenment is allowing all aspects of life's experience, or all aspects of the lighted vibrational experience, to enter our being and simply go through our "netting."[7]

That netting is consciousness. The clarity of union with the "light behind the world" happens only by connecting the subconscious and conscious minds with the superconscious mind, symbolized by the akua such as Laka, the goddess of the hula, who is also the goddess of knowledge. *Laka* is usually taken as meaning "to attract"; the goddess knows how to attract knowledge. One chant sung at her altar after it has been lovingly decorated with her fronds, the fruits of the forest, goes:

Hoʻāla ana oe,
O ʻoe o Hālau lani,
O Hoa lani,
O Puoho lani.

Thy spirit my soul may inspire,
Altar-dweller,
Heaven-guest,
Soul-awakener.[8]

The dancers are aiming to become "inspired" (literally, "imbued with breath"), to stimulate the gods and become fully conscious beings. The hula—with its techniques to open up consciousness—provides the path. The dance is indeed a "soul-awakener," offering one way of moving from the pō, the dark chaos of the subconscious, to the ʻaumakua, the superconscious Mind of Light. This is why ʻaumakua also means to "ask someone to hula." That invitation is "dancing the dream awake"!

THE COLOR OF LIGHT

Color is the most sacred element of visible things.

JOHN RUSKIN

We may think a color is only a color. We may prefer certain colors to other colors, but think that the color itself is in no way significant. So if we prefer pink and someone else prefers green, it doesn't really "mean much." That view is not necessarily true. Color therapy is becoming widely used in institutions of the West as a result of scientific experiments demonstrating, for instance, that hospital patients become much angrier in a room with red walls than they do in a room with blue walls. Many traditional peoples regard colors as possessing mystical attributes. To the Ndembu of Africa, colors have a "power and a mystical quality." In the Upanishads of India it is written that each color is a god, and associated with a particular aspect of existence. Color is very important to the Hawaiians too. Each color may be a sign of god, of emotion, and an indication of the stages of the spiritual journey to greater light.

We can explore the ways color is associated with consciousness by taking the example of one color. There are many Hawaiian words for the color we know as yellow, and each of the words for yellow has other meanings too. One word, *'ama,* is "a very light yellow." 'Ama also means "talkative" and "unripe." *Pualena,* which means "to appear yellow," as said of the dawn or muddy water, also means "lazy." *Nā'u,* "pale yellow," also means "sighing deeply." *Melemele* is a blond yellow and is the name of a star or hidden island. *Pula luhiehu* is a golden yellow. It also means "ripeness" and implies a more developed consciousness. *Lena,* an orangey yellow, also means "to sight or aim; to bend as a bow." *Mālena,* a turmeric yellow, means "tight or taut" and describes the string of a bow. *Pula 'ehu* is "reddish yellow" and also means "spray, foam, or mist" and "someone who has reached his target."

In the meanings of yellow we see a kind of progression through the "spectrum of yellow" from pale to bright. A light yellow is "unripe" and "talks too much." A color that only "appears" yellow is "lazy." A pale yellow opens up to take in mana by breathing deeply. A certain yellow begins to sing and a darker yellow is ripe. An orangey yellow aims like a bow; a turmeric yellow tightens the bow; and a reddish yellow has reached the target. The progression is toward consciousness: the increasing brightness of the shades of yellow is a sign that one is growing closer to the light.

Huna teaches—and science confirms—that each color has its own vibration or pattern. That's why, in Hawai'i, colors are always represented as being glittering and shining, never still. In the hula, the dancers "make color" through their techniques, each of which is related to a color. For example, *akalewa,* "to sway the hips daintily," is close to *ākala,* the word for pink. *'Ulī'ulī,* "the shaking hula rattles," is similar to *uli,* "the deep blue of the sea." *Poni,* to "anoint or consecrate," an important purpose of the dance, is the word for purple. This list could go on and on.

The dancer is making light and the color that appears is said to depend on the particular "vibration" of the dancer, which is a combination of technique plus consciousness. *The dancer creates the color.* The *way* the dancer does it creates the hue. The more integrated the body, mind, and spirit of the dancer, the brighter the color. We know the Hawaiians were consciously aware of this concept, because the names of the dance techniques relate to the means of lightening oneself, such as we have seen with the name for the very first movement, *hoaka.*

In Huna, there can be no word for *color* divorced from the concepts that underlie it. That is why there is no one Hawaiian word that just means "color." Instead, there are many, many words for color, depending on the context. They include *wai,* which also means "water" or "semen"; *waiho'olu'u,* "to impart scent"; *pa'a,* "a firm foundation"; *'Ano,* "beginning to clear"; *hulu,* "a fishhook"; *'a'ai,* "vivid color" or "a net"; and *kala,* "clear color" or "to forgive." It is very significant that the connotations of all these words for color include references to ways of "catching color." *Wai* shows the life-bringing aspects of color and *waiho'olu'u* its capacity to attract. *Pa'a* means "a firm foundation" and *'Ano* "moral qualities." A firm foundation of moral qualities is vital in the journey toward the light. *Hulu,* "the fishhook," refers to the capacity of color to act as a lure to catch something; *'a'ai,* "the net," refers to the ability of a bright color to bring in the catch. The clear color of *kala,* or forgiveness, refers to the capacity of the dancers—and we are all dancers in consciousness—to clear themselves. That is what we shall look at in the next section.

OPENING THE DANCER

Dance makes the world of the great powers visible.

SUZANNE LANGER

We have seen how the words describing the shades of yellow all relate to growth. So does the symbol of the dancer herself. The dancer is like an uncarved block of stone and the goal of the dance is to carve, and to free, the angel inside. The dance does that by freeing the emotions that surround the undifferentiated block. The hula dancer learns how to "unwrap" the block through the application of focused consciousness, as described by the poet T. S. Eliot in these lines from *The Four Quartets:*

> *From wrong to wrong the exasperated spirit*
> *Proceeds, unless restored by that refining fire*
> *Where you must move in measure like a dancer.*[9]

These words were spoken by a "bringer of old knowledge." As he spoke those words, "the day was breaking": knowledge brings light and the bringing of light helps to restore the wrongs the "exasperated spirit" feels.

In order to focus her consciousness, the dancer first has to clear herself, then open herself up, reflected by the double meaning of the word *pohala,* the word for "regaining consciousness," which also means "to open as flower petals." In this dance to increase consciousness, every element that *can* be opened *is* opened. The body is first opened in the gestures of the dance and then more fully in the breaking of the sexual taboo; the voice is opened by chanting; the colors of light are opened in the movement of the dance; and the emotions are opened by focused chanting, which in turn breaks up the undifferentiated sky.

In Hawaiian wisdom, just as in many other cultures, emotion is represented by the element of water. Water brings life: Thales of Miletus wrote that moisture is the soul of the world, the "universal essence." All living things, including seeds, contain moisture; no dead thing does. In Huna the "water of life" is represented by *ka wai huna o Kāne,* "the hidden water of Kāne." Kāne is, if you like, the *source of life.* But the waters of our emotions can take different forms that block our connection with the source. If the sky (or our mind) is filled with clouds, for example, they need to be "struck" by focused consciousness and broken up so the sunlight can shine through.

Waves and clouds both signal the presence of Kū, whose domain is the subconscious. Clouds are frozen water or frozen emotion, whereas the waves are like surging emotional disturbances. The *hula puaʻa,* or "pig dance," illustrates how both intense emotions and fixation on an object of desire interfere with growth. Pele, the goddess of volcanoes, had an affair with Kamapuaʻa, the lawless hog deity. The emotionalism of their torrid affair is shown by its setting: a volcanic bubble! The characters fed their passion in the unreal world of that volcanic bubble. But later, when the misshapen Kamapuaʻa attempted to visit Pele in her home, the fiery cauldron of Kīlauea, she was disgusted, and repulsed his advances with a hot lava flow. Kamapuaʻa had to flee, and the pig dance re-creates his reluctant admission that the presence of cloud signals shows he should leave Pele alone:

Koʻi maka nui, ike ia na pae ʻōpua.
A pepulu, a pepulu, a pepulu
Ko ia lā huelo! Pili i ka lemu!
Hū! hū! hū! hū!

I've read the cloud-omens in heaven,
It curls, it curls! His tail—it curls!

Look, it clings to his buttocks!
Faugh, faugh, faugh, faugh, uff![10]

The dancer enacts the realization that dangers—even when not as obvious as Pele's lava flows—are always lurking in the strong waters of the emotions. The rebuffed hog-god goes to live elsewhere, leaving both Pele's pleasures and her red-hot displeasures behind.

The *hula manō*, or "shark dance"—performed sitting down without an instrumental accompaniment—graphically illustrates what happens when the dancer lets the subconscious mind take over. The emotions are so strong they turn the very water of emotion to blood. It begins:

Auwe! Pau au i ka manō nui, e!
Lala-kea niho pā-kolu.
Pau ka Papakū o Lono . . .

Alas! I am seized by the shark, great shark!
Lala-kea with the triple-banked teeth.
The stratum of Lono is gone . . .[11]

The dancer has lost the "stratum of Lono," or conscious reason. Without the god of consciousness, the unwary dancer calls out as he is finally eaten up:

Kai uli, kai ele,
Kai pōpolohua o Kāne,
A le'ale'a au i ka'u hula,
Pau i ka manō nui!

O blue sea, O dark sea,
Foam-mottled sea of Kāne!
What pleasure I took in my dancing!
Alas! Now consumed by the monster shark!

The pleasure he took in his dancing doesn't matter; he is utterly consumed, consumed by his own emotion. The shark dance is a warning to be wary of allowing emotions to take over, and to instead choose a path of greater consciousness. The hula teaches that answers are to be reached by self-control, demonstrated by the following chant:

'A 'ohe īkā lele pali
'A 'ohe e ho'i ka wahine
'A 'ohe īkā he'e nalu
'A 'ohe e ho'i ka wahine
Make ka ili ike anu
A ō 'oe i ka hula
Ho'i ka wahine ia ka poli o ke aloha.

If you lose a loved one
and you jump over the cliff,
your woman will not return.
If your wife leaves you
and you surf to ease the frustrations,
your woman will not return
and you will die from the cold.
If you learn to dance the hula
your woman will return to you.[12]

The increased consciousness accessed by dancing the hula will ensure that the dancer's lover will return, for the hula deliberately builds up mana.

The passage from the pō, the murky darkness of the subconscious, to the 'aumakua, the bright superconscious, can be completed only through Lono, the conscious mind, represented as the pillars that join heaven and earth. The dancers make their spell by climbing up the pillars—by directing their consciousness correctly. They are aided in this by Lono's wife, the youthful and elusively beautiful goddess Laka—sometimes spied in the mists of a forest clearing—who is the most danced-to goddess of all.

"Taming oneself," one meaning of Laka, is the way of clearing the emotions. To do that, it is necessary to be aware of one's boundaries and act within them. Laka is represented by an uncarved block of wood with an open mouth, wrapped in beautiful tapa cloth. The wood must be from the *lama* (meaning "light") tree, and be wrapped in tapa cloth beaten clear like the moonlight. The dancer's goal is to become bright like the moon, *malama*. Malama plus lama means "enlightenment." *Mālama* has another meaning, which is "to take care," such as by being guided by taboos. In the context of the hula, the observation of various taboos is the means of restraining one's actions within proper bounds. Although anthropologists disagree about many aspects of the role of taboos in Polynesia, they agree that a taboo is a sign that marks something as sacred, something that needs to be valued.

Taboo makes boundaries very clear, and helps the dancers know what they need to focus on. For example, dancers were traditionally not allowed to have sex until they graduated and meanwhile needed to learn complete control of every movement and word. They even learned how to control their emotions and their thoughts, enabling them to become true dancer-shamans, gaining mastery of themselves as they danced into their new reality. The importance of taboo is shown by the fact that the words for the colors and techniques of the hula dance each have a "taboo" meaning as well, which depicts something the dancer should not do. For example, Uli—"the dark blue of the sea" and *'ulī* "the shaking hula rattles"—is also the name of the dark goddess of sorcery, which is a warning to the dancer not to dabble. 'Ākala—the word for "pink" and "the swaying of the hips"—is very close to *akalau*, which means "many shadows" and warns against a lack of focus.

One way of expressing the ultimate goal of the dance is say it is to weave a beautiful rainbow of light, one capable of shining through the darkness of the night and reaching the knowledge of the ancestors, seen in the image of the "night rainbow" around the full moon. As Pali Lee and Koko Willis said: "There is no greater blessing on earth than the blessing of the night rainbow."[13]

The rainbow is also a wonderful image of the harmony of masculine and feminine qualities, represented by the goddess Laka and the god Lono. Laka means "to strike like the sun" and Lono is the rain: the sun and the rain together help a plant to grow and be fertile. A Hawaiian proverb goes:

I mohala no ka lehua i ke ke'eke'ehi 'ia e ka ua.

Lehua blossoms unfold because the rain treads upon them.[14]

The "water from the clouds" brings life to the land, and helps with the "opening up" of nature. Similarly, a free-flowing quality of emotion, where nothing is blocked or exaggerated, is a signal that the dancer's consciousness has opened up and the restraining taboos may be broken.

The next chant describes how the prepared land—and the dancer—becomes fertile. This chant is from the *hula kilu,* performed in a shadowy, flowered hall, when the time for taboo was over and the dancers' bodies were allowed to open. Players would spin a coconut, which aimed to hit a piece of wood in front of a player of the opposite sex. When the desired piece of wood was hit, a forfeit of an embrace would be claimed:

A uwēuwē ke ko'e a ke kae;
Puehuehu ka lā, komo inoino,
Kākia, kahe ka ua ilalo.

Now wriggles the worm to its goal;
A tousling, a hasty encounter,
A grapple; down falls the rain.[15]

Rain was considered blessed and is called *kahiko o ke akua,* "the adornment of the deity." But Huna offers access to a realm beyond the clearing of emotional blocks and the falling of the nourishing rain: that of the superconscious, signaled by the sparkling rainbow of Kāne, called the "eye of the heavens." The dancers dance toward the harmony of light found in the rainbow. When that shimmering rainbow appears in the skies, it is a sign they have cleared the way to let the light within themselves shine through.

I experienced firsthand the power of the hula to evoke the super-conscious when I visited Hawai'i's most famous hula ground, on the Nā Pali cliffs of Kaua'i. Rainbows constantly appeared and disappeared in the skies around me: above the shaking palm trees, above the purple sea, in front of the emerald cliffs were rainbows upon rainbows. I blinked and looked around again, because in our terms such an occur-rence simply doesn't "make sense." But in Huna it makes perfect sense and those rainbows are there.

The rainbow's appearance is the signal that the light of harmony has proved stronger than one's own heavy sky. Kāne—the light of the superconscious—is within the rainbow, which is within the dancer, who is inside each of us. We are all dancing, in our own way, and our own timing, toward the rainbow within.

FROM CHANT TO ENCHANTMENT

The artist is merely the shaman who is able to contact all phenomena.

ISUMO NOGUCHI

Through *hō'okuakahi,* clearing the way, the dancers learn to unite their fragmented selves and fragmented world (*hō'okahi,* "make one, unite"). The kind of unity the dancer achieves has been described many times, such as in Theon of Smyrna's description of the Pythagorean ideal of music: "The perfect unity of contrary things, unity in multi-plicity, accord in discord . . . its end is to unite and co-ordinate."[16] It becomes in the words of Irish poet W. B. Yeats:

*. . . music heard so deeply
That it is not heard at all,*

but you are the music,
while the music lasts.[17]

The dancers reach grace through gracefulness: thought changes the body; fulfillment dissolves the figure; the fusion is complete. And as Yeats further wrote:

O body swayed to music, O brightening glance,
How can we know the dancer from the dance?[18]

Every part of the dancers has been tested, in what T. S. Eliot called the "refining fire" of the dance. They have survived their long, long spiritual initiation and have come out of it with the ability to control their emotions and their thoughts, and with the knowledge of how to have fun, as the next chapter on making love will make clear.

The dancers have become shamans, casting their unseen net over the whole of nature. When they tug on one section of it, such as through a chant, another section of it will be influenced. The dancers have had to grow enormously, both emotionally and spiritually, to be able to influence the weather, to call forth rain and rainbows through the power of their consciousness. The dancers, for a moment in time, have succeeded in their quest. Their call to Laka has been heard and answered, because they are ready for the answer.

E Laka, e Laka, e!
E maliu mai!
A maliu mai 'oe pono au . . .

O Laka, O Laka,
Hark to my call!
You approach, it is well . . .[19]

One famous kumu hula called the hula "action and reaction on the way to enlightenment." The dancer acts and Laka reacts. The result is fulfillment and peace in an enchanted moment. The self-control inspired by Laka has helped the dancer reach Kāne, the god of peace. Beyond the hula ground on Kaua'i, in full view of the dancers, there is a violet islet called Lehua, or Ka'ula. One proverb describes it thus:

Ke lei maila 'o Ka'ula i ke kai.

Ka'ula wears the ocean as a lei.

The purple island and its surrounding ocean have been enchanted to peace by the flower bearers. The island is known as *kaulana-o-Kāne,* or "resting place of Kāne." Thus the greatest god of all is at peace. At last the dancer-shamans may rest too. And so may you, unless you would like to "wake up" to the next chapter, on making love.

7
Making Rainbows:
The Huna of Lovemaking

Even the rainbow has a body
Made of drizzling rain
and it is an architecture of glistening atoms
built up, built up . . .

D. H. LAWRENCE

Making love in Hawai'i—unlike sex in the West—is part of the sacred. In fact, Huna makes explicit the connection between making love and "making consciousness" or "making rainbows." In this chapter we will explore the Hawaiian knowledge and practices of sacred sex, a topic that has never been written about before. We shall see how children are taught how to make love, how the art of love is carefully controlled, and how it is related to the emotional and spiritual development of the individual.

Although the sacred aspect of sexuality has been largely lost in the West, the exuberance of Polynesian sexuality is almost legendary, such as in the descriptions of the *arioi* troupe of Tahiti. This dance troupe—whose name, arioi, means "to excel in leaving a mark"—was much revered and difficult to get into. The members had to have a talent for singing, dancing—and making love. They would travel from island to island, standing naked and oiled in the prow of the canoe, and, after certain ceremonies, make love with the natives of each island.

The Christian missionaries who came to Hawai'i couldn't understand the lack of embarrassment among the Hawaiians, for whom sex was a completely natural act. And, as one missionary complained, the Hawaiians had "about twenty forms of illicit intercourse, and twenty words for each one," so if he forbade one, it left the impression that the other nineteen were still permitted! Certain Hawaiians still said to each other: "Do missionaries get *keiki* [children] by praying?"

The Hawaiians knew, as Don Blanding—an American writer of the 1920s who sailed around the islands—wrote: "A woman is made so, and a man is made so, and they are made for each other as a tree is made to root in the earth." There was no idea of sin, and it took the missionaries quite some time to inculcate the concept of sexuality as sinful. They have still been only partially successful, for, as we have seen, sexuality permeates the language itself. The hidden sexual meanings in Hawaiian words even made it difficult for the missionaries to translate the New Testament into Hawaiian. Every word they used had its sexual meaning, leading to the experience described by Mary Pukui: "When all the Hawaiians start giggling, then you know it means something else."[1]

Perhaps what's surprising isn't that the Hawaiians have so many techniques and ideas about making love, but that we in the West have so few. We do have sex therapists, to be sure, but they are typically seen as being for people exhibiting "abnormal behavior." *We are not normally taught how to enjoy ourselves sexually.* We are expected to learn "on the job," so to speak, without, of course, telling our lover or our friends we are actually learning! It is common to pretend we have either more or less experience than we actually do (more experience for men and less experience for women). Basically we expect sex to happen "naturally," but social conditioning, saying sex is sinful, tends to militate against it.

In Polynesia the social conditioning was of a different sort, and much of it had to do with increasing enjoyment of life's pleasures.

Westerners have traditionally found it difficult to understand other views of sex as a natural part of life, and as a result they have described the islanders as promiscuous. On the first journey of non-Polynesians to the islands, one of the men on Captain Cook's ship wrote that the dancers visiting the ship wanted sex so much they "used all their arts to entice our people into their houses, and, finding [the sailors] were not to be allured by their blandishments, they endeavoured to force them and were so importunate they would take absolutely no denial."[2] The writer was certainly unaware of the long period of taboo the hula dancers would have gone through before they were allowed to make love with whomever they chose. Sex was delayed gratification, delayed until the person was ready for it. That is because the body, like the rainbow, must be "built up, built up . . ."

GROWING INTO LOVE

The infant was treated like a malleable form whose
features and form could be modeled, like a
sculptor molds clay . . .
MARY PUKUI, ON BRINGING UP A HAWAIIAN INFANT

Huna teaches that life begins at the moment of conception, which, as we have seen, is called aka, the word for "the first glimmer of moonlight." Conception was an incredibly joyful act, in which the participants were absolutely aware that the sublime surge of orgasm would result in new light, new life. Conception of a child was a conscious act, shown by the phrase *au moe laua a i laila ko'u,* "they slept together and life came." *Moe* means "dream," as well as "sleep," and a child is believed to arise out of the "shared dream" of a couple.

Soon the mother knows she is *ua kanaka,* "with person." As the fetus beginning to develop limbs is mana, the parents knew they must be diligent about directing their consciousness. Hawaiian parents were traditionally very careful of their thoughts toward their unborn child. They would sing to it and tell it stories, and be careful not to feel negative emotions such as anger and jealousy, believing that the fetus picks up the emotions around it—and modern science is beginning to prove them right.

The parents would be careful about sex, too. Gutmanis recorded this chant that was done by a pregnant woman before she made love:

Ke haha ia hei au ke aloha,
Ke a'e hei au maluna
Alia wale ani ai 'a
A kau maluna o kahi ali'i
He pūhala, he pūhala ali'i
He kū noi.

Now groped for by me is love,
I get on top,
I simply wait to have hip movement;
And get on top of a royal one,
A pandanus tree, a chiefly pandanus tree,
A standing indeed.[3]

She gropes for love, confident that her mental preparation is bringing mana in the form of the "tree" of her partner's erection, as well as in the development of the limbs of the fetus to be strong like a chiefly tree.

Birth itself was usually performed in a squatting position, and was often over very quickly (Pukui talks about mothers carrying out their ordinary household tasks the following day). When a baby was born, a feast was held. The menu for the feast—which had to include seafood such as *kala* (seaweed), *'a'ama* (crab), and *mahiki* (shrimp)—has deep Huna meanings. *Kala* means "to clear," showing the necessity for clearing the minds. *'A'ama* means "to loosen a hold or grip," in terms of difficult emotions; and *mahiki* means "to peel off like removing fish scales," referring to the necessity to reveal the higher minds. From the very beginning the infant is shown the path toward life, light, and the superconscious, by being celebrated with foods that help clear the way.

Hawaiians were not ashamed of the sexual aspects of a newborn's body. The body was considered a "sacred plant" and the parents' task was to make the child's body ready for the sacred acts it would perform. Among these sacred acts was sexual intimacy, and preparation for it began at the earliest opportunity.

Physical preparation took many forms. Genitalia were important, kept covered because they were seen as a person's "precious possessions," not because they were intrinsically dirty. A mother would daily squirt milk into her tiny daughter's vagina, to moisten it for future sexual intercourse. The labia would be pressed together and "the *mons veneris* rubbed with kukui nut oil and pressed with the palm to flatten it and make it less prominent. The molding continued until the labia did not separate."[4] The penis of a little boy was blown into every day in preparation for an operation that would take place when he was about eight years old. (I don't advocate following these practices today. The climate of society is different now and such actions would probably lead to allegations of sexual abuse.)

The operation done on young boys is called *kaha ule,* or "slit penis" in Hawaiian and "subincision" in the West. Unlike in circumcision, the whole foreskin is *not* removed; a longitudinal cut is made in the foreskin instead. This operation is designed to *increase* sexual pleasure, whereas circumcision makes the penis *less* sensitive. Both Jews and Muslims require young boys to be circumcised. Some Muslims say the operation is performed because it *decreases* sexual pleasure, so the youth can give more to God. This is consistent with the belief, common among the major religions, that enjoying sex takes away respect for God.

As far as I know, subincision is not practiced anywhere in the West. However, it is still carried out in the shady groves of the islands of Polynesia. The operation traditionally would be performed by a kahuna on a sun-warmed rock in public when the boy was seven or eight years old, the age when he—as one proverb says—is:

Kokoke e 'ā ke ahi o ka 'aulima.

Almost ready to make fire with a fire stick held in the hand.

The kahuna would slice into the foreskin of the "fire stick" as he chanted:

E kiʻi ka ʻohe i Homaikaohe.
Eia ka ʻohe lauliʻi a Kāne.
Oki a i ka maka o ka mai.
Ua moku.

Bring the bamboo from Homaikaohe.
Here is the small leafed bamboo of Kāne.
Cut now the foreskin.
It is divided![5]

The kahuna would then slip a clean morning glory blossom over the penis, and the young boy would go swimming in the sea. Then the new initiate would join the kahuna and his friends and family in a feast to celebrate the widening of his world.

The name of the goddess of sex in Hawaiʻi—Kaha ʻUla—is very close to the name of the subincision operation, kahe ule. *Kaha* means, among other things, "to mark" or "to cut open," and *ula* means both "blood" and "red." Thus we can see in her name a reference to the passionate power of sex. Another name for the operation is ʻoki poe poe. *ʻOki* means "to cancel" and *poe* is very close to *pō*, the beginnings of life: the operation is a symbol for canceling the power of the subconscious. This interpretation is given weight by the fact that the boy's foreskin is cut with the "small leafed bamboo of Kāne." The child needs to be molded to grow in a conscious way: toward Kāne, the superconscious.

As we have seen in the case of the preparation of the hula dancers, part of the process of growth includes restraint until the limbs of light have grown firm. This is reflected by one proverb describing a boy or girl who desires to make love and is still too young:

Hauna ke kai o ka moa liʻiliʻi.

Unsavory is the soup made of little chickens.

Preparation for intercourse involved far more dimensions than the physical. As ever, it was important to increase the mana. One of the ways this was done was by chanting. In Hawai'i there were even *mele ma'i,* genital chants, composed especially for the genitals of little boys and girls. Marshall Sahlins described some in his book *Islands of History.* Here is one reported by a certain Samwell, a sailor on one of Captain Cook's voyages:

An ule *[penis], an ule to be enjoyed:*
Don't stand still, come gently,
That way, all will be well here,
Shoot off your arrow.[6]

And yes, the shooting of the arrow does mean what you think it means!

Most of the genital songs we have a record of were sung to royal organs. Queen Lili'uokalani's chant sings of "frisky, frolicking genitals that go up and down," whereas her brother King Kalakaua's chant goes:

Your lively ma'i *[genitalia]*
That you are hiding—
Show the big thing,
Hālala, to the many birds.[7]

These songs were chanted daily to increase the mana of the royal genitalia over the years. It is easy to imagine such highly praised organs responding well to the demands made on them!

In addition to the chanting, training in sexual techniques was also given when the children were older, usually on a beach at night. Young men, for example, were taught certain techniques from women with the appropriate mana. Pukui wrote: "Among the chiefs a boy was trained not only in warfare and government but when he was grown physically, a matured chiefess was chosen to train him in sexual practices. This was part of his education."[8] Then the girls would say:

I nanea no ka holo o ka wa'a i ke akamai o ke kū hoe.

One can enjoy a canoe ride when the paddler is skilled.

Girls were taught skills including the *'amo'amo,* the contracting and relaxing of the paravaginal muscles, to greatly increase both the man's and the woman's sexual pleasure. It is compared to the wink of an eye, and its opening and shutting increases the shudder of each new awareness. *'Amo'amo* also means to "sparkle, glimmer, or twinkle." The same light is represented by the evening star, which, *once spotted,* can always be seen in the dark sky. The metaphor of a light that has *always been there* and simply needs to be accessed is an apt description of the Hawaiian understanding of female orgasm: it is traditionally assumed that *everyone* has the capacity to have an orgasm—it just needs to be brought out by techniques such as those taught as a part of hula training.

The purposes of these techniques were to increase response, to increase the ability to feel pleasure, and to increase awareness. But technical preparation was not enough to prepare a young person for full enjoyment of sex. Many emotional dangers lurk like sharks under the subconscious sea, ready to devour the unwary. It is very, very easy to make love the wrong way and most people have experienced it, a dilemma captured by W. B. Yeats when he said, "The tragedy of sexual intercourse is the perpetual virginity of the soul." While there are many "wrong ways" to make love, there is only one outcome: when the body, the mind, and the spirit are not integrated, it results in fission, not fusion. The sexual act is an act of great power and it can lead to a lot of chaotic, splintering energy. The rainbow is broken. That is why Huna also included instruction about when to make love and when not to make love. Those teachings can be summed up as being a matter of perspective.

A FRESH PERSPECTIVE

From two miles distance no seafarer could have guessed
that Bali Hai existed. Like most lovely things, one had to
seek it out and even know what one was seeking before
it could be found.

JAMES MICHENER

What are we seeking in the West? We don't have the advantage of a system we can follow to learn how to make love. So we learn by trial and error. The process of learning often leads to confusion about the ideal and reality. We all know what the ideal is because we watch movies and television, see advertisements, and read books, magazines, and newspapers. Their focus is on romance, romance, romance. The West now has the highest divorce rate in history, and I suspect it's because we're trying to live up to that ideal, which is something like: a beautiful male and female, free and unencumbered, falling in love over a glass of wine at sunset (preferably somewhere of fabulous beauty like Hawai'i) and living happily ever after. The reality is: "Who does the washing up?" So then we go out with someone else and don't realize that the cute redhead wears old underwear she dries on the side of the bath. We are disillusioned, but "Hey, our neighbor is really attractive . . ."

Perhaps that's why our relationships tend to be those of serial monogamy, even though the ideal is to be with one person. There may be a lot of guilt and uncertainty, mixed in with Christian ideas of sex being sinful, and a tendency to suppress our emotions and retreat into work or fantasy or both. It's difficult to know what we are really feeling, let alone communicate with our lover about it. We are unclear because we don't understand. And what we don't understand are the unspoken messages.

Romantic love has been associated with industrialization and a widespread lack of meaning. Increasing industrialization meant we lost much of our integration on a daily level. When the ideal of romantic love spread around the world, depression was found *for the first time.*

This is because the ideal is so different from the reality of daily life. Suddenly the interdependent system that previously constituted reality is separated out and the individual is seen as a separate island. Even the surrounding sea is no longer one of faith. The loss to us, and the cost to us, is immeasurable.

I believe the most important quality in a mate is faith, for if that person believes in something greater, then that person is more likely to believe in him- or herself—and in you. Having faith means someone is more likely to be faith-full or faithful, very important in a committed relationship. Having faith means knowing that love sometimes means letting go and "letting God." It means believing that a relationship breaks up for a reason, and believing that there will be someone else in the future. There has to be, because that's what we create through our own power. Meanwhile, it's a wonderful and exciting world out there.

The lovely islands of desire, and its fulfillment, beckon to us. But to reach them, as with the legendary island of the Pacific, Bali Hai, we must know what we are looking for. We are seeking the hidden islands of Kāne, the lost continent of the Higher Self, *not* the personal islands of the subconscious. In other words, the trick to attaining a truly satisfying relationship lies in being attracted to someone with your Kāne and not with your Kū!

Certain Hawaiians have a dramatic, and unusual, way of putting it. They compare a bird's-eye view to a fish's-eye view. Of course a "bird's-eye view" is much higher than the "fish's-eye view" from within the sea. Fish are compared to the beginning of humanity and birds to our highest consciousness. The waters of our subconscious provide a suitable element for fish, whereas the superconscious has finally developed the capacity to see from a new vantage point.

Young people in ancient Hawai'i were expected to control where and when to make love themselves, but first they needed to learn. There was usually freedom to do so, experimentation often beginning quite young. There were no particular taboos against same-sex relationships. Although it was expected that a child would usually choose a mate of the opposite sex, there was no particular censure if they did not, or if they carried on being promiscuous. It was just assumed they needed to learn about sexuality. The stringent taboo was against incest, which was never permitted in ancient times; the punishment for it was banishment and never having your name spoken again. However, as mentioned earlier, in later centuries, incest was allowed among royal families to prevent dilution of the royal mana.

Young people were expected to eventually choose a mate with whom it felt *ao,* or "right." The meanings of *ao* also include "to regain consciousness," a wonderful definition of meeting one's lover from one's Higher Self. What's "right" is what works. If love doesn't "work"—if it doesn't have the structure of power—then it's not love, known to the Hawaiians as *aloha.* Serge King told me that one very important meaning of *aloha* is "to be happy with." The structure of personal power arises from *within* the person, inevitably attracting people with the same level of mana. Just as there is no absolute "right" or "wrong" or "good" or "evil" in Huna, there *is no one right person for another.* It all depends on one's level of perception.

In Hawai'i some lovers are compared to fish: *he i'a no ke kai kohola* means "a fish of the shallow sea," a person who is easy to seduce. Other lovers are like the *he mālolo,* or "flying fish." A flying fish is also *ka i'a lele me he manu,* "a fish that flies like a bird," which means a fish that is attempting to be something it is not. It is also said of a person who goes from lover to lover. A promiscuous woman can also be known as a *haka kau a ka manu,* "a perch on which birds rest": the birds only rest on her (they don't fly with her). She can also be called *he 'uha leo 'ole,* "a thigh over which no word is spoken." Without words, of course, she has no mana, and she will stay a temporary perch.

When a person is looking for love in all the wrong places, the saying is:

Heaha kau o ka lapa manu 'ole?

What are you doing on a ridge where no birds are found?

To find the ridge where the birds are—or attract them to *your* ridge—requires a bird's-eye view, the higher perspective of the super-conscious, and an activation of mana or love magic. When we value ourselves, then we can truly value another. The Hawaiian word for "vagina" is '*amo hulu,* or "esteemed sparkle." *Hulu* also means feather, continuing the bird imagery, for as we shall see, birds truly show the way to the Higher Self.

LOVE MAGIC

Me he lau no ke Ko'olau ke aloha.

Love is like the fingertips of the Ko'olau breeze.

HAWAIIAN PROVERB

In a sense love *is* magic, for it embodies and evokes miraculous quali-ties, qualities stronger than anything else on this earth. It comes as no surprise to learn that, in Hawai'i, magic can be used to direct love to a person. To understand Hawaiian love magic we need to go back to Dr. Brigham's definition of the three things necessary to make magic effec-tive: consciousness, force, and substance. True love is like a bird that needs to be snared. To one who has learned self-control, as opposed to controlling others, this does not seem too difficult an undertaking.

The most important factor in this pursuit is controlling our thoughts, because thoughts go into the aka and attract substance. The word for thought is *mana'o.* We know the word *mana* already, and *o* in this context means "there." So when you think a thought, "there is mana." Our thoughts attract other bodies to us. A person needs to attract the right partner, with the right mana, as expressed by a Hawaiian proverb:

Nānā no a ka 'ulu i pakī kēpau.

Look for the gummy breadfruit tree.

In other words, look for a person who has substance.

But we won't be able to attract the substance unless we *have* the substance. We need to affect the world around us through our growing consciousness. Here is part of a chant made to Lono, the god of consciousness, when offering food to a family god. The chant provides one way of directing focus and lifting ourselves out of our soupy subconscious:

O kai Kāne, o kai wahine
O kai lu'u, o kai ea,
Kai pili'aikū e, ua puni
Ua puni na moku i ke kai
O hu'ehu'e kai e Ka'ele-i, e Ka'ale-moe,
E ka 'ale hako 'iko 'i e i Kahiki
O kalana au a Kahiki ia 'oe la-e, e Lono.

O sea of the male, o sea of the female
O sea of submersion, o sea of arising,
Cramped sea, sea all around
The islands are surrounded by sea
Twisting sea, great waves, waves of calm sea.
O the agitated waves in Kahiki
O releaser of the current from Kahiki, it is thee, O Lono.[9]

Hawaiians had many rituals and prayers to increase "love consciousness." There was even a special "love kahuna," *kahuna hana aloha,* or "kahuna make love." The love kahuna would pray to Makanikeoe, the god of love, on behalf of a smitten man or woman, chanting the following words over a stalk of *manu lele,* or "flying bird" sugarcane:

Makanikeoe
Hono o lele
Lele ke aloha
Pili ia [inoa]

Ilaila 'e pili ai
A moe 'ole kona pō.

Makanikeoe, Love God
joining flies
the love flies
this pertains to [insert name]
There it will be in contact
And sleepless are his/her nights.[10]

The love kahuna would then blow in the direction of the desired person. This would contact the love god, who could take the form of the wind and bear the mana along until it gently touched the desired one, who would fall in love with the sender of the magic.

According to the excellent research of June Gutmanis, there were prayers to get love, prayers to sever love, and prayers to say thank-you for love. The kind of sugarcane used was important. The "flying bird" sugarcane captured the bird or attracted new love. The *pili mai,* or "stick to me," sugarcane was used to make love cling. The *laukona,* "hardhearted," sugarcane was used to sever love. The *pāpa'a,* or "overdone," sugarcane brought back love when used with a particular prayer dedicated to Uli, the dark blue goddess of sorcery. She was the goddess most familiar with the dark nether regions, the hunting ground of the lost loves.

However, I do not recommend using these kinds of prayers. It's said, for instance, that a lover attracted by the "love prayer" is very passionate and intense, but not one we will be able to grow with. This will lead to great frustration in the future. By saying prayers for a particular person, we get in the way of his or her free will. Developing our mana truly means letting go, just like in the prayers we've seen previously.

One prayer to say thank-you for love is for females. It begins by praising the natural features of the island of Hawai'i and the goddess of the volcano, Pele. Then the chanter poignantly gives thanks by saying she desires a great beauty like that.

Ho'okahi no a'u 'oi Hawai'i moku o Keawe
Kilohana he'ike iho i ka nani o Mauna Kea
A ke kela o Mauna Loa
Hou pili o Hualalai
Kahiko Kīlauea i ke ahi a ka wahine
He wahine mai nowau
He ukali no ka makemake
Makemake au i ka nani
Maika'i o ke 'ala, ke 'ala o ia pua
Koni au a ko omou.

One is my foremost Hawai'i island of Keawe
The greatest if you behold the splendor of Mauna Kea
And Mauna Loa is excellent
Close companion of Hualalai
Kīlauea is ancient with the fire woman
I am a woman after her
A following of the desire
I desire the beauty
Time is the fragrance, the fragrance of the flower,
I kiss and continue on.[11]

Even in this prayer of gratitude for love, there is also letting go. Perhaps this is because it is natural to find love all around, even when love is represented by one particular person. It is not a license for unfaithfulness. It *is* an acknowledgment that love is everywhere, even in the breeze that blows. To hold on to it, one has to continue to grow and be prepared to let go. The power to let go comes from the acceptance of a worldview in which we create our world and have ultimate responsibility to ourselves. Love is found not in one particular person, but in the archetypal essence that permeates everything: "I desire the beauty." But meanwhile, one must love and express that love: "I kiss and continue on."

LIMBS OF LIGHT

I manai kau, i pua hoʻi kaʻu, Kui ʻia ka makemake
a lawa pono.

Yours is the lei-making needle, mine the flowers, so let us
do what we wish.

THE GODDESS HIʻIAKA ON EMBRACING HER LOVER LOHIʻAU

Making love is the fun part, the bright result of growth. It is the time when pleasure, so long prepared for, can at last be experienced. The hula dancers' graduation ceremony—which shows the significance of the breaking of the taboo—can be seen as a helpful model for us all.

The night before the ceremony, the dancers contemplate their learning so far and pray for guidance, then are consecrated by the kumu who waits at the door of the hālau hula and sprinkles every neophyte with holy water. Then, just after midnight, the initiates plunge into the ocean to remove any lingering impurities they may have, journeying to and fro completely naked: "nakedness is the garb of the gods." The next day they recite a taboo-removing prayer in front of Laka's altar:

Ua Ku ka maile a Laka a i mua
Ua lu ka hua o ka maile
Noa, noa iau ia Kaha ʻUla.

The maile of Laka stands to the fore.
The maile vine casts now its seeds.
Freedom, there's freedom to me, Kaha ʻUla.[12]

Notice the recurrence of the word Kaha ʻUla: the freed dancer is moving toward the goddess of sex. The fledgling dancers, who are about to fly, then gather around a perfect black hog. The kumu touches it and the dancers lay their hands upon their teacher's hand. The kumu tells them that if they consecrate themselves to their work with sincerity and true hearts, then the songs will stay in their memory. If they are heedless, *regardless of their vows,* the songs they have learned will fly away.

We can understand several things from this final speech. First is how important it is for words and thoughts to be in alignment for mana to stay. Sincerity and true hearts are necessary. Otherwise mana will "fly away" just like a bird. That bird, of course, is the bird of love. The dancer-shamans have learned how to align their three minds, so when the intent is there, they not only will attract love, but they also will attract a powerful type of love. The dancer lives with integrity and does not say one thing and do another. The dancer is faithful to self and to others. The dancer has developed limbs of light.

The limbs of light do not sprout out of the weak, controlling feeling that is sometimes called love. Lovers may cling together for all sorts of reasons, such as need, guilt, and compassion, but these are not what Huna regards as love. Virtually everyone in the West subconsciously worships at the altar of the god of romantic love. But because the worship is *sub*conscious, we don't stop to think about just who—or what—we are prostrating ourselves to. We don't realize that our god of love exhibits a certain lack of awareness: Cupid, the brave archer who shoots his arrows of love, is blind in one eye.

Love is not subconscious in Hawai'i, where increasing consciousness was both the prerequisite for and the bright result of sexual intimacy. The multiple meanings of the Hawaiian word for consciousness, *'ike ho'omaopopo,* reveal this connection between growing consciousness and the ecstatic enveloping of limbs. *'Ike* means to "know sexually" as well as "to perceive." There is a similar meaning in the Bible where *know* stands for sexual intercourse. Perception is key for a couple to experience the full depths and heights of sexual pleasure, and for the development of that kind of sexual knowledge that widens consciousness beyond the realm of sexuality. The Hawaiian symbol for that link between making love and consciousness is light. The love song and dance *Pili Aoao,* "the stickiness of the light-light," describes a couple who begin to touch each other lovingly as the sun rises:

O ka pōnaha iho a ke ao.
Ka pipiʻo malie maluna,
ʻIke ʻoe i ka hana mikiʻala,
Nowelo i ka pili aoao.
Maikaʻi ke aloha a ka ipo—
Hana mao ole i ka puʻuwai,
Houhou liʻiliʻi i ka poli—
Nowelo i ka pili aoao.
A mau ka piliʻna olu pono;
Huli aʻe, hoʻoheno mālie,
Hanu liʻiliʻi nahenahe
Nowelo i ka pili aoao.

Outspreads now the dawn,
Arching itself on high—
But look! A wondrous thing,
A thrill at the touch of the side.
Most dear to the soul is a love touch;
Its pulse stirs ever the heart
And gently throbs in the breast—
At the thrill from the touch of the side.
In time awakens a new charm
As you touch and gently caress;
Short comes the breath—at
The thrill from the touch of the side.[13]

The kind of light that appears signifies the kind of love given out. A tender light is a response to a gentle love, as these verses describe. We can see another example of light representing love in the *hula o niu,* an informal dance where a top is spun and the dancers caper around. The dancers sing about how to recognize the approach of passion:

A Lohiʻau-ipo i Hāʻena lā.
ʻEnaʻena ke aloha, ke hiki mai.

Lohi'au, the lover, prince of Hā'ena
Love glows like an oven at his coming.[14]

We know a passionate kind of love is coming when glowing color is coupled with the meaning of Haena as "red hot." But love has all kinds of colors. It has the golden glowing certainty of relationships to the older members of your family; it has the blue light a young baby carries with it; it has the pink glow of your soul-mate connection; it has the green gleam of your love for nature. Next we'll tune in to the rosy colors of fulfillment in love, the colors which blend the red of the root chakra with the white of the Higher Self.

LOVE

He kēhau ho'oma'ema'e ke aloha.

Love is like cleansing dew.

HAWAIIAN PROVERB

It is appropriate that the one Hawaiian word everyone knows is *aloha,* the word for love. Polynesian society is based on the principle of love, which is seen in the very weft and warp of the fabric of this world and beyond. But this concept of love is not *wai o kaunu,* "the water of love," or "the thrilling effects of being in love" when a person is wrapped in sensation. In that kind of love, the person is prompted by the subconscious to see only what he or she wants to see. A beautiful Hawaiian proverb describes how the look of a lover changes, *just because he or she is the person being made love to:*

Hele a luhiehu i ka ua noe.

Is made bright by the misty rain.

Love is not sex, for sex without love is also of the subconscious. Love that continues after all the initial "rainy" passion clears is the only eternal and valuable thing, expressed by this saying:

O ka ua o Hilo e mao ana, o ke aloha i ka ipo, mea pau ʻole.

The rain of Hilo clears, the love of a sweetheart is endless.

However, in ancient Hawaiʻi, love was also not marriage. There was no marriage in ancient Hawaiʻi, although many Hawaiian-Christian writers say there was. But there *was* commitment, and there was a ceremony to celebrate it. When you met someone with whom making love felt ao, right, that was it: you stopped making love to other people. Remember that *ao* also means "light" and "consciousness regained." Again, this shows us the importance of the role of faith.

The following extracts are from the prayer that was recited during the ceremony called *Hoʻāo*, the commitment prayer *(hoao)* that calls on the power of internal sovereignty.

E ʻele mimo ka lani
ʻUweʻuwehe ke ao hoʻokikiʻi
Kikiʻi ke ao ʻopua lani e
ʻOlaʻolapa ka uwila . . .
Oʻimiʻimi, o nalowale a loaʻa
Loaʻa hoʻi ka hoa e . . .
Pili ʻolua e—
moku ka pawa o ke ao
Ke moakaka nei ka hikina
Ua hiki hoʻi.

The sky is covered with darkness,
The tilting clouds begin to part,
The leaning bud-shaped clouds in the sky.
The lightning flashes here and there . . .
There was a seeking of the lost, now it is found—
A mate is found . . .
You two are now one,
The darkness has begun to depart,

The east is beginning to brighten
For day is here at last.[15]

Love, light, and consciousness in a passionate relationship eventually concern commitment. A commitment made in love mirrors a person's commitment to his or her own growth. Infidelity was frowned upon, particularly if a person deliberately set out to ensnare someone else's mate, because it blocked clear vision. That's why such an act was called *pō'alo maka,* "scooping out the eyeballs." Commitment is represented by sharing the same *tapa* mat or bed. Sleeping and waking, the lovers' lives are inextricably intertwined. Then they are both:

Ua ia ia ka manai ho'okahi.

Strung on the same lei needle.

The correct consciousness must be in place for a couple to stay like that. Each must always realize that it might be necessary to let go, for love is like life: it constantly changes. If a Hawaiian (or a Tahitian or a Cook Islander) didn't feel his or her lover was the best thing for him or her anymore, then he or she was traditionally free to leave. Love, in essence, *was* freedom. Separation was ideally not judged because there was a recognition that such a difficult decision would have come only from the superconscious Mind of Light, not from the subconscious or conscious mind. But more celebrated was the path of two lovers flying *together* toward the "thousand torches" of paradise, just like in this beautiful Tahitian chant:

Let the winds of space blow through
The sailing paths of the Tahitian ships,
So that we shall fly
Higher, further, lightly, birdlike.
From the earth sphere's bone and weight
To Temehani's thousand torches,
To the sunset glow of Taaroa.

To reach this place we need to have traveled through the emotional turmoil of our subconscious mind. We need to have traveled through the weighty judgments of our conscious mind that tie us to the earth. Then we can leave our earth-weight behind and fly away . . . away, toward the hidden islands of our desire and its fulfillment.

The Greek sage Periander's epigram "Tranquillity is the most beautiful thing in the world" could also be said of this view of love. When the turbulent currents of emotion have been quieted, the higher red-gold consciousness is in control. Held in that sunset glow, we are at peace. We are traveling toward the hidden island of our desire and its fulfillment. Its sign is said to be a flock of birds hovering over it. These pellucid seas are very attractive to love:

A malama ke ka'ao o kou aloha.

And clear is the tide of your love.

That tranquillity has been attracted through inner peace. A strong structure has been developed and it is time to let it go in faith and love. One of the most joyous ways of doing that is through orgasm.

THE COSMIC ORGASM

Oh God!

FREQUENT CRY AT THE MOMENT OF ORGASM

In Polynesia, the word for orgasm, *le'a*—which also means "flowing like the sea"—was compared to waves crashing on a beach, mimicking the movement of the vulva. It also means "joy, pleasure, happiness, merriment." *Le'a le'a* is the name of a prayer to Kū, Lono, Kāne, and the 'aumakua, making it clear that in Huna, orgasm is seen as a way of breaking through to the land of the gods. According to Marshall Sahlins, the verb for "to have an orgasm," *ho'ole'a,* also means "to extol or praise as in 'Praise the Lord!'"[16] The enjoyment of orgasm in

Hawai'i is related to the *acknowledgment of faith:* an orgasm, like faith, is an allowance of something greater in our life. To reach it, we must have the faith to "let go."

As we have seen, the technique for the "winking" of the vagina, *'amo'amo,* also connotes shimmering light. The connection of making love to light—and thus to greater consciousness—can also be seen in the fact that there is even a special "star of joy" that stands for the orgasm: Arcturus, or "the evening star." That star, as we might expect, is very bright. Ptolemy called it a rich golden red. The Roman Tibullus named it Stimulus! Arcturus is the zenith star above Hawai'i, the one navigators still follow to find their way home. *'Ike le'a,* "to be like le'a," means "to see clearly."

In the cosmic orgasm there is no separation between light and love and the brightest consciousness. This kind of orgasm is completely different from the type where you are still aware of your own body and your own reactions, almost as if you are "watching yourself." The Tahitian calls the throes of this type of orgasm *navé navé,* meaning "the beauty that quivers inside and out." All of you implodes into thousands of tiny sparkling atoms. Light is in your body and your body is in light.

This kind of orgasm requires preparation and it can be taught. I know of a certain kahuna who specializes in giving people the experience of this state of "making rainbows" together. Still, it can "break through," when a person is unaware, causing his or her skin to expand into the great sky of the universe. Regular experience of this ultimate orgasm in making love to a loved one is a sign that a person is moving along the rainbow path to the gods, that the person's consciousness has truly opened up.

The bejeweled path of Huna includes many other facets that help us weave again the ancient rainbow of light; they relate to concepts of time, space, death, creativity, and sacredness. All of these may brighten and open as we allow more light to fall out of the trapdoor of the skies.

8
Lights on the Beach at Night: Beyond Time and Death

Lapalapa: *Phosphorescence on the beach at night,*
believed by the Hawaiians to be the souls of the dead,
signs of another reality.

HAWAIIAN DICTIONARY

The rhythms of star and sky, dark and light, day and night are all within us. We are each a microcosm of the universe. The interplay of the sub-conscious and the superconscious, expansion and contraction, consciousness and dreaming, life and death, clarity and the unseen, knowledge and separation—all of it is inscribed within. We repeat and repeat, and try not to repeat, the universal pattern.

The pattern is in its proper place, and we too are in our proper place within it. But it is often difficult for us to realize that, even when we are reminded by signs such as the glimmering phosphorescent lights on the beach at night. Those coruscating sparkles are said to be the souls of the dead. Their gleaming light is a sign of connection, implying that although the dead may be separated from us by space and time, they are not separated from us by *consciousness*. Their light is a signal of their continuing soul-life.

We often are unable to transcend the dimensions of space, time, and death that separate us, not only from the dead, but from the full light of consciousness as well. As we shall see, our very concepts of time blind us to our full reality. But the ancient wisdom of Hawai'i offers us a perspective of time that can guide us to see our place as part of a universe of light.

The traditional Huna knowledge in which that perspective is encoded has never been written about before, but in this chapter, I present the two Hawaiian astrological cycles and show you how to find your place in them. One is of the stars, which corresponds to the "star signs" of the zodiac. It gives clues about how earthly time and desire are built up in a system of attraction and creation. The other is of the moon: the particular night of the moon we are born under reveals things about our character, showing as well "where we are" in the universal pattern.

JOINING TIME

The final question of time [is] whether we shall live
together or die together . . . The West has been in love
with its successive linear image of time . . . it has con-
demned the past to death as the tomb of irrationality and
celebrated the future as the promise of perfectibility . . .
we shall know each other or exterminate each other.

CARLOS FUENTES

The Western concept of chronological time is fixed into hours, days, and years, stretching into the future on a "timeline" that suddenly ends. A human being can't impact it; the best we can ever do is use it well. From this perspective, time seems to be something abstract and unchangeable, as expressed so famously by Omar Khayyám in his *Rubáiyát*:

The Moving Finger writes; and, having writ,
Moves on; Nor all your Piety nor Wit
Shall lure it back to cancel half a Line,
Nor all your Tears wash out a Word of it.

The idea of a line of time is intimately related to Christian beliefs, which begin the measurement of time from the year of Christ's birth, 0 B.C. (0 Before Christ), from which it marches along in a predictable one-way procession. The concept of linear time moving in one direction—until death, when "our time is at an end"—also comes from Christianity. Jesus was able to "rise again," and for that reason he is called "the prince of time": *he is able to rule time*. The rest of us are not: time rules us. At the end of our allotted span, our time runs out. Until then we are always aware that "our life is but a brief span" and we have to make the most of it. Otherwise, we are wasting time, *which we can never get back*.

This is why even our beautiful memories are bittersweet. We worry that we can never recapture the beauty we remember. Rupert Brooke sailed away from the South Seas, longing to recapture his life with the Polynesians under the Southern Cross:

> And they're laughing and kissing and swimming and dancing beneath it. But for me it is set. And I do not know that I shall ever see it again. It's queer—I was sad at heart to leave Tahiti, but I resigned myself to the vessel, and watched the green shores and rocky peaks fade with hardly a pang. I'd told so many of those that love me, so often, "Oh yes, I'll come back . . . next year perhaps: or the year after . . ." that I suppose I'd begun to believe it myself. It was only yesterday, when I knew that the Southern Cross had left me, that I suddenly realized that I'd left behind those lovely places and lovely people, perhaps for ever. I reflected that there was surely nothing else like them in this world, and very probably nothing in the next: and that I was going far away from gentleness and beauty and kindliness and the smell of the lagoon and the thrill of that dancing and the scarlet of the *flamboyants* and the white and gold of other flowers.[1]

Brooke was indeed never going to see the Southern Cross again. He was killed in the First World War, on April 23, 1915. To us that's it:

death is the tragic and inevitable conclusion to our idea of linear time.

It's difficult to understand *how much effect* our view of time has on us because it is virtually always with us. Even when we're enjoying ourselves—at a party, for example—a little part of us is aware of what time it is, until finally: "Is that the time? I have to go. I have to work tomorrow." One of the unfortunate results is living our lives by arbitrary measurements. The physicist Buryl Payne wrote:

> We learn to associate happenings and internal subjective experience with our external awareness of calendars and clocks. We learn when it is time to eat, to sleep, to yell, to have ice cream, to get married, or to work—regardless of how we think or feel. We are rewarded and punished in terms of "tomorrow," "next week," "next summer," or "later." We gradually grow up to see the world through the screen of man-made time and to fit the richness of our own thoughts, feelings, sensations, and loves into the square mesh of seconds, minutes, days and years.[2]

This sense of time makes it difficult for us to be completely present at a given moment. Even our holidays get divided up into segments of time, for tours, excursions, travel, getting a tan. Perhaps deliberately, we leave ourselves very little free time, *because then we "don't have time" to think about our lives, where all our (limited) time is going, and if we are doing what we really want to do with it.*

In my opinion, the linear view of time is necessary for the "work ethic" to be as strong as it is. The work ethic is usually traced back several centuries to a branch of Christianity called Calvinism and the rise of free trade. Now it is prevalent almost everywhere, although there are variations depending on regional cultural beliefs: it is stronger in Britain than Italy, for instance, and stronger in the States than in Britain. Calvinists say that success in work means you have been chosen by God, and the work ethic incorporates that philosophy of achievement and success. There's a belief that time to relax is not essential, because this takes away from the time spent working (note the correlation to the belief that time is limited). The most successful people in worldly terms often work virtually all the time. Margaret Thatcher, the longest-serving British prime minister of the twentieth century, survived on only three or four hours of sleep a night. Media magnates, industrial giants, and other top businesspeople are famous for the amount of work they do. Products of this ethic often worry that if they take a holiday, they'll "fall behind" and be seen as not sufficiently committed to their job. This concentration on work to the exclusion of all else leads to many stress-related illnesses.

Perhaps the linear view of time also keeps us separate, such as when we use being "too busy" as an excuse not to see our long-lost friends and relations or not to take time off and go traveling. We have our "career plans" and don't want other people to get "there" first, wherever "there" is. When we do travel, we may use our linear view of time to keep ourselves in a nice, safe, protected capsule—like a car or a bus—because it enables us to see more places in less time. If, in the process of keeping ourselves safe, we don't encounter people with viewpoints different from our own, well, we "had a great trip." And if we still feel a bit frustrated at work, then we can look forward to our holiday "next year." The trouble is, it's a long "time" to wait.

Along with this goes the sense that the past is unalterable. Western literature is absolutely *full* of the power of the past over the present, from Proust's *Remembrance of Things Past* to Shakespeare's *Hamlet*. That concept has led to some great literature, but writers were often not very happy. Seeing our past as fixed leads us to blame the past for our problems today, like blaming our present relationship problems on what happened with our parents when we were children. That doesn't help us to lead a happier life now. We are still repeating the old patterns.

According to Hawaiian belief, we can change our past *as well as* our present and future. But how can we possibly "change our time"? We can do so because the past exists *only in our thoughts;* it does not exist in itself. The synthesist Gregory Bateson wrote that only *ideas* about pigs and coconuts exist in our head, not the pigs and coconuts themselves. Similarly, our *ideas* about time exist in our heads, not time itself. We change our past when we change our ideas about it.

Maybe it's the power of the ocean, constantly beating and circling all the islands. Maybe it's the brightness of the land, or the way the sunlight flames out at dusk, or the path of the phosphorescence in the sparkling ocean. But whatever it may be, time seems different in Hawai'i—slower, more languorous somehow, altogether less important. In Hawai'i the work ethic is less strong than in the rest of the United States. Mary Kawena Pukui—the matriarch of contemporary Hawaiian scholarship and one of its most respected authors—said there are far more words in Hawaiian for food than time. Priorities are different. Even many of the non-Hawaiians in Hawai'i feel less pressure to work hard for its own sake. There are no kudos whatsoever to be gained in putting off having fun until tomorrow. There is a feeling that there is plenty of time for everything, including fun.

There's a sense in which time is a flexible quantity, dependent on awareness. Here's a description of the periods of the day, from David Malo's book, *Hawaiian Antiquities:*

> When the stars fade away and disappear, it is *ao,* daylight; and when the sun rises, day has come, we call it *lā,* and when the sun becomes warm, morning is past. When the sun is directly overhead it is *awakea,* noon; and when the sun inclines to the West in the afternoon, the expression is *ua aui ka lā.* After that comes evening, called *ahiahi;* and then sunset, *napo'o ka lā;* and then comes *pō,* the night, and the stars shine out.[3]

Each of these words concerns light. *Ao* is light in terms of daylight and "to regain consciousness." Perhaps that's why it also means "world." It's also the word used in the commitment prayer, *ho'ao,* or "making light." *Lā* is the word for "the shining sun." *Awakea* is the word used for the effulgence of the sun at midday. *Ua aui ka lā,* "the rain turns aside the sun," aptly symbolizes the sun inclining to the West. Evening is called *ahiahi,* "the little fires of evening." *'Ehu ahiahi,* evening twilight, was often used to describe old age. The word for sunset means the "sinking," *napoʻo*, "of the sun," *ka lā*. Pō, the night, as we know, contains unrealized light. That's why the Hawaiian "day" began with nightfall, not dawn. Everything begins with the hidden light and is light all the way through.

Time is thought of not as being limited—a linear, one-way trip to extinction or heaven—but as being so abundant that it exists in many dimensions at once! Serge King wrote that Hawaiians perceive all time, including the past, as *always being there*. Within this multidimensionality, people "pick up" time through certain antennae of awareness, on the same principle of a television set picking up signals. Out of all the signals in the air, a television set picks up only those signals whose specific rate of vibration it is attuned to. *And so do we.* Time exists in many dimensions at the same time. *We are just not aware of them.*

Even when we are not aware of all the dimensions of time, they continue to exist simultaneously and we slip in and out of them. Time *changes* with awareness. Think of when you have been in an emergency situation, dependent on your split-second reaction. Time suddenly expands and "there is all the time in the world" to make your decision. When I skied off a cliff when I was about fifteen, my whole life flashed before me in milliseconds. I was infinitely more aware than "normal." As a counterpoint, there are those times when I'm less aware, such as when I'm trying to wake up in the morning. I look at my alarm clock after what seems like minutes, but hours have gone by. My soporific state meant that I "lost time."

Time exists in spheres, called *reva* in Tahiti, which surround us in concentric circles. We move between these reva. When we are in our Higher Self, our deepest center, we truly know each other and connect on a deep soul level. When we are in the outer spheres, such as the subconscious, then we are limited by the dimensions of that sphere. We are dependent on our perception, and that can always be changed, hence we move in and out of those spheres at will.

And there is most certainly a place *beyond* time, one that we apprehend in our visions and our dreams. It is a land of our awakening, a fairy-tale land of crystalline clarity, a vision of color, a bright land of paradise. Every culture has a record that talks about this eternal land, the land beyond the sea, the land beyond time. In order to reach it, we have to build up our power. Huna teaches us how to do this by utilizing the power of the moon in ritual and astrology and being guided by the stars. Then new stars *shall* burn into ancient skies and, as Fuentes wrote, we shall truly know each other. So let's see a little "moon magic."

MOON MAGIC

There's a misty, murky magic in the bright Hawaiian moonlight
It has tricky, wiki-wiki, sort of hula-hula gleams,
It's a liqueur full of bubbles and it dissipates your troubles.
Oh, it's amorous and glamorous and fills you full of dreams.

DON BLANDING

The moon is the closest body to planet Earth in a vibrant and growing cosmos, where subjects and objects create and reflect. In Hawai'i the moon seems much closer than it does elsewhere, hanging like a great shining ball in the sky. The moonlight has a sticky quality to it, almost like you can scoop it up with a spoon. On certain nights the moon seems so all-pervasive that perhaps it is no wonder Hawaiians saw special significance in the moon phases and named each day of the changing moon. Records of those names have been kept and are known to a few. The moon was seen as the reflected light of the gods and certain days of the month were dedicated to particular gods.

The days dedicated to a certain god were generally a time to honor the form of that god within one's self, by doing certain activities and refraining from other ones. For example, the time of Kū was for feeling emotion and the time of Kāne for connecting to the Higher Self. Every day was also associated with different taboos, related to the god that the day was dedicated to. Taboos—as we saw in the chapter on hula—have to do with boundaries. If, for example, a day was under the taboo of Kū, then root vegetables should not be planted on that day; that activity was reserved for the days of Lono.

Of course, in ancient Hawai'i—before the taboo system was instituted—activities were ordered not by taboo, but by an understanding about when certain things naturally would be fostered. Just as in ancient Britain and many other parts of the world, certain nights of the moon were traditionally used to plant different foods. It was considered that each one would grow better at certain times, as the moon's light reflected and increased each individual quality. Likewise, the light of the moon symbolizes certain qualities of the "sacred plant" of humanity, determined by the night of the month a person is born.

All four Nui Akea (major gods) are represented here, going in a procession from Kū to Lono to Kanaloa to Kāne, mirroring the expansion of our mind. The taboos are one way to learn, but not the only way, which is shown by their not being valid at all in the joy and pleasure of the months of the Makahiki!

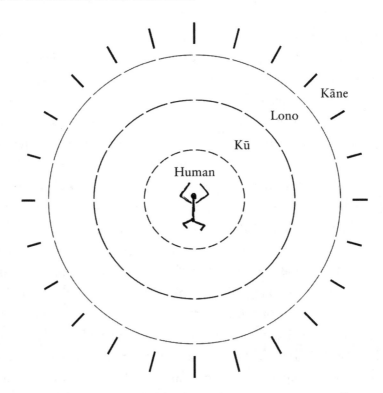

The body surrounded by the Gods (source R. A. Morrell)

A person born in the first three days of the moon's cycle belongs to the god Kū, meaning "standing," which in this context means "to be pregnant." This is the fallow period when seeds germinate in the warm earth. Hilo ("slender, twisted") is the first day of the moon's cycle. Hilo also means "a faint streak of light," and is when the first silvery sliver of moon appears. A person born on this day has more work to do to manifest his or her light than those born closer to the full moon. The next night is Hoaka. According to Scott Cunningham, author of *Hawaiian Religion and Magic,* Hoaka is an excellent night for healing, and a person born then needs to harness his or her power in that direction. The third night, when the moon is thicker, is called Kū Kahi (*kū,* "standing," and *kahi,* "first"). Traditional wisdom holds that someone born on this day does not find it too difficult to make his or her way in the world, but needs to be careful of too much independence and of making the same mistakes.

The next morning the Kū taboo is lifted. First comes the night of *Kū Lua (kū,* "standing," and *lua,* "double"), meaning "pairing off," as of mates or twins. Metaphorically, an image of light-as-reflection is being made. The primary life task of a person born at this "degree of light" is to "create" a mate. Her symbol is "a taro plant with two shoots." Kū Lua also means "standing in a pit," which is related to Pele, the goddess of volcanoes, implying that a person born on this day needs to watch out for the passion and anger of the pit.

The waxing moon is then called Kū Kolu, which means "the number three"; it is also "a thorny, weedy shrub." The primary task of these growing people is to prune themselves. According to Cunningham, it is a good time for gathering seaweed, which is taken from the beach toward the land. This relates to clearing the subconscious mind, with its fruits of the sea, and moving toward the land of the conscious mind. The next night is Kū Pau, the "finish," *pau,* of Kū, "the qualities of war." The people born under this moon may experience the war-bringing nature of Kū early in life, but have the chance to overcome it.

Next are the three "zero" nights, 'Ole Kū Kahi, 'Ole Kū Lua, and 'Ole Kū Kolu. *'Ole* means "zero, nothing or without," so those nights

THE HAWAIIAN MOON CYCLE[4]

Night 1	Hilo	first night of Kū taboo
Night 2	Hoaka	second night of Kū taboo
Night 3	Kū Kahi	third night of Kū taboo
Night 4	Kū Lua	
Night 5	Kū Kolu	
Night 6	Kū Pau	
Night 7	'Ole Kū Kahi	
Night 8	'Ole Kū Lua	
Night 9	'Ole Kū Kolu	
Night 10	'Ole Pau	
Night 11	Huna	
Night 12	Mōhalu	first night of Lono taboo
Night 13	Hua	second night of Lono taboo
Night 14	Akua	"kapu," or generally taboo
Night 15	Hoku	
Night 16	Māhea Lani	
Night 17	Kū Lua	
Night 18	Lā'au Kū Kahi	
Night 19	Lā'au Kū Lua	
Night 20	Lā'au Pau	
Night 21	'Ole Kū Kahi	
Night 22	'Ole Kū Lua	
Night 23	Pau	
Night 24	Kāloa Kū Kahi	first night of Kāloa, short for Kanaloa taboo
Night 25	Kāloa Kū Lua	second night of Kāloa taboo
Night 26	Kāloa Pau	
Night 27	Kāne	first night of taboo of Kāne
Night 28	Lono	second night of taboo of Kāne
Night 29	Mauli	
Night 30	Muku	

are considered unlucky. The moon is still growing, but more light means more shadows, so it is necessary for great care to be taken (as we have seen, *malama*, the word for "moon," also means "to take care" in the form *mālama*). People born on one of these nights are more judgmental and less fertile than others. This is also the period when the horns of the moon are growing. Then we have the tenth night, 'Ole Pau, or "the finish of nothing." Apparently, people born on that day often say too much.

The eleventh night of the moon is called Huna, "hidden," because the moon's horns are finally hidden. Huna, of course, is also the hidden wisdom of Hawai'i, a major focus of my life work, so when I discovered that I was born on this night, it certainly endorsed the validity of this way of learning more about ourselves! People born on this night that stands alone are likely to be very independent and to know a lot they don't say. Cunningham says there's fine fishing then, and it's a good time to plant root vegetables and gourds. For these vegetables you need to *kilokilo*, "dig deep," in the earth, hence they are very valuable. Interestingly, one type of kahua was known as kahuna kilokilo, which means "a kahuna of star-gazing," implying that by digging deep for our "food" of knowledge, we are also reaching high.

Next come the two bright nights of the Hua taboo, meaning the fertility after the gestation period of Kū. These nights are sacred to Lono, the god of consciousness. In *Hawaiian Antiquities,* Malo says the moon was called *hua* at this point because it was "quite egg-shaped." *Hua* means an "egg," and also "fruit, seed, to bear fruit, or to bear a child." The "pregnant" era of Kū is over, because *hua* also means "result." It's considered a very good time to be born, as personal change is relatively easy. The twelfth night is called Mōhalu, meaning to "unfold as a flower." This is considered to be a fine time for planting flowers, because they will grow round and perfect like the moon. The thirteenth night is called Hua, and people born at this time may well be very "light." To be born then is most auspicious for spiritual transformation. My shining friend Janine, to whom this book is dedicated, was born then.

The fourteenth night, the night of the full moon, is most sacred. It's called Akua, which, as we have seen, is the word for god. Akua can mean "agent" *a,* "of the high place," *kua.* Its appearance is a sign humans are doing well in building up their light. But this time is actually a more difficult one than Hua to be born, because a person born in Akua often has lots of resistance to change. Change will come anyway, however, for being born then means embracing a life of transformation! The night of Akua was *kapu,* not under the taboo of any god, because it is the very form of god. Hence, this was a time for remembering yourself as complete and pure, rather than focusing on any qualities of yourself you might still need to work on.

The next night is called Hoku, or "star." One implication of this word is that the consciousness of Kū has been transferred, *hō,* as the moon is declining. The cycle continues with the necessity to grow back to the light through one's Kū. Perhaps this is why in Huna, in common with other astrological traditions, it is considered harder to be born when the moon is declining. In general there is less information available about this part of the moon phase. On the night of Hoku, though, the fishing is still good: a good time to catch the fish of one's subconscious, perchance! The next night is Māhea Lani, which means "hazy," as in moonlight. Clarity is beginning to be lost and there is a sense that people born under this moon need to get back to what they once knew.

The seventeenth night of the now waning moon is a repeat of the fourth night, Kū Lua. This is because the moon's size is the same. It's a slightly easier time to be born, as it is no longer under the Kū taboo, so people born then are less driven by their emotions, which live in Kū. The eighteenth night is known as Lāʻau Kū Kahi. *La* is "the sun" and *ʻau,* "to swim or travel by sea," and *lāʻau* means "tree, plant, strength, rigidity, hardness, or the male erection." *Kū* is "standing," and *Kahi* "first." Together they imply a great ability to stand secure in the water of the sun and be successful in the material world. A person born on this day has to watch out for being too judgmental and living a life *too* full of individuality, for this moon shows its sharp horns.

The next night shows the moon declining further and is called Lāʻau

Kū Lua. Here *lā'au* means "standing second" or "twice." Those born under this moon, like those of Kū Lua, have the primary life task of "creating" or imagining a mate and they need to be careful of negativity. Then we have the twentieth night of the moon, Lā'au Pau, which means the time of lā'au is finished, a good day for planting and gathering.

The next stage is three nights of "nothing" as the moon further declines. These are 'Ole Kū Kahi, 'Ole Kū Lua, and 'Ole Pau. These are the same nights as in the period of Kū, but the influence of Kū is no longer overshadowing, for the moon has moved on. The twenty-first night, 'Ole Kū Kahi, can also be understood as "first without Kū," and 'Ole Kū Lua, the twenty-second night, is "second without Kū." Those born under these moons have to learn how to shed what they don't need to know. 'Ole Pau—the twenty-third night—means "the period of nothing is finished."

Then it's the time of Kāloa, which Malo says is short for Kanaloa, the god of the oceans. Kanaloa means "secure, firm, unconquerable." If you were born in the days of Kanaloa, you don't find it difficult to establish yourself in life. The twenty-fourth night, Kāloa Kū Kahi, is the first night of that taboo. Kāloa means "to create" (*ka,* "to strike" and *loa,* "length and distance"). Perhaps the universal spread of Kanaloa gives a clue about why people born at this time are said to be particularly in touch with shamanistic abilities. On the twenty-fifth night, Kāloa Kū Lua, natives are said to have the ability to imagine a mate for themselves. Cunningham says Kāloa Kū Lua is a good time to plant plants with long stems such as bananas and sugarcane. Bananas are associated with Kū, and sugarcane has many uses, including love magic, implying that a person born on that day has the ability to make magic.

Next is a time of relaxation: a night without taboos, the twenty-sixth, Kāloa Pau. The moon is safely duplicating and the period of nothing is finished. People of this moon are likely to lead a relatively trouble-free existence in this life, and they may well find they don't need to look for transcendent answers. On Kāloa Pau, the light is more distant, so if you were born then, you may well need to make a lot of effort to get what you want.

Now comes the last taboo—the taboo of Kāne, which covers the next two days of the month, when the moon is dying but the seeds of rebirth are there. Likewise, Kāne is associated with death and rebirth, as well as *wai ola,* the eternal water of life. The twenty-seventh night, when the moon rises at the dawn of day, is the night of Kāne. People born then find it "natural" to communicate with their superconscious mind. No planting or fishing was allowed on this day, reinforcing the idea of remaining in the superconscious mind (Kāne) and not the other two minds (Kū and Lono). The twenty-eighth night, when the moon rises only as the day is breaking, was known as Lono. If you were born then, your conscious mind is a naturally good communicator. It is a good time to plant gourds, which are great repositories of sacred knowledge, and to practice healing.

The taboo of Kāne was lifted on the morning of the twenty-ninth day. That day is known as Mauli, which Malo translates as "fainting." The moon isn't actually visible in the sky, because its rising is delayed until daylight. It's interesting to notice that Hawaiians also refer to death as "fainting" and understand it as the time when the soul (the essence, the aka) is there but not visible. Mauli also means "life," "heart," "spirit," and "the sea of life," perhaps giving clues as to how life can be restored. Cunningham says it is a good day for marriage and "fishing is good."

The final night, when the moon can no longer be seen for the light of the sun, was called Muku or "cut off." This isn't the best night to be born, because *mu* means "silent" or a "public executioner." Muku also means "a section of broken wave" as well as "amputated." It's the darkest night of all, and people born then are said to be the least likely to ask questions. But then the moon dips her face in the waters and begins the cycle anew, and the next night is once again Hilo, the first gleam of light. Hilo is also the name of a town on the east side of Hawai'i (the east represents the beginning of life).

Of course, these days of the moon are the same all over the world— although they have rarely been named or studied as they have been in Hawai'i—and it is possible for each of us to learn what moon we were born under. (If you want to contact me via my Web site, www.hunalight.com, I'll help you find your "moon-day." You can have some fun with it!) But, as with all astrology, it's important not to be too deterministic. It's surprising how often people say to their astrologer, "Is that good or bad?" The answer is "There is nothing good or bad in itself; everything is just a force, a power." Whether it presents itself as good or bad in your life depends on the power of your mana. That power is entirely up to you. One way we can build it up is by *imaging* the "sky light" that already exists. Imaging means reflecting. I sometimes compare it to imagining, which is putting "in" your own energy. Like the Hawaiians, I like puns!

A "moon ritual" traditionally held on the central island of Moloka'i and told to me by kumu hula John Ka'imikaua is a wonderful example of how imaging can be used to grow our light toward the gods. Only women participated in it, and they sat in a circular hut, with a hole in the roof. The full moon would shine through the skylight into a gourd shell, which was in turn full of water. Then the "moon circle" of women would chant and ask for what they most desired. The moment when the full moon was completely reflected in the full gourd was the time of most mana, the time when prayers were granted. This ritual was based in the knowledge that the full moon has the power to grant all desires when the consciousness of the women has helped their light to grow, through their individual understanding and interpretations of the teachings of Huna. Using moon power appropriately can most certainly can help us image, and grow, our own light.

The names of the phases of the moon show the power of reflection. Every month is divided into three periods, each called 'ano, meaning "type," "image," or "color." The doubled form of the word is 'ano 'ano, which means "the seed." Just as with the hula dancer, power must be built up. The seed germinates and sprouts and the moon cycle of desire and fulfillment carries on.

And now let's look at an even greater cycle, one that happens month by month, the cycle of the stars, for moonlight acts as a focus for growth, and starlight as a guide.

THE LIGHTING UP OF TIME

Local time, it's coconut time, man.

A HAWAIIAN

We are told that at the end of our time line comes death, the finish. But what if it isn't true? What if the world is more like the round coconut and we can plunge through it to different states and tastes? We know already that time was not thought of as linear in ancient Hawai'i, so death could not crown the end of it. What if the hard shell of the coconut, which we know as life on earth, was just that—a hard shell— yet full of ripe inner life and sweet flesh and juice? What if we can learn how to plunge through the inner dimensions, the dimensions where the dead are truly alive? This is not impossible in Huna! The "dead" become our 'aumakua, our guiding spirit, our Higher Self. There are many stories about communicating with spirits in Hawai'i, such as when 'aumākua come to help their descendants in times of need.

We all have an 'aumakua, even though ours may not be passed down through our families like those of the Hawaiians, and can all find our own (more information about my set of 'Aumakua Oracle Cards is on my Web site). I teach the knowledge of how to communicate with the "dead" in my courses on Hawaiian shamanism, in the United Kingdom and elsewhere, and some people have powerful experiences of messages from their loved ones. Likewise, if we are in need of help, our 'aumākua will suddenly appear and help us.

The 'aumākua are the spirit of the owls, sharks, turtles, and other beasts, as well as the birds, angels, godlings, gods, goddesses, and the whole procession of paradise. Kamakau had this to say about their realm:

> In the 'aumakua world were a rolling heaven, a multiple heaven, a multitudinous heaven, a floating cloudland, a lower cloudland, the immovable standing walls of Kāne, the horizon line enclosing the flat surface of the earth, the depths of the ocean, the beauty of

the sun, the brightness of the moon, the glories of the stars, and other places too numerous to mention which were called the 'aumakua world. Many were the gates by which to enter the 'aumakua world . . . And it was said that those who were taken to the floating cloudland and the multiple heaven and to the other heavens had wings and had rainbows at their feet. These were not wandering spirits . . . these were the beloved of the heavens . . . Those of heaven are seen on the wings of the wind and their bounds are above the regions of earth and those of the ocean are gathered in the deep purplish blue sea of Kāne, and so are all those of the whole earth belonging to the 'aumakua world; all are united in harmony.[5]

We can all tune in to our inner realms and access those realms of paradise. One day I was walking with some friends by the ocean to Ka'ena Point on O'ahu, and decided to test this faculty. I sat on the rocks at the end of the land on my own and meditated. Suddenly the ocean became bright white and I saw "the souls of the dead" gathered together, pulsing, like lines of tulip bulbs, in the shining chambers of the ocean. "Soul-shine, all light and fire." This spot is where the spirits of the dead leap back into the ocean that embraces us all. That vision was shortly followed by another one, of a beautiful rainbow guiding our journey home. It was particularly poignant because my grandfather had just died, and I had recently been to Australia for his funeral. It's said the rainbow represents the opening out of the spirit on death and the dead become our 'aumakua, our guiding light. Death is an opening, not a closing.

There are always signs for those with eyes to see, songs for those with ears to hear. The souls of the dead are winking and blinking as the sparkles of lapalapa on the beach. The word for "phosphorescence" sheds some more light. *Lā* is "the sun" and *pa*, "an enclosure." There is a sense of building something to enclose the light of the sun. The causal form is *ho'olapa*, meaning "to excite or flare as of a light." *Ho'olapa* also means "to form a ridge." *Lapalapa* is "steep-ridged."

The dead, whose home is in the inner realms, whose souls are eternal, have the ability to contact us on the lighter, higher levels. Those lights on the beach at night, right where the land meets the sea, are signs of the "lighting up of time."

STAR MAGIC

If thou follow thy star, thou canst not fail to find a glorious haven.

DANTE

The light of the stars, like the light of the moon and the sun, is "shared light," light that all humanity, all beings on planet Earth, share. The clues to the stars' shamanistic meanings in Hawai'i lie in the hidden meanings of their names. Although star names vary from island to island, the underlying nature of the interpretation is the same. I'm using names prevalent on the island of Hawai'i, according to Samuel Kamakau, where *each name of a star is the same as the name of the month it represents.* It shows a system of creation based on imaging and attraction, a metaphor for one's own journey into the Higher Self. "Imaging" shows the way you should grow your own power—by reflecting the heavens—whereas "attraction" shows the way you do it—through pulling on desired qualities.

There's a sense in which "Star Time" means "Start Time." The months "seed" or replicate themselves as they go through their natural progression. This is because they are being imaged through consciousness. The bright star provides the consciousness to replicate. Every male star images its female mate, the month, carving out the Hawaiian sky, like a great gourd of consciousness. It's the time of the "lighting up of time."

The symbolic meanings of the names of the stars offer insights about the way the humans born at a certain time or "star sign" can best grow back to the gods. Every human being has his or her place in the celestial zodiac and you can easily place yourself, and your loved ones, in the following cycle and benefit from Huna's guidance.

THE HAWAIIAN ZODIAC[6]*

Scorpio	ʻIkuwā	Clamoring creature
Sagittarius	Welehu	Fish of the deep seas
Capricorn	Makaliʻi	Creature of the Pleiades
Aquarius	Kāʻelo	Wet one
Pisces	Kaulua	Doubling one
Aries	Nana	Spreading one
Taurus	Welo	Fluttering one
Gemini	Ikiiki	Small and humble one
Cancer	Kaʻaona	Attractive one
Leo	Hinaiaʻeleʻele	Moon goddess toppling down
Virgo	Māhoe Mua	First twin
Libra	Māhoe Hope	Second twin

* I have taken the Hawaiian after Malo (*Hawaiian Antiquities,* 33) describing the measurement of time on the Big Island. The interpretations are my own, as is making ʻIkuwā the first month.

The year was divided into two seasons, *Hoʻoʻilo,* "winter," and *Kau,* "summer," divided by the rising of the constellation Pleiades above the visible horizon, which happens at the beginning of winter. In the *Kumulipo* we saw how light came out of the darkness; this is reflected in the Huna belief that the day starts with the evening and the year starts with winter. *Hoʻoʻilo,* the winter, means "to germinate or sprout" and *Kau,* the summer, "to place, put, rise up, or appear." A period of germination is necessary before light can appear. Those born in the winter need to be careful of different kinds of potentials in their psyche, and must be sure to allow only desirable seeds to flourish. If you were born in summer, it's a bit easier, for the weather is calmer then. Yet the transfer of the seasons is a progression, and each month, also known as a generation, is believed to mate with the one before and seed the one that comes after it.

The year was believed to start a month before the rising of the Pleiades. The star month called ʻIkuwā begins at the end of October and corresponds to the Western zodiac sign of Scorpio. It is a noisy month, named after the roar of the surf, thunder, and cloudbursts prevalent in Hawai'i at that time of year. The clamoring of the weather corresponds perhaps to the reverberations of the emotions of those born in this month, similar to the attributes of those born under Scorpio, who are noted for a particular quality of emotional intensity: ruled by Mars, the god of war, and Pluto, the god of the underworld. To grow, they need to lose that emotional intensity, remember they have many loves, not just one (but *not* in the sense of promiscuity!), and become brighter and lighter.

The first month of winter is Welehu, or Sagittarius. This is the time when the Pleiades first appear. Welehu means "Fish of the deep seas," and is the first Creature appearing on earth. Perhaps the sea represents the "deep sea" of memory. *Wele*, according to the Hawaiian dictionary, is the same as the word *waele*, "to weed or clear," and *hu*, "to rise as in waves." A person born in Welehu tends to excess, much like those born in Sagittarius. Yet the name also holds the necessary clues to clear the way. A certain selectivity is essential to select the contents of the billows of emotion, by "weeding" out unwanted ones and clearing one's way toward the light of the superconscious, represented by the stars.

The next month, called Makali'i, or creature of the Pleiades, is the month that corresponds to Capricorn. *Maka* means "eye" and *li'i*, "thin." The Pleiades are growing brighter and make a thin light in the sky. This is a time of great growth, as expressed by the proverb *Kupu ka lā'au ona a Makali'i:* "The leaf of the plant grows in the time of Makali'i." *Makali'i* also means "a small-meshed net," implying the net of consciousness that is needed to catch the fish of subconscious emotion lurking in the sea. Those born in the time of Makali'i need to go beyond their attention to detail and to the material to see, and then convey, the bigger picture.

Next is Kā'elo, Aquarius. *Kā'elo* means "wet one." Unlike the Western meaning of Aquarius as "the water carrier"—often represented as someone who is not in touch with his or her emotions—the person born under Kā'elo is seen as having the capacity to feel very deeply, and thus to image or reflect creation correctly. This person grows her own power by actually leaving her head and daring to feel. The infusion of emotion is the very quality she needs to create correctly, for that cannot be done from the head.

Then comes Kaulua, or Pisces. *Kaulua* means "to put together as in a pair," "to double in quantity." The single fish of Welehu has now become two! Another fish has been created through making an image in thought form (aka) and then imbuing it with mana. People born then need to "place their mate"—in other words, not become overwhelmed by emotions of attachment. Rather, they need to acknowledge their mate as part of the bright spiritual design of wonder. Just as for those born in Pisces, the quality of detachment is needed for true growth. The appearance of "twins" shows that the light is growing stronger, also implied by the Polynesian association of Kaulua with the bright star of Sirius.

Next is Nana, or Aries, which can mean "to spread" or "a variety of fish." Differentiation is occurring. Another meaning of Nana is "quiet," "restful." The emotions are being transcended. This is quite dissimilar to the interpretation of Aries as being the heedless first sign in the zodiac cycle, represented by an infant or a ram. The person born then needs to not put "all his eggs in one basket," but to remember the peace and tranquillity that is behind all. The way to grow into his true power is to stop rushing around and reconnect to the true source of power. *Nānā* also means "to seek."

Welo, corresponding to Taurus, means "to flutter, float, or stream, as in the wind." The fish is rising, leaving the deep sea below. The wind stands for love in Hawai'i, and the little fish-bird is fluttering. This is a little like the meaning of Taurus, ruled by Venus, the planet of love, although Taurus the Bull is far "earthier." The Welo character, like the opposite, 'Ikuwā, or Scorpio, needs to learn to rise above his emotions to stream in the universal wind of love. The journey may be slightly easier for the Welo person, however, as welo is also the name of a strong purgative; hence, it is easier to let go. The stars of the Pleiades are held in this constellation, and *welo* also means "progeny" or "ancestry."

Then come the first months of summer. Ikiiki, Gemini, is the time of "stifling heat and humidity, acute discomfort, pain, grief." The small fish-bird is being challenged by the pressure of the new environment. The person born then often needs to learn the lesson of being smaller (iki), or humility, hence the name "small and humble one." Like those born under the constellation of Gemini, they often have the attributes of being airy, light, and challenging. They can grow best by realizing they are only a small part of a much greater design.

Ka'aona, Cancer, means "attractive one" and "reddish brown, due to being smoked, especially of a fish." The creature is being appropriately "cooked" and—just like with the hula dancer—color is beginning to develop. The little fish-bird, as a result of the application of heat and pressure, or the growth of consciousness, is beginning to be noticed in the world. *Ka'aona* is also "the stem of the sugarcane tassel used as a dart." The sugarcane was used in love prayers sent on the wind, implying that a child born in this time is a messenger for love, similar to Cancer being associated with love. A child of this constellation can best grow by really moving a lot *(ka'a)* and allowing herself to attract others *(ona)*. Children of this sign are believed to be particularly attractive and lovable.

Next is Hinaia'ele'ele, or Leo. Hina is the moon goddess, yet this name also implies "a murky color": *hina* is "gray," *ele'ele*, "black." *Hina* also means "to fall, tumble, topple over from an upright position." The creature is beginning to walk on land, but unsteadily. A person born then must learn to stand steadily on his own and really weave his own belief system, rather than taking on that of others. *Hina'i* means "a basket," and this could be one of woven thought-forms, made to retrieve the unwary creature as it falls in its first steps on land. Hina also means "to blow in a straight course, of wind." By following the wind of love, one may direct oneself appropriately. Here one is beginning to learn new things and must be careful to navigate properly toward the superconscious.

Next come the last two star generations. Māhoe Mua (first twin) is associated with Virgo and Māhoe Hope (second twin) with Libra. *Māhoe*, the word in common, means "twins" and it refers to two native trees of Hawai'i (*Alectryon macrococcum* and *A. mahoe*). Trees, a wonderful sign of consciousness, are able to grow on the land where one has only recently learned how to walk. *Mā* means "to perceive" and *hoe* means "to move or travel"; *māhoe* thus implies that those born under these two signs have traveled through the dimensions appropriately and at last perceive a sense of unity. *Mua* means "to progress" and *hope*, "result" or "conclusion." Taken together, Māhoe Mua and Māhoe Hope can be understood as the mate mirroring itself, or the earth mirroring the star of origin. For example, some Hawaiian tales-that-may-be-true tell of earth coming from the Pleiades. Now those on earth need to learn to mirror the qualities of joy and compassion that shine in the faraway light of that star system. The twins indicate that as we learn how to shape time, progression leads to result: one thing follows another, to a harmonious conclusion. All we need to do, to find our own glorious haven, is to carry on following our star with love: we need to reflect back the attributes of the particular light that is mirrored in us by our birth sign and moon sign, as well as shine with a more universal light.

THE PLEIADES

Canst thou bind together the brilliant Pleiades?

FROM THE BOOK OF JOB

As we have seen, the Pleiades, or *Makaliʻi*, are particularly important in Hawaiʻi. Some Hawaiians say we all come from the Pleiades, and that "Star Men" originally seeded Hawaiʻi, a topic I explore in my next book, *Star-Seeding Hawaiʻi*. The "sweet influence" of the Pleiades is found all over the world, as expressed by the poet Milton—one of my ancestors on my mother's side—in his description of creation in his epic poem *Paradise Lost*:

The grey
Dawn and the Pleiades before him danc'd,
Shedding sweet influence . . .[7]

Many classical writers also allude to this group of stars. The Pleiades were known in Greece as the Seven Sages. Hippocrates, just like the Hawaiians, divided the year according to them. The Aborigines of Australia celebrate the reappearance of the Pleiades with dances in honor of the Seven Stars. The Hindus of India hold the festival of light, Diwali, in their honor. The pagan Arabs saw them as the seat of immortality, as did groups as diverse as the Dyaks of Borneo and the Berbers of North Africa. The Barasana of South America regard them as the center of the universe.

All around Polynesia, the appearance of the Pleiades over the horizon was welcomed with dancing, feasting, and making love. They marked the time known as Makahiki, when war and sacrifice, and even paying taxes—all aspects of the imported system of taboos—were forbidden. Even though that system became much stricter over the last few hundred years, there were no taboos in the last few months of the year, when the Pleiades were in view, which goes back to ancient wisdom. Makahiki was the period between the passions of Ikuwa and the peace of Kaulua. As we've seen, even the worship of gods was not necessary then: it was a time for just having fun! *Maka* means "eye" and *hiki* means "can, may, and to be able." The Makahiki festival pointed the way to the superconscious mind-in-the-sky. It was considered to be the time of great consciousness, or "the enabling of the Great Light," when many things were encouraged *to be done in the correct way,* meaning with and for love.

Of course these qualities of light and love were also found in Hawai'i for the rest of the year, but the very qualities of paradise were brought down to earth by loving behavior for these four months. The qualities of light and love of the Pleiades—a dimensional state one can slip in and out of at will—were celebrated by dancing on the beaches to welcome the visibility of that great constellation.

The Pleiades are also known as Na Huihui O Makali'i, or "the nets of Makali'i." The gossamer light matrix of the net symbolizes the threads of aka, interwoven with our body, and needing to be tuned in to the greater light. One reason we need to do this is taught by the legend of the god Makali'i, who was worried about food shortages. He put all the food of the earth in a great net in the sky to ensure that he would not go hungry. But the rest of the beings did. Both animals and humans (for this was in the days of conscious communication) held a meeting to decide what should be done. Eventually the rat offered to climb up to the stars, which he did on a rainbow; he bit several holes in the net, and the net, the rat, and the food fell back to earth. It fed the Hawaiian people and taught Makali'i that he needed to learn how to deal with his selfishness.

Just like the god Makali'i, we need to learn to share what we have. Otherwise we end up with the way the world is at present, with some people of the world having too much to eat while the rest of the world does not have enough. Or—as in London—humans mostly having enough to eat while wild creatures go hungry. We need to learn to give in order to choose the right capacity of food that is appropriate for ourselves.

Likewise we need to learn how to give in order to really enjoy our food, literally and symbolically. The nets of Makali'i are nets of consciousness, needing to be re-magnetized through our connection to our universal sense of being. Then we have the ability to tug on the nets of the universe, abolishing all time and distance and separation. That is how we bind together the brilliant Pleiades.

THE LIGHTS OF THE NIGHT

Stars are the eyes of the night.

VICTOR HUGO

The role of the stars is to guide us. *Hōkū,* or "star," can also mean "to give," *hō,* "the arriving," *kū.* One thing they give all over the world is light, fine light that pours down upon us from light holes placed at various points in the great fabric of the night sky. The giving of light and love provides a template we can follow in the growth of our own light.

That is why some very special centers for training in mystery and magic in ancient Polynesia, including techniques for fertility and growth, were called star schools.

The stars are wonderful representations of the light of the superconscious. Perhaps their very light and height is one reason why many kahuna guide their magic toward them, through dedicating their rituals and star-chants to them. Perhaps the "fullness of light" they embody was why chiefs were given "star names." Like the chiefs, the stars also guided the Polynesians in a very real sense and were the basis for their navigation of the Pacific. Stars are indeed "the eyes of the night."

It is said that the eyes of the glowing chief Tahaki were so beautiful they were "too sparkling to lose forever" and are now stars in the sky. Symbolically, the "lights in the night" represent consciousness achieved, revealing the light that is already there, "the light behind the world." If one thinks of the amount of light-years it takes starlight to reach us, we realize that the light revealed thereby may be very ancient indeed. Another revelation of ancient light is Hawaiian myth, which we will look at in the next chapter.

9
Gods Sliding Down Rainbows: Myth and Magic

O Rainbow sun-bridge!
The purified colors of all being,
O Rainbow, bridge that unites,
The reflection of the creative spirit art thou.

POLYNESIAN CHANT

The rainbow plays a huge and dewy role in representing Hawaiian knowledge. The beauty of a shivering rainbow always has an uplifting effect on the spirit. Huna is also a thing of beauty, containing the power to help the spirit raise itself. The rainbow is a sign of harmony, because in it all the colors of visible light are presented together, flowing into one another. Hawaiian knowledge is also ultimately about harmony: the harmony of the three minds—subconscious, conscious, and super-conscious—working together instead of against one another, and the harmony of the individual in relation to all other aspects of creation.

The rainbow is also a sign of discovery: Luomala reports that one of the canoes the Polynesians used for discovering their islands was called "rainbow"—"and some say it was a real rainbow."[1] Huna is about discovery, too, disclosing inner lands that are normally hidden. The rainbow is a "bridge that unites," reminding humans how to connect to the bright lands of light, such as in this fabulous chant, taken from Kamakau's *Tales and Traditions:*

O ke anuenue ke ala o Kahaʻi
Piʻi Kahaʻi, ko i Kahaʻi
Aʻe Kahaʻi i ke koʻiʻula
Aʻe Kahaʻi i ke anahā
He anaha he kanaka ka waʻa.

The rainbow was the pathway of Kahaʻi
Kahaʻi ascended, Kahaʻi pushed on
Kahaʻi tread the rainbow-hued trail of Kāne
Kahaʻi tread along the reflected light
The man like a canoe on the reflected light.[2]

The trail along the glimmering path of the reflected light is the path of return to the distant, yet familiar, land of the gods, which is the superconscious source of light. Thus, in Huna, the appearance of the rainbow is a sign of the opening up of consciousness into the spiritual dimension. The world is no longer seen on the level of the lower self that divides things into either "This is the way it is" or "That is the way it should be." As Pali Lee and Koko Willis say: "When men say they believe this or that they put blinkers on themselves. Blinders hide the beauty and majesty of what we are a part of."[3] When new meanings are apprehended and included, the self, like the rainbow, will open out into gradations of light. It will be able to function more creatively.

As we have seen, Huna points the way to the creative spirit in many ways such as through the hula, through chanting, and even through making love with consciousness. In this chapter, we will look at yet another profound teaching method of Huna: the ancient myths of Hawaiʻi. First we will discuss in detail the myth of Pele and Hiʻiaka, which offers clues about ways to free our light from the grip of our subconscious urges and blocks. Then we will explore the intertwined metaphor of rock and light to understand more deeply our essence as light, even when it seems to be imprisoned by the rigidity of fixed ideas. Finally, we will look at the myths of the goddess of the moon and the goddess of the snows, which depict two different ways of releasing oneself, either through properly channeled emotion (Poli'ahu, the snow goddess) or the importance of focusing on a new pattern (Hina, the moon goddess).

Although we will closely examine only a few myths, at a certain level all the myths of Hawai'i interpenetrate and weave a canopy of light, reminding us of our capacity to receive answers to all the questions of life from the superconscious. A deeper look into the symbolism of the myths helps us to become alive to many meanings. On the vehicle of myth, we more easily travel to the place of no distance and simultaneous time, where we are able to go wherever our consciousness chooses: we too can slide up and down light.

NEW LIGHT, NEW MEANING

New islands, new lands, new seas, new peoples and what
is more, a new sky and new stars.

PEDRO NUNES

Mythology, all over the world, shows us new ways of being. It opens us up to worlds where fairies communicate with mortals, animals talk, and humans swim between dimensions. Hawaiian myths are no different. They contain an abundance of amazing beings, interacting with each other and even with humans. In these myths, the humans are often extra-ordinary, in the sense of being beyond themselves. Just as in the mythology of other cultures, Hawaiian myths depict struggles between the light and the not-so-light, the visible and the hidden.

Myths can be interpreted in many, many ways. They can be understood as entertaining stories, recapitulations of geologic history, psychological studies, and revelations of spiritual dimensions, among many other possibilities. They also contain fascinating guides for unlocking our emotions, as well as being a coda to the sacredness of the landscape.

That is why Claude Lévi-Strauss described mythology as "that huge and complex edifice which also glows with a thousand colours as it builds up before the analyst's gaze."[4] The very same myth can express all these layers of meaning simultaneously, a truth captured by August Strindberg when he wrote:

> *Meaning is in the play, an interplay of light.*
> *As in schizophrenia, all things lose their boundaries*
> *become iridescent with many-colored significances.*
> *No things, but an iridescence, a rainbow effect.*[5]

The "rainbow effect" of higher knowledge is found in many Hawaiian tales, which sparkle with the "thousand colours" Claude Lévi-Strauss talks about.

Myths usually contain warnings about what not to do, and they often concern our emotions. The power of our emotions to take away our light may reflect an origin-al problem. Wākea, the sky god, made love with Papa-i-ka-Haumea, the earth goddess. Then, from their love-making, the earth came into being. But the sky was solid and there was no space for light to enter the world. Kāne had to pry Wākea and Papa apart from their cosmic lovemaking and attachment to each other, like two halves of a giant clamshell. Then, according to Luomala, he "decorated the sky with twinkling stars, great stars, the moon, the sun, the lunar rainbow, the rains, the winds, the clouds."[6] This shows how the destructive power of passion and emotions can be transformed into higher consciousness.

Another myth that warns about the destructive power of emotion is the myth of Pele and Hi'iaka, one of the most important myths in the Hawaiian Islands. The version below is taken from an account by Nathaniel Emerson; the paraphrasing and interpretation are my own. In this myth, we can see the gods and goddesses taking certain paths, and the inevitable consequences of their choices. They offer us vivid guidance as we make our own choices in life. The two goddesses, in my view, represent two possibilities: Pele sometimes uses destructive power to get what she wants, with chaotic consequences, while her sister Hi'iaka learns to use directed consciousness and so creates more appropriately.

THE MYTH OF PELE AND HI'IAKA

Kāne-pō, ho'oulu mai!
He hiamoe kapu kou ho'āla ana.

O God of the Night, inspire me!
Thy sleep needs a sacred waking.
FROM *PELE AND HI'IAKA*, TRANSLATED BY NATHANIEL EMERSON

Pele, one of the Hawaiians' favorite goddesses, was born of the union of Wākea, the sky father, and Papa, the earth mother. Each of their children represents a different aspect of nature, like the sea, the volcano, and the rain. Just as happens in the best of human families, there were a lot of rivalries in the godly one, but the rivalries of the gods and goddesses were played out in the creative and destructive forces of nature. This particular myth dances between the southernmost and northernmost extremes of Hawai'i: the volcano Kīlauea on the Big Island and the Nā Pali cliffs on the north coast of Kaua'i.

As we have seen, Pele—sometimes represented as having flying red hair—is the goddess of volcanoes. She had huge problems finding a home for herself and her family. Her early experimentation with fire necessitated her leaving her parents' home in far away Kahiki, one homeland of the gods. Pele reached the Hawaiian archipelago and tried to find an island to live on there. But her jealous sister, the sea goddess Namakaokaha'i, kept driving her away from whichever island she tried to settle on. Pele was in despair until she came to the last island, Hawai'i. In the following chant she "lets go" of the other islands, and welcomes the one on which she intends to live:

Aloha o Maui, aloha, e!
Aloha o Moloka'i, aloha, e!

Aloha o Lāna'i, aloha, e!
Aloha o Kaho'olawe, aloha, e!
Ku mākou e hele, e!
O Hawai'i ka āina
A mākou e noho ai a mau loa aku.

Farewell to thee, Maui, farewell!
Farewell to thee, Moloka'i, farewell!
Farewell to thee, Lāna'i, farewell!
Farewell to thee, Kaho'olawe, farewell!
We stand all girded for travel:
Hawai'i, it seems, is the land
On which we shall dwell evermore.[7]

Pele and her family eventually chose to settle in one crater of the Big Island, and evidence of their stay remains today in the world's most active volcano.

One fine day, Pele fell asleep. Her spirit became restless and left her body, lured along the islands by the ghostly sound of Kanikawī, "the nose flute," and his companion, Kanikawā, "the whistle." Eventually her spirit reached Kaua'i, where she saw the handsome prince Lohi'au dancing the hula on the sea cliffs. Pele fell passionately in love with him and decided to make Lohi'au fall in love with her too. She projected her spirit into a beautiful earthly form and chanted to him. They feasted together, and

... when they rose from the table he led her, not unwilling, to his house, and he lay down upon a couch by her side. But she would favor him only with kisses. In his growing passion for her he forgot his need of food, his fondness for the hula, the obligations that rested upon him as a host: all these were driven from his head.[8]

The situation continued thus for three days and three nights, after which Pele left, promising to find a home for them. Lohi'au was inconsolable with grief, and—without realizing he had fallen in love with a *projection*—he killed himself.

Pele was dreadfully disconsolate when she heard this news, back at her home in her crater on the island of Hawai'i. Her youngest sister, Hi'iaka-i-ka-poli-i-Pele, dreamt she would be asked to go on a journey of rescue and, when Pele did ask her, she agreed. Pele gave Hi'iaka "weather mana" to protect her. She "called upon the Sun, the Moon, the Stars, Wind, Rain, Thunder, Lightning." Then Hi'iaka and her maidservant and friend, Wahine 'Ōma'o, began to travel throughout the islands. The pair needed to use every bit of mana they had, as they were beset by dangers such as dragons in disguise, sorcerers, lizard-witches, and enchanted sharks. But Hi'iaka chanted and sang, always remaining alert, and the pair managed to vanquish those who wished them ill.

After many trials, the brave pair reached the north coast of Kaua'i where Prince Lohi'au used to live. There, they saw his ghostly form high up in a cave on the cliffs and found his lonely spirit wandering desolately on the beautiful Nā Pali coast. Hi'iaka chased it and finally managed to capture it in a flower. However, she still needed to restore Lohi'au to life by calling on the other godly beings and uttering many prayers. Here is her final desperate prayer:

O Hi'iaka kaula mana e;
Nana i ho'uluulu na ma'i . . .
Eia ka wai la, he Wai ola, e!
E ola, ho'i, e-e!

Thus toiled the seer Hi'iaka;
For hers was the magic of cure . . .
Here's water, the Water of Life!
Grant life in abundance, life![9]

This restored a bewildered Lohi'au to consciousness. Hi'iaka's work of healing was accomplished. Then there remained only the task of conducting Lohiʻau to Pele. The journey began easily enough when three rainbows arched "conveniently at their feet," and the goddess, her handmaiden, and the prince slid down them, back to Lohiʻau's old home at the base of the cliff. They all cleansed themselves in the ocean and, to quote Emerson, "with this cleansing each one of them seemed to have a new birth of physical perfection. As they came up out of the water their bodies seemed actually to glow with a fresh and radiant beauty."[10] Lohiʻau was so joyful at being restored to life that he went surfing at once in the high, purple waves. He was still in love with Pele and happy to go back to her.

However, when the three reached the island of Hawaiʻi, Hiʻiaka discovered that a calamity had happened. Her beloved *lehua* trees had been destroyed by one of Pele's cindery outbursts, and her friend Hōpoe, whom Pele had promised to look after, was dead, due to a fit of Pele's jealousy. Hiʻiaka vowed revenge. As they reached the flank of the caldera, in full view of Pele, Hiʻiaka wove Lohiʻau a lei of scarlet flower blossoms, sang to him, placed the lei around his neck, and kissed him, first gently, then passionately, as he responded to her.

Pele was absolutely furious. Things had not gone her way. She gave the order: "Ply him with fire." Hiʻiaka's elder sisters were reluctant, but then they "put on their robes of fire and went forth." Once they reached Lohiʻau, they found him to be of such surpassing beauty that they exclaimed:

Mahina ke alo,
Pali ke kua.
Ke kū a ke kanaka maikaʻi . . .

Front, bright as the moon,
Back, straight as a mountain wall:
So stands the handsome man . . .[11]

They dropped a few desultory pieces of cinder around Lohiʻau and left him, but Pele, fuming, sent them back to do the job properly.

Lohi'au cried out in despair as he was suffocated by the encircling fires, comparing his own death to the turning of nature itself away from the "natural order" of things:

Wela ka hōkū, ka Malama;
Ua wela Makali'i, Kā'elo Ka-ulua . . .
Iki'ki i ka uwahi lehua;
Pāku'i ka uwahi Kanaka . . .
Pua'i hanu, ea 'ole i ke po'i a ke ahi.

The stars are on fire, and the Moon
Cold winter is turned to hot summer . . .
I choke in this smoke of lehua—
How pungent this smell of burnt man!
I strangle, my breath is cut off . . .[12]

The poor "burnt man" soon perished and was afterward turned into petrified rock by Pele. Hi'iaka was desolate but calm, saying very little to her sisters. Then Pele discovered that the girl Hi'iaka—whom she had always thought of as nothing but a little sweetie—had magic so powerful that she had been able to restore Lohi'au to life. She also discovered that Hi'iaka had not touched Lohi'au until she realized Pele had broken her word. Finally, Pele agreed that Lohi'au should be brought back to life again. After some more adventures, this was done by Pele's powerful elder brother, Kānemilohai, Kāne of the spinning of tales. But Hi'iaka did not know, as she was away visiting a hula court on O'ahu. Lohi'au secretly waited there, hidden under a pile of tapa cloth. Hi'iaka sang sadly and Lohi'au was moved to respond to the familiar sound of that beloved voice. He revealed himself; the pair were in rapture; and Lohi'au entered into "'Hi'iaka's encircling arms, lovingly extended to him."[13]

So Emerson concludes the myth of Pele and Hi'iaka. It is said that Lohi'au, handsome as the full moon, and his Hi'iaka still live in the hula ground at the base of the Nā Pali cliffs. They are so happy with each other that only sometimes do they need to dance in order to refocus the light of their superconscious. Pele herself is not quite so "at home" in *her* home, the volcano, as the constant red movement of the lava shows. These larger-than-life figures are examples to be aware of, or beware of: the choice is up to us.

There are many messages contained in this myth. One speaks of the need to grow correctly by directing one's consciousness. The first journey through the islands was performed by the goddess Pele. She could be a careless goddess: her unbridled, fiery emotions were twice responsible for the death of her beloved Lohi'au, symbolic of the disruptive results when we act according to the promptings of the subconscious mind and think only about what we want. The next journey—made by the goddess Hi'iaka and her maidservant, Wahine 'Ōma'o—restored Lohi'au to life. Hi'iaka accomplished this through her chanting, which, as we have seen, is a powerful way of focusing consciousness.

Another difference between the journeys of Pele and Hi'iaka is that all of Hi'iaka travels (not just her spirit, but her body too). Therefore Lohi'au fell in love not with a projection, the way he did with Pele, but with a whole person.

Hidden meanings within the names of the goddesses convey similar teachings. The shading in Pele is black *('ele),* the color Pele turns the land after her rampages. The land is covered in fresh lava; nothing can grow. This is like the blocked state of a person whose consciousness is burned by intense emotions surfacing from the subconscious and then frozen by hidden fears and obsessions. In contrast, Wahine 'Ōma'o means "lady in green," the color of regenerating nature. Hi'iaka means "carrier," *hi'i,* of "the potential for consciousness," *aka.* Hi'iaka is a carrier of consciousness, just as we all are. Hi'iaka and Wahine 'Ōma'o help bring life to the land and to Lohi'au. This is because they know how to focus their light of being.

There are no "happy ever afters" in Hawaiian myths, however, no static endings of a prince and princess returning to their castle. This is because the world is constantly moving, constantly being created, so there cannot be "an ending." Even though some of the characters do find contentment—like Prince Lohi'au and Hi'iaka living together in the hula ground—they have to keep dancing the hula to maintain their enchanted state. In other words, they need to keep re-creating their consciousness.

The great god Kāne is the only god who rests in his form Kāne moe awakea, or Kāne-sleeping-in-the-great-light. He is the ultimate archetype, the ultimate expression. He represents the peace of the rosy superconscious light, the goal toward which each of us—gods, goddesses, humans, animals, plants, and rocks—must journey. He uses signs, found in the weather, for example, to adorn our personal skies and offer us guidance.

We begin our journey from the realm where, like Pele, we can be ruled by our subconscious urges, the dim and dusky land of pō. Our senses in this particular world are so much dimmer: our sense of touch is only a shadow of the touch we will feel in the future; our sense of vision only an outline of the brightness that is to come; our sense of hearing merely an echo of a distant harmony; our sense of smell a mere waft of the fragrant lands beyond. These myths show us how to use consciousness, ao—which also means "to grow light," "land" or "world"—to grow toward the lands of brightness where the gods and goddesses reside.

THE ESSENCE OF LIGHT

I was fascinated by golden figures in streams or on the sea-shore.

PAUL GAUGUIN, ON POLYNESIA

Lapalapa, the phosphorescent flicker on the beach at night—which we looked at in the last chapter—can be seen as representing the essence that absolutely everything in the cosmos is composed of, whether plants, planets, or people. It is the flicker of our soul, the most basic quality we are born with, and the quality we take with us when we leave. It is our eternal component. Our essence is eternal because it comes from the pō, and the pō is everywhere. The pō is the home of the gods who do not need the material reality of our world. One Hawaiian thinks of the dead as dancing the *hula 'ōlapa,* feasting on shadowy food and leading a drowsy existence. The gods feed on essence, as demonstrated by the feast that was held for the gods after Hi'iaka returned Lohi'au to life. Emerson described it like this:

> No speech, no human voice, only the gentle clash of wooden dishes, the rustle of leaves, the gurgle of deep potation and the subdued sounds of gestation came from the place in which the human foot or eye dared not intrude.[14]

After the gods had eaten their fill, they left:

> The coconuts unbroken, devoid of meat, the bananas were found to be but hollow skins . . . the substance, the essence had been filched away by some inscrutable power.[15]

Perhaps this explains why the Hawaiian grace is: "Yours is the essence, O God, ours the material part." The gods thrive on essence because they *are* essence. That essence can be understood as the essence of light, shown by the description of the infant offspring of the gods as "sparks of phosphorescent animation glittering in baby shells of etheric substance finer than the finest glass."[16] The phosphorescence of the ocean is seen as the footfall of the stars and a sign that the gods are active. On the nights when the tops of the waves shine with a glistening light, it is said that the gods have joined in the sport of surfing.

Humanity is also made up of this essence of light. Huna teaches, as Melville wrote, that emerging souls are "tiny effervescent sparks scintillating with phosphorescent brilliance."[17] Our growth can be measured in terms of light, and many Hawaiians believe our souls leave this plane in a blaze of effulgent light. The souls of the dead go into the path of the setting sun: "a splendid crimson aura streaked with rays of gold—the brightest light in the world, yet the most glorious and soothing to behold."[18]

In fact, *everything* is made up of the essence of light, because everything is made up of glimmering aka. We are surrounded by "patterns of essence." Buryl Payne described them as being "invisible, waiting to become manifest like the radio waves that imperceptibly bathe us, unseen and unheard until we turn on the TV and tune it to the proper channel."[19] The essence of light exists in every dimension at once. It transcends all boundaries, even the boundary between life and death. Huna teaches that the difference is illusory: the body may be gone, but the *essence* of the person is still there, as expressed by the Upanishads: "The body is mortal, always gripped by death, but within it dwells the immortal Self."[20] Although that essence cannot normally be seen by us, we can widen our consciousness to allow the flicker of night light to break through to our world of ao, daylight.

The light of the dead—both the light they developed here on earth and the light they have become—is freely available to us if we know how to access it. A strange concept, but is it really so strange? Payne wrote that essence provides the raw material for reincarnation:

> Formulating essence (our inner sparkle of joy and life) as a meta-pattern, although not yet demonstrable by modern scientific inference, provides a logical basis for life and death and occurrence of successive reincarnations, *for a pattern can exist independently of the material which manifests it* [my italics]. Just as a musical score may exist as black, patterned marks on lined paper, as wiggles in a phonograph record, or as magnetized spots on a tape, so essence seems to exist independently of physical bodies.[21]

Einstein reduced the terms *space* and *time* to mere words, not to be taken as things in themselves, but only as indications of an underlying wholeness. We apprehend that underlying wholeness by increasing our knowledge and our open-mindedness. In Huna, rocks can symbolize our resistance and, paradoxically, provide a means to overcome it, enabling us to glimpse Gauguin's "golden figures" on the edges of our consciousness.

ROCKING INTO THE LIGHT

It is the jester's truth
Lead crystal makes me sick and this
Is a water world.

KERI HULME

From the beginning of creation—when darkness slipped into light, when hot and glassy matter erupted and flowed, only to become solidified—two polarities have existed: the material and the spiritual, familiarity and change, the rock and the light. We experience life as a constant struggle between the two polarities, a conflict mirrored by Pele, who overwhelmed the land when she got annoyed, and Hiʻiaka, who made it green again. If we understand burning rocks as representing the fixed ideas of our subconscious, we can see more clearly how holding on to certain ideas interferes with the new, green growth of consciousness. But Huna shows us the intriguing truth that the very form of the universe makes the struggle easier. Everything is made up of aka (the potential for consciousness), so light is *always* trying to break through everything, including rocks.

Rocks are not conceived of as solid; they are seen as being made of frozen light. Their heaviness is like that of the sky, which the Polynesians conceived of as solid. But the solid sky can be cracked open to allow the light to shine: Hiʻiaka, "the carrier of consciousness," is also known as Hiʻiaka waiwai lani, which means "Hiʻiaka who breaks the skies open." The medium is consciousness, the director of all things. Like the sky, rocks can be made lighter and made light. The following description gives a very clear expression of the dynamic between rock and light:

Each child born has at birth, a Bowl of perfect light. If he tends his light it will grow in strength and he can do all things—swim with the shark, fly with the birds, know and understand all things. If however, he becomes envious or jealous he drops a stone into his Bowl of Light and some of the light goes out. Light and the stone cannot hold the same space. If he continues to put stones in the Bowl of Light, the Light will go out and he will become a stone. A stone does not grow, nor does it move. If at any time he tires of being a stone, all he needs to do is turn the bowl upside down and the stones will fall away and the Light will grow once more.[22]

Each rock added to the Bowl is a fixed idea, seen in Hawai'i as *he kui nao hemo 'ole i ka kala,* "a screw that the screwdriver cannot remove." Fixed ideas surface as emotions like anger, vividly expressed in the Hawaiian description of someone who is very angry as having "gone into tending the red-hot stones," *hele a kahu ka'ena.* Another instance of fixed ideas are *obsessions,* which are also well represented by rocks and stones, such as when Pele burned Lohi'au and then turned him into a rock for loving another. Obsessions are "frozen emotion" and cause a blockage in the currents of our subconscious sea. As the anthropologist and synthesist Gregory Bateson, husband of Margaret Mead, wrote "a rock is a rock because it resists change."[23] Perhaps because they are so good at holding, rocks are universally seen as representing our difficulties in letting go. The French writer Gaston Bachelard said: "The consolidation of meaning makes idols. Established meanings have turned to stone."[24] Those "established meanings" are frozen light, or unquestioned knowledge. Luckily, there are many dimensions to the knowledge that the stones hold. There is always hope, no matter how fixed someone's opinion is, because there is always light waiting to be released from within everyone and everything, even stones!

Hawaiian ways of transcending obsession all concern "unblocking emotion" and making contact with the superconscious by first making contact with the subconscious. One traditional way was to sing to certain stones placed at points where sea currents divide. For instance, there are a number of stone sentinels at Kumukahi, the easternmost point of Hawai'i. As we have seen, *au,* the word used for "the current of the sea," also means "the flow of time." At the point of division, there is a *choice* about which way to move. Huna teaches that chanting to these stones helps a person to release fixed ideas. The chants include requests that the stones reveal the rainbow of Kāne and Kanaloa. They are based on the premise that the material is formed out of the spiritual, and the understanding that creation begins with the voice, such as in the creation chant of the earth.

Another traditional way is to choose a sign or object—such as a particular rock—to represent the subconscious, and then to take care of it. Transforming a particular symbolic object in this way helps us transcend the blocks of fixed ideas in ourselves, attract the desired energy, and increase our power. We can understand better how to do this by taking a close look at the unique relationship hula dancers have with special stones known as 'ili'ili. Every serious hula dancer in Hawai'i has her own personal "hula stones," which she clicks like castanets while dancing. The stones must be flat, thin, and waterworn to a particular shape, and measure about an inch and a half to two inches across. These stones are kept clean, rubbed in kukui nut oil, wrapped in tapa, and stored where they will be handled by no one but the dancer. For hotel performances of the hula—known as "good-time" excursions—the stones are not specially prepared. For other hula performances, however, they are. As the famous kumu hula of Kona, Hawai'i, Iolani Luahine, said: "If you take care of what you have, what you have will take care of you."

Every aspect of this tradition has meaning in relation to the movement of consciousness. The name of the stones, 'ili'ili, makes it clear that they relate to the breaking of boundaries: 'ili means "skin." The dancer is using the stones to help break through his or her skin, the boundary between self and the world. In the movement of the dance, the world is depicted as shifting this way and then that way, because it is ever in the process of being formed. The constant beating and reverberation of the stones helps attune the dancer's emotions to the fluid rhythms of creation. As water represents emotion, waterworn stones are chosen for their symbolic capacity to help the dancer overcome his or her subconscious blocks and emulate their smoothness. They imply that for all of us emotion needs to be felt, and then integrated, because only in this way can creation happen appropriately. Only then can tiny golden threads of consciousness shoot out from us and connect us to the world around, like the hula dancer connects her every movement to the rhythms of the music. The kukui nut oil stands for enlightenment and the tapa cloth for being wrapped in consciousness. This technique joins with the others we have learned about that help transform the dancer into a shaman, one who is able to apprehend the creative nature of reality and influence it consciously.

Now for a glimpse of another way of releasing our light, the power of focused consciousness. Words are the most famous example of this power, which is so strong that it can change our experience of solid stone. This truth is recognized by the following Tahitian chant to an ax:

Hold!
That it be taken out enchanted,
Made light;
That it may produce sparks . . .
The ax will become sacred . . .
To unite act and handle,
To make light the ax,
To consecrate the ax,
To impel the ax,
To complete the ax,
To give power to the ax.[25]

Even the hardest rock will produce sparks when struck in the right way by the right instrument. The ax is only a symbol here; the power is focused consciousness. We can often see that power at work with practitioners of Huna: Roselle Bailey—the former curator of the hula ground at Kēʻē, Kauaʻi—said she always chants to rocks before she moves them so she will "carry the stone, but not the weight of the stone." One curator of the Bishop Museum, Alexander McBryde, tried to move a stone called Kauai Iki:

It was so heavy it proved impossible to budge it by any known means. Mr. McBryde was told that he must find an old chanter who could *oli* (chant) the hula *Kaua'i-iki* and "talk" the rock into a moving mood. An old chanter, *Pihaleo,* was found; and sure enough, as he chanted its special *mele,* the stone grew lighter and lighter, and thus allowed itself to be removed to the McBrydes' old home at *Waialoa.* It was taken there on an oxcart. A rainbow arched overhead above it.[26]

The word itself brings light, and the light brings life. That is why chanting is said to give life. Hi'iaka chanted to the "rocky" soul of Lohi'au on top of the cliffs of the Nā Pali coast after he had died. The hula's original enchantress crouched over the revived Lohi'au in the cave on the cliffs, calling forth in triumph:

O Hi'iaka au lā, o ke kaula, a ke kahuna,
Nana i hana, nana i ho'oulu,
Aho'oulu au i ke ola, a he ola no!

Hi'iaka, prophet and priest, am I,
It is mine to inspire, to perform,
I have striven for life and life came![27]

Hi'iaka is so effective in bringing life because she has learned how to focus her consciousness without restriction, allowing her mana to flow through a clear channel.

To rock ourselves into the great light of being, to create appropriately, we need both a steady flow of emotion and focused consciousness. Then we are able to produce our own light, a light that glistens with water droplets. There is a word for that light when it is manifest to other people. That word is *rainbow.* It is considered blessed to see a rainbow because it represents the power of the spirit to unite separate spheres, including life and death. A rainbow is a symbol of someone's passing, such as the rainbow that appeared when my grandfather died, giving an assurance of his continuing life. The opening of the colors of light represents the expansion in consciousness that happens when the spirit is freed. The rainbow is a visible bridge between the physical and spiritual, and death is merely a slide from one state to the other.

The essence of light remains, as expressed by a beautiful quote from *Tales of the Night Rainbow:*

> We are all born with the perfect power to do and be all things. We have the right to do with it whatever we wish. If we keep our bowl free from rocks, we can go forward and backward in time, walk with the angels, climb the heights and live in paradise. It is everyone's own decision, where and what he is. We are all one, each part of the eternal whole. There is no line that divides one from another or those in body from those in spirit.[28]

The eternal light has always been there, will always be there. Yet our knowledge helps it to expand, for we are also creators. The light is our beacon of hope to a new world.

SKY LIGHTS TO THE LANDS OF LOVE

Come forth
Come forth rainbow-encircled
with lightning flashing in the sky,
and the multitude crowding around!
Hail to the chief!
Hail to the ancestor of chiefs!
TUAMOTUAN CHANT TO THE GOD KĀNE

Mythology provides us with several patterns to follow to allow our Kāne, our Higher Self, to blaze forth. The gods and goddesses each teach certain specific qualities. Poli'ahu, the goddess of the snows, for example, teaches the value of well-placed emotion and Hina, the goddess of the moon, shows us how to increase our focused consciousness.

Poli'ahu's home is on Mauna Kea, "the mountain of clarity," one of the Big Island's most sacred mountains. It is the site of the most brilliant light in Hawai'i when sunlight reflects off the snow-covered cairns of rock. Poli'ahu found her home near the summit: her hair is the glimmering icicles hanging from the rocks, her raiment the shining snows. In a time long ago, the beautiful snow goddess was involved in constant battles over men with her sister Pele. Pele would overwhelm the land with fire and then Poli'ahu would retaliate by covering it with ice and snow. This is correct in geological detail: the strange, conical shapes on Mauna Kea are the ancient cinder cones caused by eruptions through the ice caps. But Poli'ahu is now peaceful: there has not been an eruption on the mountainside for over ten thousand years. Mysterious Lake Waiau, near the summit, has no freshwater springs, yet is never dry. It is said to be fed by the eternal spring of the crystalline goddess.

Each aspect of Poli'ahu's home, as with all place-names in Hawai'i, is rich with symbolic meaning. Unlike Pele, Poli'ahu no longer needs to erupt in avalanches of passion. The hidden meanings of her name show how she managed that great feat. Poli'ahu means "bosom goddess" and "to caress." She has learned to reach out with love and nurture—poli means "heart," "breast," and "arms." She has also learned to overcome the waters of motion and emotion, allowing them to flow into one central pool. That pool is Lake Waiau, which means "waters of the current." Poli'ahu is beyond time. That's why the spring replenishing Lake Waiau is eternal. The goddess Poli'ahu knows how to create the clearest light in Hawai'i, through the nurturing nature she achieved by focusing her emotions. She also lives on the highest point of the land of Hawai'i, and Mauna Kea is said to be the highest mountain in the world when measured from sea level.

The next way of reaching the bright land concerns the necessity to continually focus, represented by the goddess Hina-i-ka-mahina, or "Hina-of-the-moon." Her legend says that she originally lived in a village on earth, and was married with children. One version says that she found a beautiful type of sweet potato from the moon. She grew so fond of it that she decided to visit the moon. Another version says she decided to visit the moon because her children made so much excrement. Whatever the reason, she set out on her rainbow sky canoe one night when the moon was full. Hina, like Laka, is the wife of Lono and he tried to stop her flight to the moon—tried to "cut off" the development of her consciousness—by cutting off her foot and separating her from her canoe. It is said that if he had not done so, she would have gone all the way to the sun.[29]

When Hina finally reached the moon safely, she liked it so much that she made it her home. Luomala wrote:

> The people of many Polynesian islands . . . believe there is a woman industriously beating *tapa* in the moon and her name is Hina. The white clouds are the *tapas* she has set out to air on the blue stone floor of the sky.[30]

In this myth are the keys to transformation. Hina travels by the light of the full moon, symbol of the divine superconscious. Her perception, her consciousness, is so great she is even able to make her home in that brilliant light. But this myth also contains a warning. Lono tried to stop Hina from making a greater connection of consciousness by splintering her away from her personal rainbow, which she could use to reach the moon and even the sun. Lono in this context is called Lono moku, or "amputated Lono": although he cut off Hina's foot, the effect was that of amputating himself. It's worth noting also that *moku* means "island." This myth is a symbolic way of teaching that Lono, our conscious mind, is insufficient in itself; it is also necessary to open to the superconscious by taking risks.

Although Hina now lives in the moon, she does not rest. She "industriously beats tapa." Clouds represent the subconscious mind, as we saw in the pig chant of chapter six. Yet they have the blueprint of a higher design within, like the ancient Hawaiian tapa cloth. The meaning of the tapa clouds is revealed by a Hawaiian proverb that says *Ola i ka wai a ka'ōpua*, or "There is life in the water from the clouds." And Tahitians on the island of Raiatea, still the most sacred island in Polynesia, talk about "the sacred cloud of learning." Another Hawaiian proverb is *He hō'ailona he ao i'ike'ia*, or "Clouds are

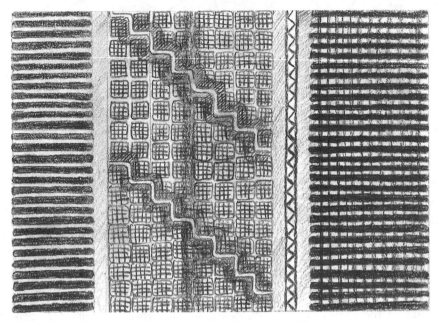

Tapa cloth (source R. A. Morrell)

recognized signs." Hina's continual beating of the tapa cloth shows the importance of focus and repetition to maintain one's desired state.

Hina has created (not without trouble) her own higher designs of light, and uses them to point the way to the denizens of the ao. The goddess Hina is beloved all over Polynesia. For example, the Maori of New Zealand say her glistening hair makes up the mesh of a silvery net. The net is the nest of consciousness, and provides a gleaming choice of filmy cords for us to activate.

The gods and goddesses have reached their apotheosis, and it is now up to us to follow the signs they have left behind, found through myth, language, prayers, songs, and many other ways. As we have seen, *akua,* the word meaning "god" or "goddess," is the same word as the one for "night of the full moon." Hina's most blessed sign is the rainbow around the full moon. It has an important meaning:

There are many kinds of rainbows. The night too has rainbows . . .

Na Pō Mōkole is seen by only a few. It is the spirit rainbow. The rainbow that holds our ancestors. When it is seen it is a great blessing from all our family who have gone out of flesh. Many healings take place at this time for our spirit family knows our needs and tries to help us. They give us knowledge and rekindle the light when it is weak. It is a time of unity.[31]

When we consciously take on the signs these bright beings have left behind, life is so much easier, for then we are creating from a much higher place, far less troubled by the waves of emotion and the islands of separation. Then we are bringers of the old knowledge of harmony.

RAINBOW EFFECTS

Apo ka lani
Apo ka pō
apo ke ao

He has spanned the sky.
spanned the night
spanned the day

HAWAIIAN CHANT

In many cultures, the rainbow is a sign of a connection to the superconscious Mind of Light. It may signal a promise from God to man, such as when the God of the Old Testament told Noah there would never be another flood:

And God said, "This is the token of the covenant which I shall make between you and every living creature that is with you, for perpetual generations . . . and it shall come to pass, when I bring a cloud over the earth, that the bow shall be seen in the cloud and I will remember my covenant . . ."[32]

In Hawai'i too, the appearance of the rainbow is a sign of successful communication with beings of higher consciousness, who exist on a
normally invisible wavelength. After the flood of Kahinali'i, Kāne
promised that forever afterward the sea would be separated from the
land. This extremely powerful chant shows the Hawaiians asking for a
sign that the contract had been agreed to:

A ha'ina ae ana ka mana o ko akua iwaho lā, e ha'ina
E kūkulu ka pahu kapu o ka leo,
E ho'ohi kanawai akua, Kai'okia
He ala muku no Kāne me Kanaloa.

Reveal the mana *of your god out there, reveal it*
Set up the sacred drum of the voice,
Make binding the kanawai *of the god, the Kai'okia,*
Show us the rainbow of Kāne and Kanaloa.[33]

The rainbow of Kāne and Kanaloa is a sign of eternity. *Kai'okia*, or
"promise," means the "cutting," *'oki*, of the "sea," *kai*. The sky-sea of
time, of emotion, of separation on earth, has been transcended.

We are all treading the rainbow-hued trail of Kāne. Our consciousness is light imaging itself, represented by the rainbow, in which
light reflects through substance and produces form. The form of har-
monized consciousness is symbolized by the ability to slide up and
down rainbows.

Through myth, our ancestors give us light. That light can be represented by the rainbow light of traditional knowledge, now shining
around the world again and illuminating our night skies. Whatever our
race or culture, we each need to be a bringer of the old knowledge of
harmony. Rainbow light is the light that leads to the shine we all dimly
remember, the sheen behind the world.

We have looked at some different ways to access it: the dance, making love, a new understanding of time and myth. Let's now see how pilgrimage offers another way to reach that shining place.

10

Brightening the Trails: A Pilgrimage through Hawai'i

With a kiss let us set out for an unknown world.

ALFRED DE MUSSET

In our time of disenchantment, we have lost a lot we don't even know we've lost, except for a little, disregarded voice inside. One of the things we've lost is the knowledge of how to find an unknown world. Getting really inspired by traveling is quite unusual in this day and age, because we *do not know how to travel.* Travel used to be (and in some parts of the world still is) a sacred journey, where places were visited to gain sacred inspiration from them. That was known as "going on a pilgrimage" and the inspiration was used by the returning pilgrim to change the quality of daily life at home. Today, however, our society encourages us to see traveling as a complete contrast to our routine, as "getting away from it all" for a couple of weeks. Travel advertisements linger and play on isolated beaches with pink-and-gold sunsets. They present traveling as a trance, not a vision. But traveling as a pilgrimage is much more special, because it is "going toward" knowledge and consciousness, not "getting away" from the boredom of our daily lives. That is why we need to "set out for an unknown world." And we need to do so with-a-kiss, for that is letting go with real love and feeling.

TRAVELING LIGHT

Most sacred is my person
Untouched has been my person
I will go to the Sacred Isle.
HINA'S CHANT WHILE BEING BEATEN BY HER PARENTS AND
DETERMINING TO LEAVE

Traveling through the magical beauty of the Hawaiian Islands gives us the chance to create our own consciousness. The journey does not have to be made literally, although it is likely to be a powerful experience if it is. Travel can make us much more conscious of our Higher Self, by first making us aware of the subconscious baggage we need to let go of. When we are literally in a new environment, among new people, but find that we experience similar reactions to and from the people we meet, that can help us to realize that we are creating the world we see. And we can observe our different reactions to places, particularly if they are very powerful.

Two entries in the visitors book in a cabin at Mauna Loa make it clear that the very same place can attract or repel. The first one says: "The entire trip has been a religious experience, the summit trail is very hard but worth every minute." The other one says: "This is the most God-forsaken wasteland I've ever been in. Heading for Hilo for a beer."[1] We can only speculate about what was going through the mind of the thirsty guy at Mauna Loa, but what usually get in the way of our being at one with the greater mind of nature are our addictions or our emotions. As we have seen, once we understand that we have created our own world, we have the power to change it to any world we want. Like the moon goddess Hina, with her glimmering hair spread throughout the night sky, we can learn how to activate the meshes of our consciousness. But like Hina, we need to begin somewhere.

Hawai'i as locus for a sacred pilgrimage may seem surprising, because it is not like the sites that are the focus of the world's major religions. Mecca is the holiest site for Muslims; Varanasi or Benares, the

"City of Light," is the most auspicious place for Hindus. Lourdes is beloved by Catholics, and Lhasa, the "forbidden city," is the sacred dream of Tibetan Buddhists. In all these cases, only particular places are considered sacred, whereas in Hawai'i, the sacred land can be found all over the Hawaiian Islands. It can also be discovered in ourselves as our own land of light.

TUNING IN TO THE SACRED

The South Seas are heaven—and I no angel.

RUPERT BROOKE

There are several keys to turning a holiday in Hawai'i into a pilgrimage. One is to choose a sacred place, guided by perception of the hidden meanings of its name. Places were named very carefully, because the constant repetition of a name brings out certain qualities in a place— and in those who repeat its name. Certain Hawaiian places help us on our individual journey because they are *consciously associated* with certain emotions through the names the Hawaiians gave them. Another key to making a pilgrimage consists of "tuning in" to the energy of those sacred places. It is very helpful to visit them if we want to come to terms with the role of that emotion in our lives.

To demonstrate how this helps us, I'm going to talk about two particularly sacred areas, both very popular with visitors. One is Kīlauea, known as "the volcano," in the extreme southeast of the southernmost island, Hawai'i. The other is the Nā Pali sea cliffs, at the northwest of the northernmost island, Kaua'i. Hawai'i and Kaua'i are geographical and geological opposites, and form the two ends of the Hawaiian rainbow. The color of Hawai'i is red, associated with passion. At the other end of the island chain, the color of Kaua'i is purple, the highest vibration of the visible rainbow, which is associated with the ability to transcend emotion.

The journey from the south to the north of the Hawaiian Islands can be seen as a metaphor for our journey from the subconscious to the superconscious. Throughout, the link is the place-names, which have left their resonance in the sacred land of Hawai'i. The first area, the volcano of the Big Island, offers lessons about letting go of our subconscious blocks and clearing our path. The second area, the Nā Pali of Kaua'i, reminds us that we need to increase our consciousness, like Hina and Hi'iaka, through focused repetition and directed consciousness. We shall see how we can travel from one consciousness to another by clearing the colors of our emotions. Then we can reach the other side of the rainbow.

CREATING HAWAI'I: THE RED ISLAND

There are certain places on the planet where the very
universal laws of nature that you have come to depend
upon simply do not apply . . . legend and folklore herald
them as doorways.

PILA

The Big Island of Hawai'i is one of those magical places where laws "simply do not apply." It is a very special place, even among the Hawaiian Islands, for it's the only one still exploding! It has such intense energies that they can be felt by those with no knowledge of them—I heard of one lady who got off the plane at the airport, having arranged to spend some time on the island, but who immediately hated it and got straight back on the plane again! In fact, its energies are so powerful that Pila called the island "the major doorway of the hemisphere consistently held ajar by the grace of Madame Pele."[2] It is an island of great extremes: from the snowy contours of Mauna Kea, to the black lava deserts of Ka'u, to the rolling green hills of Waimea, to the lush rain forest of Hilo. It has almost every climate imaginable; if the weather in one place is not appealing, different weather can be found by driving for a couple of miles along the road. That's how strong the energies are on this unique island.

Hawaiians say the island is presently divided between the volcano goddess Pele, who reigns over the east side, and the pig god Kamapua'a, whose dominion is the west side. The tumultuous love affair between fiery Pele and the rutting hog god is said to have been responsible for many natural features, such as the vagina cave and gulches caused by the scraping of Kamapua'a's trotters, but now they have finally settled on an uneasy division of the island. And—in the synchronicity that is typical of Hawaiian "myth"—the landscape of the eastern side, the domain of Pele's scorching breath, is hot and dry, while the western side, the realm of Kamapua'a, is wet and swampy. The island's capital, Hilo, on that side has the advantage of being the most "Hawaiian" town in Hawai'i— tourism never took off because of the climate.

Hawaiians talk about Pele as if she is was the lady next door, but with great respect and awe in their voices. She has many forms, but often appears as a lone old lady hitchhiking. She is very demanding and whenever she asks for something, it must be given. If you do, she vanishes and troubles you no more; if you don't, you need to watch out. She likes to be remembered, too, even when she is not there—or else she will suddenly be there! There is a story about the eruption that recently destroyed a village in Puna, saying that all that was left was one house, whose inhabitants hadn't forgotten to worship her.

Visitors to the volcano, driving up into the rainy hills, westward from Hilo or eastward from Kailua-Kona, know they are getting close when they see a sign by the side of the road that says FAULT ZONE. The trees are usually dripping with moisture and the sky seems low and glowering as the road sweeps around, past the ticket office toward the brown logs of the visitors center. The village on its flanks, appropriately called Volcano, is about one and a half miles from the visitors center. The Volcano children have wonderful, dewy complexions, apparently due to all the rain! The village attracts people who are creative and a little crazy—as we might expect from those who choose to live "on the edge" of the world's most active volcano. The full moon in particular attracts residents down to the "flow," and afterward they sometimes have parties on the edge of the surrounding roads. Villagers have organized an amazing amount of cultural events at Volcano, from poetry meetings and plays to classes in the hula and lei making. It's a great place to stay.

Visitors are sometimes surprised that the volcano is not immediately visible. From movies, we expect a cone pouring out lava from its peak. But Kīlauea is a different kind of volcano, a basalt volcano, which has a low, humplike structure. There are two main visitor attractions. The first is the crater Halema'uma'u, circled by the Crater Rim Road, with sites of interest marked every few miles. It was almost continuously active until 1924, but it is now crusted over by congealed lava, with small parcels of steam rising up from the earth like witches' breath. This gray crust is a far cry from the brilliant lava lake that the lady explorer Isabella Bird described as "clots of living fire . . . molten metal hath not that crimson gleam nor blood that living light."[3]

Whenever I arrive at the volcano, I can feel the energy change all through my body. I usually have to rest for twenty-four hours to help my system adjust, even if I just came from another part of the Big Island. Visitors to the volcano sometimes talk of experiencing the sensation that the earth is moving. In fact, the earth *is* literally moving: it is right there, at the world's most active volcano, that the earth is being created. This particular part of the island of Hawai'i is still being formed. The evidence is all around, in the roads closed off because of cracks or piles of lava, now congealed into strange shapes. Flags mark the recent lava flows, the map in the visitors center is constantly changing, and the coastline at the eruption site is sometimes unrecognizable from one visit to the next.

The other attraction, and the one I couldn't recommend more highly, is the flank eruption—some Hawaiians say Pele goes by a road underground from her house in the crater to the shore. On the drive down the Chain of Craters Road to where the eruption is—currently twenty-three miles from the visitors center—the chances are that the "end of the road" will be covered by a syrup of glossy black lava so new that it still shines in the sun. The road, which is continually shortening as it is being "eaten" by Madame Pele, had a strange and dislocating effect on me. I was brought up to think of roads as solid things, and that when we travel along them we know where they—and we—are going. The roads themselves are the definers of the journey: they alter the landscape, they are not altered by it. In other words, the work of humans is more powerful than the work of the land. The volcano— literally—overturns all that. The area of the volcano is littered with remnants of roads that will never be open again.

A good time to approach Pele and her works is sunset, because then it is possible to see the clouds change from the whites of daylight to the luminous pinks and grays of dusk. Finally comes the greatest contrast of all, the glowing red of the lava against the dark of the night. The lava flow is on the coast, reached by driving carefully down the strange and winding road with the ever-changing ending. Pele's power is first seen in the mesmerizing cloud of gases that hangs above the ocean. There, in what the poet Tennyson called lava-light, it is possible to get out of your car and walk on the freshest land on earth, where the rocks are still sticky, past a sign that says DANGER, VOLCANIC FUMES and onward toward where the land is birthing.

The moon was full when I first approached the source—nay, the exit—of all this power, and the stars were mere pinpricks of light. The unbroken black lava fields stretched behind me, the inky ocean fringing their edge. Approaching closer and closer to the fountaining lava, across land too new to have a path, I was absolutely overwhelmed. My knees shaking, I couldn't stop myself from sitting for a moment on the *newest* land in the world. I had never seen anything so powerful in all my life. I had never even imagined such power. Looking deep within the source of the explosions—as I shook with the heat and awe and terror and shock and I-knew-not-what—I discerned a glowing block. I walked a few steps closer to view the bright red crevasse in the giant's anvil that formed the exit of the explosions.

The land felt as if it could break away and hurl itself into the volcano at any minute. As indeed it could have. I felt a great heat under my feet and, looking down, saw the magma, the liquid lava, flowing among the rocks. These liquid veins of the earth have a constant, irides- cent glow. I knew that a week later there could be dozens of different eruptions along the lava fields I was then standing on, or not—it's impossible to know. Hawaiians have long known Madame Pele as an unpredictable goddess and scientists do not know the pattern of her eruptions. As recently as the 1990s, a piece of lava on which twenty people were standing began to break away and one person died. Remembering this, I stepped backward pretty quickly, onto land where I could not see the light of the earth.

I could feel the liquid red light of the volcano vibrating all through me and the lava fields, through the sky and through the stars. An eclipse of the moon occurred that night, and as the moon was slowly "eaten" by the sun above the dark fields of lava and the bright patch of the flow, I was overwhelmed by the power in the universe. I had heard about, and thought about, the power of creation, but had never dreamed it could be anything as powerful as the scene before me. I had to agree with the comment of a French gentleman, d'Anglade: "For once reality surpasses imagination."[4] Seeing the volcano was not only different in degree from anything I had ever seen, but it was also different in kind. For the first time I felt part of the creation of the world. For days after that most incredible night of my life, I felt the energy zinging through me. I knew I could never be the same again.

Although I recommend a visit to Pele for anyone who needs to get in touch with his or her creative energy, that recommendation also comes with a warning. It's not a good idea to go to places with really strong energy—such as Hawai'i's volcano—if you don't feel ready. It is very easy to become overwhelmed by a sudden surge of energy, and if you don't know what to do with it, its chaotic force could set off a lot of unwanted forces in your life.

The domain of Pele is the ultimate example of creativity in action. It's a fantastic place, but terrifying, just like creation itself, for the outcome is unknown. Whenever we create something, whether it's a baby, a meal, or a book, we can never be absolutely sure how it's going to turn out! The unknown can be disorientating, and I certainly find the volcano the most disorientating place I have ever been. Whenever I first reach there, my head and body feel light and I lose the sense of earth.

Even when I am walking along familiar trails—whether through a forest of yellow ginger or along the black rocks of the Ka'ū desert—I often lose my sense of where I am going and what will be next. It's like the earth is no longer underpinning me, I'm "out there" in creation, among the stars. Yet in a strange way, it feels familiar.

I'm not alone in my overwhelming reaction. The people who live at Volcano live there because of the power of Pele. The photographer Brad Lewis describes what happens when he takes photographs at the flow:

> I've tried to develop the intuition, to catch the energy. Because, as a living planet, there's something out there and it is truly uncanny. I've felt it many times. It's almost like a guardian angel sometimes. It kind of says, "OK, move now, it's time to leave." And five minutes later I look back where I was and the whole coastline has exploded.[5]

The volcano has astounded Westerners right from their first view in 1823. The explorer Isabella Bird described her view of the lava lake at Halema'uma'u:

> I think we all screamed, I know we all wept, but we were speechless, for a new glory and terror had been added to the earth. It is the most unutterable of wonderful things. The words of common speech are quite useless. It is unimaginable, indescribable, a sight to remember forever, a sight which at once took possession of every faculty of sense and soul, removing one altogether out of the range of ordinary life.[6]

The power of the volcano is so great that visitors can't help thinking about God—whoever their God may be. For many it is a vengeful God. The sight of the gaping pit and hellfire inside cause many to think of the vengeance of eternal fire and the gateway to hell described by the Bible. William Ellis wrote that the volcano was the manifestation of "the power of that dread Being who created the world and who has declared that by fire he will one day destroy it."[7] In the Middle Ages, sages wrote that the fantastically shaped fragments of black lava that came hurtling and hissing out of the smoke of an Icelandic volcano were "monstrous birds or the souls of the damned."[8]

These passages provide a useful reminder that whatever we find depends on our belief system. To the Hawaiians the goddess Pele is alive and the lava flow is her dramatic appearance. Pele and her relatives live at Halema'uma'u. Among them are Kānehekeli, spirit of the thunder, her brother Kapohāikahiola, god of the lava fountains, and her brother Lonomakua, god of the fire sticks. There's a wonderful description of how the gods make their home in the boiling lava lake, from a great book on geomythology by Dorothy Vitaliano:

> The conical craters are their houses, where they frequently amused themselves playing *kōnane* (checkers), the roaring of the furnaces and the crackling of the flames were . . . the music of their dance, and the red flaming surge was the surf wherein they played, sportively swimming on the rolling wave.[9]

Perhaps the general fondness for Pele has something to do with her being a bit like us, but more so. She's always having battles of control with her family, especially her constant war with her sister, the sea goddess, NamakaoKaha'i. The evidence is in the steam cloud above the ocean, the product of opposing forces, viscous lava against billowing waves. The sea stands for emotion: *pi'i ke kai,* "the sea has risen," means "the temper has risen." Both these goddesses are in constant battle *because neither of them can win.* In this particular aspect, they are still working on the emotional level and so are doomed to war over the same old issues. The riverine lava veins of the earth continue to flow under the earth like blood.

But there are more ways to create. It's now time to look at how we can use the power of the goddesses to transcend our own issues.

CLEARING THE WAY

Ua no ka 'āina i ka puke iki, i ka puke nui,
I ka hakina ai, i ka hakina i'a,
I kou hakina ai ia Kulipe'e i ka Lua, lā.
'Eli'eli, kau mai!
Ma ka holo uka, ma ka holo kai.
'Eli'eli kapu, 'eli'eli noa!
Ua noa ka 'āina a ke Akua!

The land is fed by each hill, small or big,
By each scrap of bread and of meat—
Food that is ravaged by Kulipe'e.
Plant deep the foundations of peace
A peace that runs through upland and lowland.
Deep, deep the taboo, deep be the peace!
Peace fall upon the land of the goddess!

LOHI'AU'S PLEA TO PELE,
TRANSLATED BY NATHANIEL EMERSON

Volcano land. Land so hot it shines, a glassy mirror. What does it reflect? The looker. Let's see how the power of the land itself can be used to clear our way so we can "plant deep the foundations of peace" in "the land of the goddess." By looking at the kind of land Pele makes, we can learn how to let go of our emotional complexes, described by Serge King as being of three kinds. There are assumptions that King calls "beliefs which have been crystallized in consciousness like blocks of ice. They deal with generalities about life and self and are not easily changed."[10] Attitudes are "liquid beliefs" that are "more easily changed but change may involve emotional conflict." Opinions are "gaseous like water vapor" and are changed easily with little emotion.

We can extend his metaphor by looking at the land at "The Flow." It's easy to compare assumptions to the earth, attitudes to the sea, and opinions to the steam clouds rising above the meeting of the earth and the sea. What Pele does is *knock over* our assumptions, the way she—sometimes spectacularly, sometimes quietly—destroys the earth and makes lava land, land so new it shines. What kind of lava land does Pele make? The Hawaiians identified two main kinds of lava, and scientists all over the world now call them by those names. The glassy lava, which crunches when you step on it, is known as *'a'ā*. And the long, ropy stuff, like syrup or a chain of molecules, is called *pāhoehoe*.

We can use the lava as a "kahuna stone," or "mirror of the soul," to help us destroy what we need and create what we need. It is good to visit the clinkery *'a'ā* lava (which Pila calls the "umbilical cord to the forces of creation") when we feel the incredible energy of destruction and creation surging through us. Contacting the *'a'ā* with a part of the body is an uncomfortable reminder of the properties of anger, as this lava is very hard and jagged and can slice through even the toughest boots. A Hawaiian proverb is:

Aloha mai no, aloha aku
o ka huhū ka mea e ola 'ole ai.

When love is given, love should be returned.
Anger is the thing that gives no life.[11]

"Anger is the thing that gives no life." Expressing anger is largely forbidden in our society, particularly for women. But when anger is unexpressed, the Hawaiians say it "eats away inside." There is an analogy here with certain diseases, such as cancer, where an organ "inside" mutates and spreads throughout the body. Modern scientific research associates it with the inability to express emotions, such as anger. Anger definitely has its role; it helps us "destroy" our old land and put behind us what we need to put behind us. Our assumptions are hard like rock, and changing them—like the metamorphosis of the rock from solid to liquid—depends on heat and pressure and can never be easy. So we need to be like Pele, whose lava can be seen as the red expression of her anger. She is certainly very much alive, as her works show.

Visiting the 'a'ā can help us really feel our anger, because 'ā means "to burn" and 'a'ā is 'ā doubled, so it is even more intense, like a blazing fire. It is a place where we can safely let that feeling take us over— a long way from the nearest habitation, with no one to hear if we scream and shout! After my first visit to the volcano, I was more in touch with my anger than I have been for some years, red-hot, burning anger, which, like the lava, had to come out. I knew that I needed to transform this 'ele ao, "black light," within me, so that I would not explode later in a different context. It is essential that we clear our darkness before we can create clear light. Like all things, though, expressing anger should be done with compassion.

Pele is a lady of big appetites—the Hawaiians describe her as *Pele 'ai honua* or "Pele, the eater of land." With the amazing synchronicities of Hawai'i, I discovered that the names of the places along the coast of the eruption are associated with eating *and* with a lack of consciousness. All the places I shall describe now have suffered—or probably will suffer—the same unfortunate fate: to be eaten by Pele. Peace still needs to be made!

At the heiau, or temple, called Waha 'Ula, where the visitors center used to be, I could see—on top of the mound built up by hundreds of years of clinkery 'a'ā lava—ghostly silhouettes against the lava's red glow. The silhouetted sticks used to be palm trees. Now, with their greenery singed off and a burning smell hanging in the air, they are eerily reminiscent of the stick idols of ancient Hawai'i. The Waha 'Ula temple was founded by the priest Pā'ao on his arrival from Samoa in the thirteenth century. It was Pā'ao who introduced the system of human sacrifice and taboo into Hawai'i, which many people wrongly think of as being intrinsically Hawaiian. The name Waha 'Ula means "red mouth" and this was the very heiau at which he introduced those terrible practices, which were to spread all through the islands. Somehow this knowledge makes the sticks of palm trees more ghastly and less ghostly. The heiau where I stood and stared is in the process of being eaten by the volcano, just the way the heiau ate the people. Everything that is done returns to the doer. Indeed, at the time of publication of this book, the heiau is long gone.

Along the coast used to stand a beautiful palm-fringed campground called Kamoamoa. Villagers still talk about its loss with regret. But name-wise, it is no surprise. *Kā* means "to hit or strike" and *mo'a* is "cooked" or "burned," or "made brittle as tobacco leaves over a fire." We know that doubling the word makes the effect more intense, so it is not difficult to guess what happened there. Just past Kamoamoa is a place called Lae'apuki, which used to be a village. Its name also has to do with eating. *Apu* means "to snap, snatch with teeth, destroy, ravage, or ruin." The beach and campground of Halape used to be farther along the shoreline. *Hala* means "vice or offense" and *pē* is "crushed, flattened, drenched, or soaked." This is where both earthquakes and tidal waves happened! On Thanksgiving weekend in 1975 there was an earthquake followed by a tidal wave. Thirty-five people were camped out there and two of them were killed.

Back along the Chain of the Craters Road, traveling away from the flow toward the visitors center, the metaphors of the place-names still relate to eating. Randomly selecting some landmarks popular with tourists, we find the sea arches called Nāulu. *Nau* means "to munch" and *nāulu* "sudden shower" or "to get vexed" (reminding us of the association between weather and emotion). A lookout on the side of the mountainous road is called Ke Ala Komo. *Ke* is the definite article; *ala* means "path or access" and is a variant of *'ale*, "to swallow, engulf, gulp." *Komo* means "to enter, penetrate, or feel emotion." Here, in one place-name, we have the well-known association between eating and feeling emotion. We can guess what will become of these places in the future!

The psychospiritual geography of the volcano can be a metaphor for our own growth. The 'a'ā lava is found in blocks, unlike the pāhoehoe lava, which flows. We always have a choice, a choice about how we perceive. Through our perception we change our conception. This conception influences which of our ideas gets born. If we stay in the 'a'ā phase, we will block ourselves, because we can't "let things flow." It is the faster pāhoehoe, with its recent connection to the source, that will help us transform our complexes. Greenery settles only on the pāhoehoe lava, which is the only lava with the ability to make connections—just like our thoughts. So it is good to touch the pāhoehoe, the smooth unbroken billowy stuff, as we decree what we want to create in our life. Once our old assumptions have been overturned, we have the chance to choose new assumptions, new land.

The name of the lava also tells us just *how* to create our desired land. *Pāhoe* means to "drive fish into a net by beating rhythmically against the canoe" and *hoe* means "to paddle" or "to get to work." Consciousness is the necessary net to draw fish—which can be both certain types of people and ideas—into our span. This meaning of *pāhoe* also shows the importance of focus and repetition, such as we saw in the myth of Hina and the moon. Also, a *pāhoehoepele* is the hook used to catch turtles, and the turtle represents the land in many mythologies, including the Hawaiian.

That reminds us that we can view eruption as creation—an extremely fast transformation—rather than destruction. Brad Lewis told me: "I don't see it as a destruction, I see it as a birth. It's the very beginning of the next rain forest." Pamela Frierson, in her excellent book, *The Burning Island,* described the astonishing growth of the rain forest after an eruption.[12] A year later, she walked on a glassy layer of pāhoehoe lava, crushing to cinders a gleaming surface shot with blue and gold. Then, after a few years, the brilliant green *ama'u* fern grew out of cracks in the rock. The *ohi'a* fern was beginning to flourish and the brittle surface of the pāhoehoe was weathered and crumbled. Mixing with the vegetation, it produced a mineral-rich "soil." Ten years later it hosted a "young forest." The ferns were waist high, the ohi'a turned to shrub, and the *'ōhelo* bushes—whose berries are sacred to Pele—were everywhere. The rapidity of this process shows just how strong Hawaiian mana is.

The appearance of the color green shows consciousness is being achieved, for greenery represents consciousness, as well as creation, such as we saw in the myth of Pele and her sister Hi'iaka. When Hi'iaka (*hi'i,* "to carry," *aka,* "consciousness") followed Pele's trail, she brought greenery where once there was none. In this regard, I was fascinated to find that the name Kīlauea, usually translated as "much spreading," also means "ferny." *Kīlau* is "a cosmopolitan, stiff, weedy fern" and *ea* is "life" or "breath." Breaking the word another way, we get *kī,* "a woody plant"; *lau,* "leaf"; and *ea,* "life." The volcano brings life.

Now we'll look at how we can bring new life to ourselves. The hidden meanings of the place-names here, as with the kaona of all Hawaiian names, show us different ways to interpret our reality, and so change it. In the case of place-names, we do not need to visit the places to do this. Meditating on the names, feeling, and choosing to consciously create a different way is enough.

The biggest part of Kīlauea is the huge crater Halemaʻumaʻu. Its dry bottom covered with sulfur vents is now a long way from the "broiling hellfire" described by the observers of the last century. Its name literally means "house," *hale* "of the ferns," *amaʻu.* Hiking across another crater, Kīlauea Iki, is a popular three-hour trek for visitors. Kīlauea Iki means "in the image of Kīlauea." Creation is imaging itself through naming. This crater has ferns growing between the steam vents issuing from the earth, which are so hot that visitors can—and frequently do—cook hot dogs on them! Another crater is Puhimau. *Mau* means "always" and *puhi* means "to burn, set on fire, blow" and "uncircumcised foreskin." "Cutting off" the foreskin means you are cutting off your associated burning emotions, as we saw in the way circumcision helps a boy move into the conscious mind of Lono. This place can be considered in conjunction with an old place-name along the coast, Kahuuleʻa. *Kahu* is "to tend" or "cook," *ule* is "penis," and *ʻa* is the same as *ʻā,* "to burn or blaze." This reminds us that we need to "cook" our sexuality with burning emotions in order to make progress. Then we will be ready to travel, either figuratively or literally, to the higher consciousness represented by another, very special, island, sparkling like a violet gem in the sea of consciousness.

CREATING KAUA'I: THE VIOLET ISLE

*It was on this trail high on the Nā Pali coast that several
revelations came to me. The first was that Hawai'i is
more than the most beautiful island chain in the world; it
is a living, symbolic metaphor bridging the physical
world with the esoteric realm . . .*

PILA

Pila is referring to the Nā Pali trail along the north coast of Kaua'i, a
trail of shivering beauty, traditionally used for the initiation of kahuna.
As we have seen, one of the connections between the Big Island and
Kaua'i is through the myth of Pele and Hi'iaka. As Hi'iaka traveled
with her maidservant, Wahine 'Ōma'o, the lady in green, she sang and
the land was created. And what a green and spectacularly beautiful land
it is! But creating in such a conscious way did not come easily to the
young goddess Hi'iaka. The place-names of the Nā Pali coast mirror
her process—and those who do the three-day trek into Kalalau often
find that they mirror theirs as well.

The Nā Pali trail lies in a land of fabled beauty called Hanalei.
Hanalei has a very beautiful beach, where conical mountains rise
suddenly out of the sand, the inspiration for the popular sixties anthem
Puff the Magic Dragon:

*Puff the magic dragon lived by the sea
And frolicked in the autumn mist in a land called Honalee.*[13]

Isabella Bird raved about its beauty: "*Hanalei* has been likened by some
to Paradise and by others to the vale of Caschmir. Everyone who sees it
raves about it . . . for mere loveliness I think that part of Kaua'i exceeds
anything that I have seen." Here one can "passively drink in sensations
of exquisite pleasure."[14] Indeed! But alas, we don't usually allow things
to be that simple.

The district of Hanalei brings up strong emotions. Its very name means "hurled forth as in vented anger." *Pali,* or cliff, metaphorically means "an obstacle" in Hawaiian, and a trek up and down the cliffs makes clear why! Even *mauna,* another form of the word for "mountain," *māuna,* also means "emotional waste" or "mistreatment." However, the words for emotion in Hawaiian all have connotations of movement. The place-names also indicate what we can do to transform our emotions. Let's have a look at what happens when we begin our movement or hike into Kalalau.

The Nā Pali trail to the magical valley of Kalalau is a difficult one, with several stages along the way. It begins by the beach at Hā'ena, or "red hot." Near it, we find Hawai'i's most sacred hula ground, Kaulu Paoa, on a palm-covered bluff above the ocean. It is separated from the end of the road by a five-minute scramble over rocks to a place called Kē'ē. *Kē'ē* means "full of faults," which shouldn't surprise us when we remember the equation of rocks with things needing to be "made light." But here, in this place that is "full of faults," I discovered that it was possible to make my own magic. To kick-start my own consciousness, I took a few deep breaths and touched the stones lightly with my hand. I felt a tingling run through me as I became tuned in to the unique consciousness of the place, along with noticing rainbows appearing and disappearing in the mackerel skies above my head. The amount of rainbows there—sometimes there may be several dancing together—is a sign from the gods, an acknowledgment of all the love, dances, rituals, and "clearings" that have been given to this place over the centuries.

Above and behind me were emerald cataracts—traditionally the leaping place for the souls of the dead in Kaua'i—cascading over each other into the distance. This is the way of the Nā Pali trail. The path is steep and slippery, yet replete with unexpected visions. Distant waterfalls slide in and out of the mist, and gleaming shelves of sand come suddenly into view. The beaches provide a golden interval to the rhyming green and the sea always stretches out the melody. So beautiful! But the first couple of days I walked the trail I was amazed to find myself very angry. I wasn't alone, either: everyone I met on that part of the trail seemed to be having the same reactions. And some of them said every time they walked it they felt the same way in the same place. I didn't know then what I know now, about the importance of place-names, or I wouldn't have been surprised.

The first stop along the way is at the campground at the wide beach of Hanākāpi'ai. On one side of this golden beach there is a magical sea cave, and behind it, shivering in and out of the misty hills, is a gleaming waterfall. Hanākāpi'ai is a puzzle, beautiful yet there is something not "right." The place-name tells us what is going on. *Hana* means "worthless," "provoked" (and this is exactly what I was feeling!). *Kāpī* means "to sprinkle or scatter" (just what I was doing with my emotions). And *ai* means "to eat, destroy or consume by fire, erode, taste, bite." No wonder I was feeling the way I did! However, the vision of the waterfall blinking in the distance *did* bring me a strange comfort. Years later I found out its name is Pōhākea. *Pōhākea* means "a bursting force of light, like the dawn." It also means "white," *kea*, "stone," *pōhā*. The "white stone" waterfall represents the power of clearing our rocky complexes. The stone is white, because white is made up of all the colors of the rainbow. So white is the last color before the transcendent light bursts through.

But alas, I was still on the tough trail, and I couldn't get off it. So I had to go on. The second day was harder than the first: the forest seemed to close in on me and I was glad to reach Hanakoa, where I decided to stop for the night, as I didn't feel I had the energy to rush on to Kalalau. *Koa* means "bravery" and is one of the most enduring kinds of Hawaiian wood. This sounds good until we remember that *hana* means "worthless, provoked," so Hanakoa is "worthless or provoked bravery." *Kō'ā* also means "arid, barren, unfruitful, dry or tasteless as overdone meat" and "to be rude or nasty." It was there, at that cold and rainy campground away from the sea, that many couples seemed to have arguments!

But everything changed as I approached Kalalau. Suddenly I could hardly feel the weight of my backpack, and I felt much lighter, as if the force of the sun was within me. The clouds, scudding busily along the sky, began to shine; and some say the gleam of the clouds is the light of the gods. Kalalau is a lush valley, filled with fruit trees, even though it gets only a fifth of the rainfall of arid Hanakoa. *Kala* means "to forgive" and *lau* means "a leaf" and also "to be numerous." To enjoy this place, one needs to have learned to forgive, for kala—as Laura Yardley wrote in her book on the kahuna—is "the technique for mental and emotional cleansing of negative emotions, sins, and guilts in order to maintain one's life path clearly. Literally it is: 'restoring the light.'"[15] Interestingly, Kaua'i is the only island in Hawai'i where the purple amethyst crystals naturally occur, and these are associated with the ability to purify.

At the time, I knew little about the significance of Kaua'i and Kalalau but did feel forgiveness and a sense of release. Many people call Kalalau paradise, and if the Higher Self has a land on earth, it may well be in that lush valley. Interestingly, the boyfriend I had in New Zealand had given me a pale lei of seeds gathered from Kalalau, before I had ever heard of the Nā Pali! He was literally seeding my inner self for the necessary experience there. That lei now crowns the foundation stone for the marriage to my husband, a stone that stands next to the fire.

We have approached the violet isle of Kaua'i, which lies toward the inner circle of the rainbow, in the place of paradise. We have traveled a long way, from the red root of the rainbow to this place, the sacred isle of clearing and forgiveness. We also have had the opportunity to travel a long way in consciousness, to see how Hawaiian place-names can help us or hinder us. The point of all this is not to be clever, but to learn how to focus, and use, our knowledge, for ultimately we need to create ourselves.

CREATING OURSELVES

We all think that Paradise is a place, when all the time,
it's a State of Mind.

VILI HERENIKO

We have seen, over and over again, that the key to creation is consciousness. That consciousness needs to be spiced with motion and applied with emotion. The place-names of the Nā Pali are a clear reflection of that process. I only wish I had consciously known what I was doing when I made my journey to Kalalau, for then I would have been able to use the techniques hinted at by the place-names to save myself much pain and unwanted emotion.

In addition to describing difficulties, all the place-names describe *the way to clear them*. Hana also means "to make," and Hanalei means "to make leis." *Ke'e* also means "a stone used for adzes," the axlike tool that carves the stone out of which it was formed. This is the clue to the means of overcoming our faults—by sculpting our own consciousness. *Kaulu* means "ledge" and *paoa* "the predawn light." This sacred hula ground is the place where light is built up. *Hanakāpīai* means to "make a sprinkling" (of salt for purification); *Hanakoa* means "to make courage." *Mauna*, "mountain," is also "the kind of hard stone from which adzes were made." The mountain above Kē'ē is called Makana, which means "gift" or "reward." These high cliffs were the setting for a grand love competition. Young Hawaiian men would climb it, then throw burning sticks down to young women waiting in boats far below. The holding of a flaming stick was the signal for a union with another burning brand of desire.

Na also means "calmed or pacified," and can be a sign that the obstacle of the Nā Pali cliffs has been surmounted. *Nā*, "to be pacified" is often used in connection with Pele. Pele symbolizes the *'ele*, the dark forces within ourselves that have not yet been transformed. *'Ele* is part of *'elekū*, the priest's word for north, and it is significant that the Nā Pali cliffs are at the northern end of the northernmost island. 'Ele plus Kū is the dark subconscious mind. *'Elekū* is also a rock, coarse vesicular basalt (volcano rock!), as well as the stone polisher made from the rock. And therein lies the secret. Inside everything—however black or dark or secret—are the tools necessary to bring it into the light. A dancers' chant is:

E ho'i, e Pele, i ke kuahiwi, ua na kō lili, kō inaina.

Return, O Pele, to the mountain, your jealousy, your rage are pacified.[16]

Pele's emotions—her jealousy and rage—have been transformed. And ours can be as well. The volcanoes on the island of Kaua'i are long extinct, so instead of the monochrome colors of the new volcano country, they wear the bright colors of an old and fertile land. The volcano on Kaua'i is in a district called Ka'ū, meaning "fear" or "hesitation." However, the removal of the glottal stop and macron gives us *kau,* "to place." Kau is separated from Kaua'i by the syllable *a'i,* which is the thing that does the placing. Doubled *a'ia'i* means "bright as moonlight, fair, white, clear, pure, brilliant, shining." It describes the qualities we need for the journey into consciousness.

Standing in fair Hawai'i, we must never forget that the land is the land of the gods. The passable trail for humans might end in the radiant valley of Kalalau, but the trail of the gods does not. If we were able to travel farther in the same direction, we would reach the small settlement of Mākole, or "rainbow." Everything is in its proper place. Pele is in hers, at the other end of the island chain. Hi'iaka is in hers, forever dancing the sacred hula at Kaulu Paoa with her prince of Kē'ē. Hina is in hers, having bravely sailed to her "sacred isle," the moon. Hopefully, we are also in ours. For in the end, however much we travel, the important thing is that we feel the inner calm and contentment of being "at home." We can travel and travel and never find the land of peace if we don't find the bright land inside us. Paradise is indeed "a State of Mind." It is always there, and we can access it once we have cleared the way.

11
The Quality of Light

E ala ua ao, ua malamalama!

Awake, it is day, it is light!

HAWAIIAN PRAYER AT DAYBREAK,
BELIEVED TO DETERMINE THE QUALITY OF THE DAY

We've journeyed along the Hawaiian Islands and experienced a new way of looking at the world—a new-old kind of knowledge, which can be understood in many different dimensions. It's been quite an experience! Experience in the true sense of "passage through." The anthropologist Victor Turner defined it as:

A true psychological passage from one way of seeing and understanding to another, a passage not vouchsafed to those who hold hard to the values, meanings, goals and beliefs they have grown up with to think of as reality.[1]

Let's look at some ways of understanding our "psychological passage," our passage through the knowledge, *logos,* of our *psyche.* As ever, they depend on opening our vision and letting a fresh "quality of light" into our minds.

THE VIBRATION OF LIGHT

For the rest of my life I want to be able to reflect
on what light is.

ALBERT EINSTEIN

Even though light is the source of our life, we are able to perceive only a certain proportion of it, as described by Carolyn Bloomer in *Principles of Visual Perception:*

> All life on earth is based in wavelengths of energy called electro-magnetic radiation. What we experience as visible light is simply a tiny portion of this continuum within which typical wavelengths are about 1/50,000 of an inch long and travel at a velocity of 86,000 miles a second. Electromagnetic radiation of this wavelength activates the nerve cells in our eyes.[2]

Within this spectrum of visible light, we perceive different "vibrations" of light. We call the visible quality of differentiation of vibration "color." We perceive different colors according to their vibration and name them accordingly: "red," "blue," "yellow." These colors don't exist in the world on their own—they are simply names for light waves of different energy and frequency—but we distinguish them as if they exist independently. Perhaps, in a sense, they do: we have brought them into being.

As we have discussed earlier, *how* we see the colors of our world depends on our personal and cultural conditioning. We see only what our minds allow us to see. Living organisms are essentially creatures of habit, as Samuel Butler pointed out more than a century ago. He suggested that they inherited an unconscious memory from their predecessors.

Our closest predecessors are our parents. We have all learned about the influence of family in our life. Dr. Dennis Jaffe said:

> I often think of the family as a protective envelope, forming a first

line of defense and protection against the environment. The home is like a social skin.[3]

We usually see the same colors as our parents and repeat their way of looking at the world. We take our "social skin" into all the environments we visit. As one Hawaiian put it:

Whatever a child hears his respected elders discuss as fact makes an impression upon his subconscious mind. As he matures, the seeds grow and influence his thought later in life.[4]

That is, of course, until we choose to change them! Learning to think in a different way needs to be worked on. Buryl Payne wrote:

Dropping the cherished cloak of personality is a hard task. Your personality may have been a hindrance and an obstacle, but its operations are at least familiar to you. As you begin to shed it, you may feel very naked indeed. Nearly everything that you formerly considered to be important, may have to go. Your friends may find an unpredictable stranger in your place. We live most of our lives in aspects of acquired personality and a great percentage of it in states of negative emotions. People always criticize this or that person, or group, or nation, or complain about themselves endlessly and automatically, like broken records.[5]

We attract things into our lives according to our own "vibration of light." Jacob Liberman said it well:

There are physical laws that govern the phenomenon of attraction and repulsion in the body, because the body is an electromagnetic organism. We literally attract certain things into our lives. We need a much wiser guiding force, because the species needs to continually evolve. I believe it is the part of us that knows what we need that literally brings things in for us to experience. How we experience that determines whether we move forward in the process, or whether we have to repeat that "grade" over again.[6]

How true this is, and how very often I have wished it wasn't! Some Hawaiians say the ghosts laugh at the way we repeat ourselves. We attract the same experiences, again and again, until we say: "That's it! I've had enough! I'll do anything it takes to *stop* having that experience now!" Often it's not until then that we're willing to take action on our higher wisdom. To do that, we need to "see" in the correct way.

The way we see our experiences, and the way we look at the world, is vitally important, for this seeing "seeds" the ways we react. We visually perceive information through our eyes, as we all know. But what everyone doesn't know is that information is *processed* through our pineal gland. In many mystical traditions the pineal gland is the center of consciousness of the body. From it, information is sent electromagnetically to every cell in our body through a hormone called melatonin. What we see through our eyes affects our whole body.

People of the Western world have a high incidence of myopia (short-sightedness). That's when the eye muscles become locked into converging on a particular point and cannot relax enough to see into the distance. Sixty to eighty percent of college students in the West suffer from it. In nonliterate societies, by contrast, the incidence of myopia is much lower, between four and six percent. But this incidence increases with the amount of time spent in Western-style schooling. For instance, only two percent of nonliterate Inuit children are myopic, but sixty-five percent of their peers who attend Western schools are.

Carolyn Bloomer attributes this difference to the act of going to school. I would go further and say that it could be related to a difference of *cultural ideas,* for Western ideas are interwoven with our school system the way the flowers of the lei are twined into the string that holds them together. Those ideas "see" the world visually. We even talk about "seeing" the world, not "smelling" the world, or "touching" the world.

Western culture also pays great attention to detail. The work of college students, for example, usually requires studying a subject in terms of "topics." Sometimes there is difficulty in relating those topics into a more integrated whole. All in all, there can be a difficulty in seeing the wood for the trees. Myopia is the perfect illness that shows an over-attachment to the close. I could go as far as to say myopia also shows an overattachment to the *familiar,* including familiar knowledge.

We need to learn to "see" in a different way in order to see things differently. Trite, but true. Meaning depends on perception. For example, when people from the West go into a room for the first time, they often notice the objects in it, as we have been brought up to find "things" important. But a Japanese is more likely to notice the dominance of space, and the Japanese traditionally design rooms to maximize the space around objects. They even plan railway lines so that the stations show the most scenic views of the journey!

Our perception changes according to the amount of light we let in. Cultures differ in the way they represent light, and it is worth looking at the way some other cultures do so. A good example of this can be found in the contrast between two ways of representing light and shadow in paintings. What is called the "Eastern option" uses shading that enhances the form. This leads to "flat"-looking paintings, prevalent in some Hawaiian, Japanese, and Egyptian art. The more usual "Western option" is to use shading representing a shadow cast by a specific light source. This technique has given us the "realistic" and famous paintings of Rembrandt, Leonardo da Vinci, and many others.

The implications of these differences are fascinating. Western painters are part of a Western belief system which holds that the world we see using our *limited* sight is real. The *light* is from a specific source. In the same way, our *knowledge* is believed to be from a specific source. Other cultures, however, believe that light (and knowledge) has no exclusive source, so no object is represented above any other. Their paintings have a timeless quality, because they are not "fixed" in time and place.

The so-called Eastern techniques have been used by certain Western painters such as Gauguin, Matisse, Miró, and Modigliani, demonstrating that we have the capacity to transcend our cultural blinkers. All we need to do is open up and admit that other ways of thinking may *possibly* have some validity. Experiment and experience will do the rest! But it's surprising how rarely we do this. Our preconceived beliefs stop the light that is always there from shining through. To change our level of vibration, we must let go of our fixed ideas that hold us "in place." But if we "open up" our consciousness, we can see more colors, like the Hawaiians, who have several words to identify the many shades of the color we think of as plain old yellow. As we have seen, the many techniques of Huna are all ways of learning how to live on a *higher vibration* of light.

INCREASING OUR VIBRATION

Madam, what use is a newborn baby?
BENJAMIN FRANKLIN'S REPLY TO A WOMAN WHO QUESTIONED
THE IMPORTANCE OF HIS WORK ON ELECTRICITY

Electricity was "discovered," harnessed, and used to change the world, but before we knew about it, it "didn't exist." Similarly, our minds are a force we haven't yet learned how to exploit. As we have seen, the application of Huna is based on understanding the principle of attraction that underlies all of existence and provides the means for the various powerful aspects of Hawaiian shamanism: we attract things by way of the mana-force we project onto the world through our three minds: the superconscious, conscious, and subconscious. That mana sticks to the aka, the substance of which everything is made. Getting the results we want depends on the alignment of the three minds and the direction of consciousness.

Huna's teaching that our task in life is to move up through our minds, from the heavier subconscious toward our lighter, superconscious mind, is reflected in the general Hawaiian conception of all growth as moving upward. For instance, the "family tree" in Hawai'i shows the generations growing upward, unlike in the West, where family trees are represented as growing downward. The Hawaiian view is more reflective of the fact that we spring from a common source, with branches of our families coming out of our ancestral roots.

Huna also makes it clear that humanity, like all of nature, grows toward the light. Indeed, the survival of most forms of life depends on their capacity to detect the presence of light. The ability of one-celled animals to detect the presence or absence of light, for instance, can warn an organism of an approaching enemy or signify the presence of food nearby. Green plants need to find and absorb light in order to grow. Narai, the heroine of Sverre Holmsen's beautiful novel of Polynesia, *Singing Coral,* described the world thus:

> "All living things are akin," she thought: "All things that hunger for light strive in the same direction, all life is seized sooner or later by the same hunger and gradually ascends to higher terraces. All such as clearly reflects the colors of light reveals in so doing its kinship; both with the depths from which it is sprung and with the life of other more highly developed worlds . . . The crystal mountain of *Makatea* [her island]; *Maona's* [her lover] firmly sculptured head, the coral monoliths and the breaking colors of shoals of flying-fish in flight, over foam-capped waves . . . all these bear kinship with the ultimate origin, as with the uppermost terraces. But whichever road life strives along, to reach a higher plane it must always follow the beacon-shafts of light . . ."[7]

Teilhard de Chardin wrote that evolution has always been in the direction of increasing consciousness. Our bodies have remained the same for eons, but our use of the cortex (the center of consciousness in the brain) for self-awareness and reflective thought has increased tremendously. Applying the principles of Huna enables us to foster that process of increasing our light.

When we increase our quotient of light, we need to prepare ourselves for a lot of changes in our external world, because our external world always mirrors our internal world. For that reason, change will be quicker and more controlled if we seek internal stimulation—such as meditation and controlling our mind—rather than external change. This "inner world" is so exciting that we can even lose our taste for external stimulation!

When I discovered this, I was in an area of New Zealand where everyone loves adventure and the outdoors. Everyone around me was into sensation, talking about "how much air" he caught under his skis, or the steep rocks she climbed. Bungee jumping was even invented in a nearby gorge in Queenstown! But I had discovered that I needed external stimulus much less than I had before. I would no longer be the rappeller, the high-diver; I would not repeat the parachute jump I did at sixteen. I no longer wanted to learn to fly an airplane. I was much lonelier than I would have been otherwise—fewer parties and more nights alone gazing at the mountains and the stars—yet somehow I felt much happier. The higher vibration of allowed light made up for the lack of contact with familiar habits and people. I was more sure of myself and my place in the world, with less need to "prove" myself through the opinions of others.

I was more in touch with what was truly important, which, in my case, was the sugared mountains, the glittering lake, the way the clouds shone, the shining strand on which I gathered firewood at sunset, and the many moments I noticed them. I realized that it was my own power that had brought me to that crystalline location in southern Polynesia. I could go somewhere else. Or I could stay. In a deep sense, it did not matter, for I was far more aware of the soul-light I had always been carrying inside.

Now I am aware of the wonder of what is all around me wherever I am: the brightness of the grass, the expression of people's faces in the street, the taste of food. I do still love to travel, to get my "stimulus" that way, although I spend much more time staying in one place. I am more likely to spend time (gently) in nature, rather than go to the city for the theater and shopping, for I simply feel better when I'm outside. Indeed, I met my husband because I wanted to go to an outdoor picnic rather than an indoor concert. As you can see, I still need to move a little.

Some of the greatest sages can be recognized by their ability to stay in one place. They are perfectly content doing the same thing every day, just *being*. That is because the world they "see"—such as smelling the table and hearing the lamp—includes extraordinary sensations. But, of course, some people who stay in one place aren't sages; they are just lazy or need to control their environment. We can know who we are by how much pleasure we find in the little things, expressed by the Zen saying: "Oh how wonderful! I chop wood, I carry water!"

We are growing not toward something new, but to a new appreciation. We are growing toward the manifestation of something that has remained hidden for a long time. This is reflected in our natural preference for the "lighter" ends of the spectrum of color. Arthur Koestler noted in *The Ghost in the Machine* that baboons, monkeys, and humans prefer the blue end of the spectrum to the red. Experiments show we also perceive the blue end of the spectrum as being lighter: asked to find the balance point between two disks of color, people judge red to be the heaviest. Hence, the Big Island of Hawai'i, whose color is red, relates to a "heavier" part of the mind than the violet isle of Kaua'i, at the other end of the rainbow spectrum.

The idea of moving up through the vibrations of the color spectrum can be taken literally. The ancient Greeks also knew about the healing properties of colors and even built healing temples to them. Many medical doctors use color in their practices, including Jacob Liberman, whose work on light has been extensively quoted in this book. In Europe, the German scientist and healer Peter Mandel invented Colourpuncture. He said that beaming in necessary color at the correct point on the body—where cells take up the healing vibration and pass the altered "light information" among themselves—averts illness. Hospitals routinely use elements of this concept, such as when jaundiced newborns are exposed to artificial blue light. Exposure to ultraviolet light is used to correct calcium metabolism, and shining color into people's eyes has been found to bring about emotional healing. A recent study at the New England State Hospital showed that when people with normal blood pressure were bathed in blue light, their pressure dropped.

Thank God, we can also empower ourselves on our own. The researchers in the New England State Hospital study were particularly amazed when their subjects could duplicate the results merely by *thinking about the blue light.* To change our level of vibration, we must let go of our fixed ideas, the rocks that hold us "in place." Our consciousness can be compared to a flow of light. Normal living cells emit a regular stream of photons or light radiation, passing on information through a "language of light." We have the power to alter that information. Our *mana'o,* "thoughts," are the best signal of what our consciousness is doing. Our thoughts are so used to running along habitual paths that they won't want to run off them. We must force them to become attracted to higher mana. We need to "bribe" them to encourage them to leave their old patterns.

In the use of creative visualization, the mind concentrates so hard on a new reality that it actually creates it. This "new reality" will be higher and brighter—in other words, we will be much happier—if we have made sure all our minds are in alignment, flowing up the hidden rainbow of Huna toward the light above. To bring a certain quality into our life, we can concentrate on a color that represents that quality.

Color Therapy is based on a principle the Hawaiians have known about for eons: every color corresponds to a particular emotional and spiritual quality. The gods represent qualities and they each have their special color. Kāne is the color of flame, Lono white, Kū blood red, and Kanaloa blue. Every family in old Hawai'i would wear clothing of the same color, the color of their 'aumakua. If their 'aumakua was the owl, they would wear brown tapa cloth; if it was the shark, they would wear gray. If their 'aumakua was the shell, they would wear dark red; if it was the thunder, they would wear black. The symbol of their 'aumakua, as well as the color, would be printed on their clothing to aid their connection to their 'aumakua, their Higher Self.[8] A chant from *Singing Coral,* about the arioi of Tahiti, sings of the magical qualities of each color, and of the ultimate light as the source of all:

O rainbow sun-bridge!
Drops of rain,
Rays of Ra,
From the vault pure colors flow:
Fair red of courage and battle,
Clear blue of song and dance,
Soft green of sympathy and hope,
Wisdom's clear yellow—
The purified colors of all being.
For Ra, white blinding light
Is the source of all.
O rainbow, bridge that unites,
Bright vault of Taaroa
The reflection of the creative spirit art thou.[9]

White is the color of eternity. White is the color of those bulbs of light I saw pulsing in the sea, the souls of the dead. White is the color of the Taj Mahal, the world's most famous tribute to the passing of a beloved spouse, which is so pale and unearthly that it looks as if it is about to float off into the Indian sky. White is a "clear" color, exposing deficiencies. For example, "dirt" shows far more on white than on any other color. The polar explorer Robert Swan said being surrounded by unbroken white meant he felt he had "nowhere to hide." Antarctica's all-white landscape appears featureless and pristine. No judgment of distance or direction is possible—just as with our Higher Self, the source of which is white.

White is "the source of all": science has shown it consists of all the other colors put together. Hawaiians call all the colors put together *maka'āinana*, "the eyes of the land." The center of our eye is known as the iris, the old word for rainbow, for the harmony of the rainbow knows how to see.

UNDERSTANDING CONNECTIONS

*And the cosmos is a mystery wherein every sound
however small
And every thought however feeble, reverberates and is
loudly heard everywhere so that there is no such thing
as privacy.
And everything is recorded . . . is never destroyed . . .
and is always repaid in a befitting manner. And the endless
struggle between man's ego and his higher self goes on.
And he constantly ponders what he should attempt to
save . . . Others? Himself? Or the world? But first he
must consider the many worlds within himself.*

KRISTIN ZAMBUCKA

Everything in the world is connected and *every*thing in our life is there because it is attracted to our "sphere of influence." Once there, it sounds, and reverberates, and tugs on the great fabric woven with aka. It is then activated, bringing things into being on that level of vibration. Our glowing world becomes our "going world." The trick is to attract the aka from our Higher Self, not our subconscious mind. To change our aka, we do need to consider, as Zambucka says, "the many worlds" within ourselves.

The concept of "spheres of influence"—first "discovered" in the West in the 1840s by Faraday and Maxwell—is far more important than it might seem at first. Unlike every traditional society in the world, people in the West are used to looking at events as "things in themselves." We don't see how they are connected to the pattern running through everything. When we *do* see how every event is a hologram illuminating the whole field, rather than an individual point within it, our consciousness expands enormously. We begin to see how aspects of our life we thought were unconnected—such as our relationship with our boss and our relationship with our mother—*are* all connected to each other. And *we* are always the "focal point." No getting away from it, the patterns repeating themselves *are not* just coincidence. They are there for a reason and *we* are the reason. Payne wrote about the We-Field:

From the field point of view, we are not separate from the universe which spawned us, but are instead multidimensional beings consisting of complex knots of organic fields, patterned structures of proteins, fats, carbohydrates, and minerals connected to the vegetable and animal kingdoms . . . our living and choosing form parts of fields . . . that transcend space-time, extending to all the realities that were, are, might have been, or will be. We extend in all directions, into all dimensions and are all interconnected. The We-Field comprises the entire universe in one whole.[10]

Although this may seem a bizarre or "far out" notion, it carries more validity than the viewpoint held by most people. We cannot separate ourselves from our world or from each other any more than time, space, matter, energy, form, and consciousness can be split asunder. Mind and universe are as inseparable as front and back.

From these considerations, the "oneness" of the universe emerges as a scientific fact. There is no need to use the term *mystical* for something so obvious and straightforward. When you understand this viscerally, you will understand how all men may be called brothers and that the golden rule, "Do unto thy neighbor as to thyself," is no arbitrary prescription, but arises quite logically from the fact that you are inextricably connected with your neighbor.[11]

Powerful stuff! And very, very true. Walter Harrison said:

The more widely we look and the more completely we see, the more intricate and all-embracing is the linkage displayed before us and which unites, not only all forms of life, but matter no less. It has been said that if a man raises a finger he creates a corresponding, albeit infinitesimal, displacement in the stars, such is the absolute and all-extending link between everything that is. On the same terms to kill a wood-louse, pluck a leaf, or cut a blade of grass must send an infinitesimal quiver through all living things.[12]

Everything we do affects the rest of the universe. One of the ways we best understand connection is through others, for even though we may appear to be separate atoms interacting with each other at random, we are really part of a greater dimension that is available to us if we can only learn to "see." Payne said:

> As I sit with my friend and talk, I sense so much more than his mere physical presence. Through him shine all the years of his life, his joys, his sufferings, his hopes, his future plans. All of this and more is there if I just look with my higher mind's eye.[13]

The ability to see the people we have drawn into our life this way means we have transcended our subconscious and our conscious minds to see them from the bright dimension of our Higher Self. Rumi put it wonderfully when he wrote many centuries ago:

> *Out beyond ideas of wrongdoing and rightdoing*
> *There is a field. I'll meet you there.*
> *When the soul lies down in that grass, the world is too full to*
> * talk about.*
> *Ideas, language, even the phrase "each other" doesn't make*
> * any sense.*[14]

There is no concept of separation in Rumi's field of unity. He was able to perceive the world *as it really is*. Being human, we can't always see other people this way, but the ability to see our friends and lovers this way, even once, will make a huge difference to how we think of them forever afterward. The direction of light will have moved upward, the shadow they cast will be less. By changing *what* we see, we will have changed *who* we see.

An extraordinary world awaits us when we know how to see, a world where we take responsibility for everything and everyone around us, a world where our vibrational energy has speeded up and so many things happen to us that we feel like we are living many lives in one! It is a world where we are constantly learning and constantly teaching—and we know it. It is world of power. A world of sound. A world of color. A world of light.

THE TRUTH

We believe, as Jones remarked, all that we can and
would believe everything if we only could.

CLIFFORD GEERTZ

Well, we're coming near the end of the book now, and can we really believe any of this stuff? What is the truth? The "truth" is: "There is no such thing as truth." It is all dependent on our perception.

We have seen that in the Hawaiian way of passing on knowledge, pupils learn by careful observation and questioning. Accordingly pupils learn only what they're ready for, and they—and we—never know how much we don't know. Our beliefs about our knowledge are different, many people believing that their way is the only true way. Asking questions can get us into a whole heap of trouble. The Greek sage Socrates said before he was ordered to die: "In another world, they do not put a man to death for asking questions, assuredly not."

In my experience of fieldwork in Hawai'i I learned that telling "the truth" occurs on many different levels, in many different dimensions. Think of the way a story changes according to the teller, think of the way a picture changes according to the light source, think of the way the shape of a flower changes with the removal of certain layers of petals. That's why there's "true" but no truth.

What is "true" is what is true for us, rather than some overarching reality. Although our souls pulse with the same light, we grow at different rates, in different ways, see different symbol-scapes. Yet somewhere we are encoded with the same bright knowledge, the knowledge from beyond-the-world, and the codes are codes of light.

Perhaps that's why the Hawaiians have so many words for the phenomenon we know as "rainbow." A rainbow fragment can be described as *ala muku* (*ala*, "path, trail"; *muku*, "cut short") or *'ōnohi*, "like an eyeball." Then there is *mākole* or *mōkole*, the "red-eyed rainbow," or *hakahakaea*, the "greenish" rainbow, full of open spaces." *Uakoko*, the "earth-clinging" rainbow, or "rain-sparkling" rainbow. This is usually red: *koko* means "blood" and *ua* "rain." The rainbow is called *lehopulu,* which means "wet cowry shell." Or a "standing rainbow shaft" is called *kahili* and a "barely visible" rainbow *punakea.* The *luohoana* is the "rainbow around the sun or moon." We all see a "rainbow," yet, when our perception brightens, we can distinguish among kinds: many representations, one bright presentation.

The colors we see outside brighten as we climb the mountain to a higher place, a higher space, always looking, always asking. The answers change as our questions change. The poet e.e. cummings wrote: "Always the beautiful answer who asks a more difficult question." Then the colors we are inside shake and glow and grow and we burst through our layers of stuff to become visible to all, in our true glory.

Except one more thing. Even now, we must remember what we don't yet see, for the knowledge that comes down to the people is of the gods. Hawaiians say there's always a double rainbow. The male rainbow is the visible spectrum, the female rainbow the invisible specter. The visible male rainbow is of the people, the invisible female rainbow of the gods. On earth, when the glens glance with a certain light, when we remember to look upward, we can see them both: the female rainbow arching gracefully below, the foundation for the light of the male.

THE BRIGHTNESS OF LIGHT

You have your paintbox and colors. Paint paradise
and in you go.

NIKOS KAZANTZAKIS

I hope I have given you an idea of just how many "colors" make up the brightness of Hawaiian light. We have moved, as it were, from the world of the pō, the "unseen," to the world of ao, "daylight," or "consciousness regained."

The more we see, the brighter is the world. Socrates had so increased his vibration that he was able to apprehend a world of great beauty and brightness:

There are many wonderful places in the world, and the world itself is not of such a kind or so small as is supposed by those who generally discourse about it . . . In the first place, then, my friend, the true earth is said to appear to anyone looking at it from above like those balls which are made of twelve pieces of skin, variegated, a patchwork of colors, of which the colors that we know here—those that our painters use—are samples as it were. Thus the whole earth is made up of such colors, and of colors much brighter and purer than these: part of it is purple, of wondrous beauty, and part again golden, and all that part which is white is whiter than the whiteness of chalk or snow; and it is made up of all the other colors likewise, and of even more numerous and beautiful colors than those we have seen . . . one should repeat these things over and over again to oneself, like a charm.[15]

My only knowledge of the colorful world Socrates speaks of comes through my contact with the 'aumakua. One scene I remember was full of vibrating points of light. I seemed to "know" that the living colors were the souls of the dead. The violet—far brighter than anything I had ever "seen" before—held the room where Janine was staying. As the incredibly bright colors—violet, red, orange—pulsed, I experienced such heat and love and light it felt like my insides were bursting with rainbows.

It was an emotion completely different from anything I had ever experienced before, the kind of emotion that brings swift understanding and makes life worth living. Einstein described it this way: "The most beautiful emotion we can experience is the mystical. It is the source of all true art and science. He to whom this emotion is strange, who can no longer wonder and stand in rapt awe, is as good as dead."[16]

The Hawaiian shamans know that we cannot find this sense of unity through drink or drugs: they call alcohol "the drink that snatches away the light." We can find it only by clearing ourselves and opening ourselves up to the eternal whole. Then the light we see will become brighter and so will our consciousness. Application of the knowledge of Huna will change the quality of our light and thus our lives. Thoreau put it beautifully: "To influence the quality of the day, that is the highest of arts."[17]

THE ISLANDS ARE REVEALED

Gleaming islands, indeed whole continents, can still add themselves to our modern consciousness.

CARL JUNG

The fragrant islands of paradise comprise the land that is hidden until we are ready to see it. We reach it through being prepared to break away from our assumptions and unwanted emotions, by increasing our knowledge and using it to consciously create our world. We are prepared to break away from the main continent and consciously create a new world. As we have seen, the process is a journey through our minds, a journey that unmasks the great light and clarity of our Higher Self. The journey to paradise is also one toward greater creativity, as described by Silvano Areti:

At the same time as it enlarges the universe by adding or uncovering new dimensions, it also enriches and expands man, who will be able to experience these new dimensions inwardly. It is committed not just to the visible, but, in many cases, to the invisible as well . . . a new painting, poem, scientific achievement or philosophical understanding increases the number of islands of the visible in the ocean of the unknown.[18]

We create, make land, make islands, make our world. How we do it—whether or not we know we're doing it—depends on what we see. I was surprised to realize that "saw" became "was," viewed backward. And "see" (phonetically, *si*) is the reverse of "is." We make our island out of our is.land, our concepts and facts. When we learn to see into the invisible, the land we perceive is our "promised land." It may be Hawai'i, the Holy Land, or some other place that is dear to us. It doesn't matter which place, for the promise was made only to us. When we find it, we will know it.

The key lies in understanding that our *huna moku,* or "secret island of paradise," resides *within us.* It is we ourselves who bring the mythical isles, the isles of the blessed, into existence. For this we need to travel. That's why the enchanted lands lie over the distant ocean, and why Hina, the moon goddess, voyages into the violet distance in her canoe called "Rainbow."

Huna is an excellent guide to bringing the colors of light down to earth. Huna offers us the knowledge we need to leave the "shallow sea" of the majority, travel over the billows of ocean and emotion, and access the purplish blue waters surrounding our desired land. The land "where the sky meets the sea" is the land of Kāne, the soul land we all share, the radiant continent of deep light and soft peace.

That's it for now; *pipi holo ka'ao,* "it is sprinkled," the tale has fled. May the wisdom I have shared in these pages empower us all to produce our own light in harmony with the bright rainbow of Hawaiian knowledge. Creating our own reality, our own land, with awareness helps tug on the totality of the universe. In the process of creating our land of crystalline clarity, we, like the kahunā, will be the ones who know, the ones who glow, the ones who hold, the ones who help. Then we will truly realize the national motto of Hawai'i:

Ua mau ke ea o ka 'āina i ke pono.

The life of the land is preserved in righteousness.

Notes

Chapter 1

1. Beaglehole, *The Voyage of the Resolution and Discovery*, part 2, 1221–22.
2. *Polynesian Odyssey*, film directed by Kieth Merrill for the Polynesian Cultural Center in Hawai‘i.
3. Goldwater, *Primitivism in Modern Art*, 66.
4. Gauguin, *The Intimate Journals of Paul Gauguin*, 19.
5. Hassall, *Rupert Brooke: A Biography*, 413.
6. London, *The New Hawaii*, 221.
7. Emerson, *Unwritten Literature of Hawai‘i*, 246–47.
8. Barrère et al., *Hula: Historical Perspectives*, 1, 2.
9. Pukui, Haertig, and Lee, *Nānā I Ke Kumu*, vol. 1, 127.
10. Sherman, *Tahitian Journals*, 80.
11. Lodge, *Paradise News*, 62–63.
12. Pila, *The Secrets and Mysteries of Hawaii*, 70.
13. Reyes, *Made in Paradise*, preface.
14. Melville, *Children of the Rainbow*, 18.

Chapter 2

1. Luomala, *Voices on the Wind*, 3, 4.
2. Beckwith, *The Kumulipo*, 298.
3. Fromm, 1976, 87.
4. Lee and Willis, *Tales from the Night Rainbow*, 17.
5. Nisker, *Crazy Wisdom*, 84.
6. Selye, *Stress Without Distress*, 27, 28.
7. Woolf, *On Being Ill*, 3.
8. Kelley, *The Home Planet*, 78.
9. Jaffe, *Healing from Within*, 224.

10. King, "The Way of the Adventurer," 31.

Chapter 3

1. Kupihea, *Kahuna of Light*, 15.
2. Long, *The Secret Science Behind Miracles*, 13.
3. Ibid., 33.
4. Ibid., 33, 34.
5. Ibid., 34, 35.
6. Ibid., 36.
7. Ibid., 37.
8. Ibid., 38.
9. Ibid., 83.
10. Ibid., 88, 89.
11. Kamakau, *Ka Po'e Kahiko*, 36.
12. Ibid., 33.
13. Gutmanis, *Na Pule Kahiko*, 14, 15.
14. Hulme, *Strands*, 17.
15. Melville, *Children of the Rainbow*, 9.
16. Luomala, *Voices on the Wind*, 124, 130.

Chapter 4

1. Long, *The Secret Science Behind Miracles*, 14.
2. Sheldrake, *The Rebirth of Nature*, 68.
3. Long, *The Secret Science Behind Miracles*, 389.
4. Ibid., 69.
5. Ibid., 16.
6. Gutmanis, *Na Pule Kahiko*, 61.
7. Ibid., 46.
8. Kamakau, *Na Hana a ka Po'e Kahiko*, 116, 117.
9. Beckwith, *The Kumulipo*, 202, 203.
10. Handy and Pukui, *The Polynesian Family System in Ka'u, Hawai'i*, 28.
11. Barrère et al., *Hula: Historical Perspectives*, 82.
12. Handy and Pukui, *The Polynesian Family System in Ka'u, Hawai'i*, 28.
13. Ibid., 34.

Chapter 5

1. Sheldrake, *The Rebirth of Nature*, 87.
2. Long, *The Secret Science Behind Miracles*, 19.
3. Ibid., 10.

4. Kupihea, *Kahuna of Light*, 14.
5. Long, *The Secret Science Behind Miracles*, 394.
6. Ibid.
7. Ibid.
8. Sheldrake, *The Rebirth of Nature*, 98.
9. Payne, *Getting There Without Drugs*, 185.
10. Auden, *Twelve Songs*, 21.

Chapter 6

1. Barrère et al., *Hula: Historical Perspectives*, 71.
2. Ibid., 70.
3. Emerson, *Unwritten Literature of Hawai'i*, 17, 18.
4. Barrère et al., *Hula: Historical Perspectives*, 36.
5. Emerson, *Unwritten Literature of Hawai'i*, 75.
6. Ibid., 41.
7. Jacob Liberman, personal communication, 2002.
8. Emerson, *Unwritten Literature of Hawai'i*, 43.
9. Eliot, *Collected Poems 1909–1962*, 205.
10. Emerson, *Unwritten Literature of Hawai'i*, 230–31.
11. Ibid., 221–22.
12. Oral tradition.
13. Lee and Willis, *Tales from the Night Rainbow*, preface.
14. Pukui, *'Ōlelo No'eau*, 134.
15. Emerson, *Unwritten Literature of Hawai'i*, 240.
16. Bamford, *Homage to Pythagoras*, 132.
17. Yeats, *Selected Poetry*, 41.
18. Ibid., 30.
19. Emerson, *Unwritten Literature of Hawai'i*, 43, 44.

Chapter 7

1. Sahlins, *Islands of History*, 18.
2. Beaglehole, *The Voyage of the Resolution and Discovery*, 1083.
3. Gutmanis, *Na Pule Kahiko*, 51.
4. Handy and Pukui, *The Polynesian Family System in Ka'u, Hawai'i*, 94.
5. Malo, *Hawaiian Antiquities*, 94, 95.
6. Sahlins, *Islands of History*, 16.
7. Ibid.
8. Handy and Pukui, *The Polynesian Family System in Ka'u, Hawai'i*, 110.
9. Gutmanis, *Na Pule Kahiko*, 22.

10. Ibid., 44.
11. Ibid., 28.
12. Oral tradition.
13. Emerson, *Unwritten Literature of Hawai'i*, 169, 170.
14. Ibid., 248, 249.
15. Gutmanis, *Na Pule Kahiko*, 45.
16. Sahlins, *Islands of History*, 4.

Chapter 8

1. Brooke, *The Collected Poems of Rupert Brooke*, 118.
2. Payne, *Getting There Without Drugs*, 21.
3. Malo, *Hawaiian Antiquities*, 13.
4. Hawaiian Moon Cycle according to Malo, *Hawaiian Antiquities*, 35.
5. Kamakau, *Ka Po'e Kahiko*, 49, 50–51.
6. Hawaiian Zodiac according to Malo, *Hawaiian Antiquities*, 33.
7. Allen, *Star Names*, 394.

Chapter 9

1. Luomala, *Voices on the Wind*, 7.
2. Kamakau, *Na Mo'olelo a ka Po'e Kahiko*, 95.
3. Lee and Willis, *Tales from the Night Rainbow*, 75.
4. Lévi-Strauss, *The Naked Man*, 694.
5. Brown, *Love's Body*, 246, 247.
6. Luomala, *Voices on the Wind*, 76.
7. Emerson, *Pele and Hi'iaka*, xv.
8. Ibid., 7.
9. Ibid., 143.
10. Ibid., 152.
11. Ibid., 192.
12. Ibid., 210, 211.
13. Emerson, *Unwritten Literature of Hawai'i*, 239.
14. Emerson, *Pele and Hiiaka*, 155.
15. Ibid.
16. Melville, *Children of the Rainbow*, 21.
17. Ibid., 22.
18. Ibid.
19. Payne, *Getting There Without Drugs*, 186.
20. Ibid., 199.
21. Ibid., 196, 197.
22. Lee and Willis, *Tales from the Night Rainbow*, 19.
23. Bateson, *Mind and Nature*, 114.

24. Brown, *Love's Body*, 246, 247.
25. Kamakau, *Na Moʻolelo a ka Poʻe Kahiko*, 76.
26. Barrère et al., *Hula: Historical Perspectives*, 21.
27. Emerson, *Pele and Hiʻiaka*, 321.
28. Lee and Willis, *Tales of the Night Rainbow*, 75.
29. Beckwith, *Hawaiian Mythology*, 242.
30. Luomala, *Voices on the Wind*, 29.
31. Lee and Willis, *Tales from the Night Rainbow*, preface.
32. Genesis 9:13, 15.
33. Kamakau, *Na Moʻolelo a ka Poʻe Kahiko*, 14.

Chapter 10

1. Frierson, *The Burning Island*, 11.
2. Pila, *The Secrets and Mysteries of Hawaii*, 71.
3. Bird, *The Hawaiian Archipelago*, 55.
4. Frierson, *The Burning Island*, 87.
5. Personal interview, 1994.
6. Bird, *The Hawaiian Archipelago*, 54.
7. Ellis, *A Journal of a Tour Around Hawaiʻi*, 131.
8. Vitaliano, *Legends of the Earth*, 128.
9. Ibid., 109.
10. King, *Kahuna Healing*, 97.
11. Pukui, *ʻŌlelo Noʻeau*, 61.
12. Frierson, *The Burning Island*, 26.
13. "Puff the Magic Dragon," by Lenny Lipton and Peter Yarrow.
14. Bird, *The Hawaiian Archipelago*, 217, 218.
15. Yardley, *The Heart of Huna*.
16. Emerson, *Pele and Hiʻiaka*, 182.

Chapter 11

1. Turner, *The Anthropology of Experience*, 203.
2. Bloomer, *Principles of Visual Perception*, 22.
3. Jaffe, *Healing from Within*, 131.
4. Oral tradition.
5. Payne, *Getting There Without Drugs*, 99.
6. Liberman, *Light: Medicine of the Future*, 221.
7. Holmsen, *Singing Coral*, 131.
8. Lee and Willis, *Tales from the Night Rainbow*, 18.
9. Holmsen, *Singing Coral*, 40.
10. Payne, *Getting There Without Drugs*, 188, 189.
11. Ibid.

12. Harrison, *The Threshold of Discovery*, 49, 50.
13. Payne, *Getting There Without Drugs*, 185.
14. Nisker, *Crazy Wisdom*, 68.
15. Plato, *The Last Days of Socrates*, 190.
16. Nisker, *Crazy Wisdom*, 31.
17. Ibid., 41.
18. Areti, *Creativity: The Magic Synthesis*, 171.

Glossary

This glossary contains selected Hawaiian words mentioned in the text. Hawaiian acts as a "secret code" to embody meanings, and each word has an enormous amount of *kaona,* or hidden interpretations. I have put down some of the ones looked at in this book. May finding their relevance set off many green connections for you.

Please note I have not put in place-names except Hawai'i; the names of the gods and goddesses are in capitals although Hawaiian was originally an oral language and they would not have been written down this way.

The transliteration of the letters was altered in a meeting of missionaries in 1822. It is my hope that eventually Hawaiian will revert to the original letters, *t* instead of *k,* and *r* instead of *l,* to make it the same as some of the other Polynesian languages, and even closer to the source. Meanwhile, a *kahakō,* or macron above a vowel, lengthens it. An *'okina,* or "backward glottal stop," gives a staccato quality to pronunciation.

The words are your wand. Enjoy your journey into Hawaiian: language of light.

'a'ā	to blaze; the first rock formed from lava, forerunner of *pāhoehoe*
'āina	land, land with plants growing on it
aka	matter meets consciousness, a fetus at the moment of conception, the essence of light; *aka* is contained in

everything; everything is capable of becoming light through directed consciousness

aliʻi	chief, often used to designate the rulers who came into power after the chief Pāʻo arrived in Hawaiʻi from Samoa around the fourteenth century
Akua	god, goddess, a creative force different from humans and nature in degree, not kind; night of the full moon, fourteenth night of the moon's cycle
aloha	love; hello; good-bye; to be happy with, to be at peace
ʻanāʻanā	form of "bad magic" in which the user tries to force outcome to conform to his or her own will
ānuenue	most common word for "rainbow"
ao	light, world, rightness (of a lover), daylight, to regain consciousness
ʻao	new shoot or leaf; also used for human birth and growth of consciousness
aoao	the prayer of the way of daylight; name of commitment chant for lovers
au	flow of measurable time, often compared to the current on the surface of the sea; action of mind
ʻaumakua	guiding spirit who often takes the form of a creature on earth, family god; they live in the realm of our Higher Self, which *ʻaumakua* also stands for
ʻaumākua	plural form, swarm of guiding spirits or family gods
hā	breath; pipe or channel for water
hale	house
hālau	long house, meeting house
hālau hula	hula group
haole	term for any white person, meaning *ʻole*, "without," *hā*, "breath"; its use is often insulting
Hawaiʻi	the string of islands named after Hawaiʻi, the Big Island, which is the southernmost island of the Hawaiian chain; one kaona is "agent," *ʻi*, "of the breath," *hā*, "of life," *wai*
Hawaiʻi nei	all of Hawaiʻi
Hawaiʻi nui	great Hawaiʻi

Hawaiian	the indigenous language of Hawai'i, often understood by speakers of other Polynesian languages; there remain dialectical differences and the substitution of certain letters by others
heiau	sacred temple—many remain today
Hi'iaka	sprightly goddess who moves consciousness, Pele's youngest sister, Lohi'au's love
Hina	the moon goddess
hina	to topple over from an upright position
hō	to give
hoaka	crescent moon; to glitter; to open as the mouth; second night in the moon cycle
hoku	fifteenth night of the moon cycle
hōkū	star
hō'onoponopono	spiritual practice of "making right," often done with your family
hōonoponopono	family conference
hōnua	earth before anything is growing on it
hula	sacred dance of Hawai'i, in its purest form a system of shamanism; the ancient form *hula kahiko* is in the midst of a revival, and I recommend you look for performances of that rather than the more modern and common *hula 'auana,* or "stray hula"
Huna	"hidden," the sacred wisdom knowledge guarded for generations, the most important remnant of Lemuria, not restricted to Hawai'i; eleventh night of the moon cycle
'ike	to see, to seem, to be like
'ike ho'omaopopo	consciousness
kā	to strike, often used for directed thought; a vine, to send out a vine
kaha	to cut into, mark
kaha ule	subincision; literally, "cut," *kaha,* "penis," *ule*
Kaha 'Ula	goddess of sex in Hawai'i
Kahiki	legendary lands, the isles of the blessed, separated from us only by our awareness; shifting our perspective to a

	higher one means we can learn to embody their shining qualities
Kahuna	one who knows how to strike out, *kā*, the hidden, *huna*, a master of consciousness; every kahuna has a different area of expertise, such as *kahuna 'ōlelo*, language kahuna; plural form is *kahunā*
kala	to clear, to forgive, to release; a type of seaweed
kalo	plant of Hawai'i; said to be the progenitor of the human race; also known as taro
Kamapua'a	the hog god, Pele's sometime lover
kanaka	human being, often used to mean "native," as in *kanaka maoli*
Kanaloa	god of the oceans, unity, one of the Nui Akea, the four major gods
Kāne	great god of peace who sometimes stands for the superconscious mind or Higher Self, perhaps the highest of the Nui Akea; twenty-seventh night of the moon cycle
Kāne huna moku	hidden islands of Kāne, they lie in a dream of beauty on the horizon; legend says they come into view when we expand our horizon and "learn how to truly see"; some say a remainder of ancient Lemuria
kaona	hidden meanings of a word
kapa	bark of the mulberry tree, also known as "tapa," from which the famous cloth of the Pacific islands is made
kapu	"forbidden"; in English we know this word by the Tahitian form "taboo;" this word is often falsely used to describe the ancient system of Hawai'i, but in fact it only describes the *imposed* system brought by Pā'ao
keiki	child, progeny; the name also means *kei*, "to glory in," and *kī*, "to aim," as of thoughts
kino	"body," "the result of," *no*, "our aimed thoughts," *ki*
Kū	God, in later times erroneously associated with war, sometimes symbolizes power of the subconscious; to stand, to be erect, to be independent; one of the Nui Akea
kua	high perspective, part of the words *makua* and *'aumakua*
kuahu	altar

kukui	candlenut tree—the white oily kernels of the nuts can be used for lights, symbols of enlightenment
kumu	root, source, main stalk of a tree; teacher—for instance, *kumu hula,* "hula teacher"
Kumulipo	"out of the source" or "the pattern of the unseen," most famous Hawaiian cosmogonic (creation) chant
kupuna	grandparent, respected person of that generation, ancestor; also means "starting point" and "growing"
lā	the sun, sometimes also Ra
laʻa kea	sacred light, sacred knowledge
Laka	goddess of the hula; tame (often used in the meaning of to tame oneself)
lani	sky, heavens
lapa	ridge, built up
lapalapa	steep-ridged; phosphorescence, signs of the souls of the dead
leʻa	pleasure, orgasm; clarity
Lea	Arcturus, "the star of joy"
leʻa leʻa	name of a prayer to the Nui Akea; have a great time
Lemuria	the "land of light," now existing only in the subtle realms; this continent predeceases Atlantis; the remnants comprise the islands of Polynesia, former mountaintops of the great land
Lohiʻau	this princeling is Hiʻiaka's eternal lover; they live together at the Nā Pali coast of Kauaʻi
Lono	god of consciousness and the conscious mind; the Makahiki festival is dedicated to him, one of the Nui Akea; twenty-eighth day of the moon cycle
mā	perceive, entwine as a vine or thought
Makahiki	the annual festival of peace and love, celebrated all over Polynesia in the months when the Pleiades were in view
Makaliʻi	the Pleiades group of stars
Makanikeoe	love god, who travels in the breeze that blows
make	to faint, change consciousness; since Western contact, has come to be used for "death"

mākia	directed consciousness; aim, purpose
makua	parent, respected person of parents' generation
mākua	parents, respected people of parents' generation
malama	light, moon, month
mālama	to take care of, to honor, to beware
mālamalama	great clarity, shining one, enlightenment
mana	creative power from within; mana is contained by every element, the force by which every element eventually becomes Akua
manō	shark, can be an 'aumakua, part of the superconscious; alternatively, manō is a sign of strength of the subconscious that needs to be moved through
Maori	the indigenous Polynesian language of New Zealand, easily understood by Hawaiians
Menehune	race of small beings, left over from Lemuria, often represented as brown goblins
moe	dream, sleep
Mū	small and hairy "people of the silence," some say visiting beings from hidden islands; *mū* means "silence"
nui	great, big
Nui Akea	the great, wide group of gods, used for Kū, Lono, Kanaloa, and Kāne
'ohana	family
'oia i'o	true
'ole	without
'ōlelo	language; *Hawai'i 'ōlelo,* the Hawaiian language
'ōma'o	green
Pā'ao	Samoan chief who arrived in Hawai'i in the thirteenth or fourteenth century and imposed a system of kapu that did much to destroy the ancient system of Hawai'i; a forerunner of the later destruction by the haole
pāhoehoe	ropy lava, more developed than 'a'ā
Papa	the earth goddess, lover of Wākea
Pele	the volcano goddess, who usually lives at Kīlauea on the Big Island

pō	the source, the unseen, the night sky, darkness; *pō* always contains an element of light
pōhaku	rock, stone; *pōhaku* also means the movement of potential, *pō*, through the breath, *ha*, of the subconscious, Kū
Poliʻahu	snow goddess, famous for her nurturing qualities; her home is on the summit of Mauna Kea, the snowy mountain on the Big Island; her name also means "bosom" and "to caress"
Polynesia	certain islands of the Pacific including the Hawaiian archipelago, as distinct from Melanesia and Micronesia
Polynesian	language group that spreads across the Pacific, and helps define which islands are part of "Polynesia," part of the Austronesian group of languages
Polynesians	indigenous people of the islands, known as *kanaka maoli* in Hawaiʻi
pule	prayer, sacred link of directed consciousness between earth and heavens
ʻuhane	the conscious mind relying on talk and reasoning, needs to be linked to the Higher Self and the subconscious
ule	penis
ʻunihipili	the subconscious mind, which needs to be encouraged not to cling to habit
wahine	woman
Wahine ʻŌmaʻo	"lady in green," Hiʻiaka's companion in consciousness
wai	water, semen
Wākea	the sky god, lover of Papa; light came into the world when Kāne pried them apart

Huna Resources

There are many resources available for the study of Hawai'iana. Here are some of my favorites:

www.hunalight.com
Author's Web site, which tells you more about the "light of huna." Has details of Sacred Travel consultations and Huna readings. The site offers Hawaiian astrology and information about courses in Huna and retreats.

www.mysticalhawaii.com
Pila's Web site, where you can go to download Hawaiian chants, buy CDs, and get readings.

www.huna-research.com
Huna research.

www.hawaii.edu
University of Hawai'i Web site

www.leahi.kcc.hawaii.edu/org
Kapiolani Community College Web site—some excellent Hawaiian stories.

www.hawaiianlinks.com
Many links to Hawaiian Web sites.

Music

There are some wonderful recordings of Hawaiian music. I recommend getting songs that have not been translated into English for obvious reasons!

Many people find drums more powerful than guitars, but a number of other instruments exist, such as the nose flute.

For a collection of general Polynesian music, I recommend David Fanshawe's *Polynesian Odysseys*.

Newspapers

The Big Island Weekly gives some interesting accounts. The *Honolulu Advertiser* and *Honolulu News* include accounts of Hawaiian cultural events.

Movies

The Whale Rider is an authentic depiction of New Zealand Maori tradition. I also recommend Vili Hereniko's *The Land Has Eyes*.

Bibliography

Allen, Richard Hinckley. *Star Names: Their Lore and Meaning.* New York: Dover Publications, 1963.

Arieti, Silvano. *Creativity: The Magic Synthesis.* New York: Basic Books, 1976.

Auden, W. H. *Twelve Songs.* London: Faber and Faber, 1936.

Bamford, Christopher. *Homage to Pythagoras.* New York: Lindisfarne Press, 1970.

Barrère, Dorothy, Mary Kawena Pukui, and Marion Kelly. *Hula: Historical Perspectives.* Honolulu: Bishop Museum Press, 1980.

Bateson, Gregory. *Mind and Nature.* London: Fontana, 1980.

Beaglehole, J. C., ed. *The Journals of Captain James Cook.* Vol. 3, *The Voyage of the Resolution and Discovery* (2 parts). Cambridge: Cambridge University Press for the Hakluyt Society, 1967.

Beckwith, Martha Warren. *Hawaiian Mythology.* Honolulu: University of Hawai'i Press, 1976.

Beckwith, Martha Warren, ed. *The Kumulipo: A Hawaiian Creation Chant.* Translated and edited with commentary by Martha Warren Beckwith. Chicago: University of Chicago Press, 1951. Reprint, Honolulu: University of Hawai'i Press, 1972.

Bird, Isabella. *The Hawaiian Archipelago.* 1875. Reprint, London and Basingstoke: John Murray Limited, 1974.

Bloomer, Carolyn. *Principles of Visual Perception.* New York: Van Nostrand Reinhold Company, 1976.

Borofsky, Robert. *Making History: Pukupukan and Anthropological Constructions of Knowledge.* Honolulu: University of Hawai'i Press, 1987.

Brooke, Rupert. *The Collected Poems of Rupert Brooke.* London: Sidgwick and Jackson, 1931.

———. *The Works of Rupert Brooke.* Hertfordshire: Wordsworth Editions, 1994.

Brown, Norman. *Love's Body.* New York: Random House, 1966.

Carr, E. H. *What Is History?* Harmondsworth: Penguin Books, 1961.

Cunningham, Scott. *Hawaiian Religion and Magic.* St. Paul, Minn.: Llewellyn Publications, 1994.

Davies, Paul. *Superforce.* New York: Simon and Schuster, 1984.

Dudley, Michael Kioni. *Man, Gods and Nature.* Honolulu: Nā Kāne O Ka Malo Press, 1990.

Eliot, T. S. *Collected Poems 1909–1962.* London: Faber and Faber, 1974.

Ellis, William. *A Journal of a Tour Around Hawai'i.* New York: Crocker and Brewster, 1825.

Emerson, Nathaniel. *Pele and Hi'iaka: A Myth from Hawai'i.* 1915. Reprint, Honolulu: Ai Pohaku Press, 1993.

———. *Unwritten Literature of Hawai'i: the Sacred Songs of the Hula.* 1909. Reprint, Tokyo: Charles E. Tuttle Company, 1986.

Frierson, Pamela. *The Burning Island: A Journey Through Myth and History in Volcano Country, Hawai'i.* San Francisco: Sierra Club, 1991.

Friery, Ned. *Hawaii.* Melbourne: Lonely Planet Publications, 1990.

Fromm, Erich. *To Have or to Be?* New York: Harper & Row, 1976.

Garcia, Shirley. "For the Life of the Land: Hula and Hawaii's Native Forests." In *Hawai'i: New Geographies,* edited by D. W. Woodcock. Honolulu: Department of Geography, University of Hawai'i at Mānoa, 1999.

Gauguin, Paul. *The Intimate Journals of Paul Gauguin.* London: Routledge and Kegan Paul, 1985.

Goldman, Irving. *Ancient Polynesian Society.* Chicago and London: University of Chicago Press, 1970.

Goldwater, Robert. *Primitivism in Modern Art.* New York: Vintage Books, 1966.

Gutmanis, June. *Na Pule Kahiko. Ancient Hawaiian Prayers.* Honolulu: Island Heritage, 1983.

———. *Pohaku: Hawaiian Stones.* Laie (O'ahu): Brigham Young University, Hawai'i campus, n.d.

Handy, E., and Mary Kawena Pukui. *The Polynesian Family System in Ka'u, Hawai'i.* 1972. Reprint, New York and Tokyo: Charles E. Tuttle Press, 1993.

Handy, E. S., E. G. Handy, and Mary K Pukui. *Native Planters in Old Hawaii: Their Life, Lore and Environment.* Honolulu: Bishop Museum Press, 1991.

Harrison, Walter. *The Threshold of Discovery.* London: Foundation Trust, 1964.

Hassall, Christopher. *Rupert Brooke: A Biography.* London: Faber and Faber, 1972.

Holmsen, Sverre. *Singing Coral.* London: James Barrie Publishers, 1951.

Hulme, Keri. *Strands.* Auckland: Auckland University Press, 1992.

Hütschnecker, Arnold. *The Will to Live.* London: Victor Gollanca, 1952.

Jaffe, Dennis. *Healing from Within.* New York: Alfred A. Knopf, 1980.

Jamal, Michele. *Volcanic Visions: Encounters with Other Worlds.* London: Penguin Books, 1991.

Kamakau, Samuel. *Ka Poʻe Kahiko: The People of Old.* Honolulu: Bishop Museum Press, 1991.

———. *Na Hana a ka Poʻe Kahiko: The Works of the People of Old.* Honolulu: Bishop Museum Press, 1976.

———. *Na Moʻolelo a ka Poʻe Kahiko: Tales and Traditions of the People of Old.* Honolulu, Bishop Museum Press, 1991.

Kameʻeleihiwa, Lilikalā. *Native Land and Foreign Desires: Pehea Lā E Pono Ai?* Honolulu: Bishop Museum, 1992.

Kanahele, George. *Ku Kanaka. Stand Tall: A Search for Hawaiian Values.* 1986. Reprint, Honolulu: University of Hawaiʻi Press, 1992.

Kelley, K. W., ed. *The Home Planet.* Reading, Mass.: Addison-Wesley, 1988.

King, Serge. *Kahuna Healing.* Wheaton, Ill.: Quest Books, 1983.

———. "The Way of the Adventurer." In *Shamanism,* edited by Shirley Nicholson. Wheaton, Ill.: Theosophical Publishing House, 1987.

Kuhn, Thomas. *The Structure of Scientific Revolutions.* Chicago: University of Chicago Press, 1962.

Kupihea, Moke. *Kahuna of Light.* Rochester, Vt.: Inner Traditions, 2001.

Lee, Pali, and Koko Willis. *Tales from the Night Rainbow: The Story of a Woman, a People, and an Island.* Honolulu: Night Rainbow Publishing Company, 1990.

Lévi-Strauss, Claude. *The Naked Man.* London: Jonathan Cape, 1981.

Levy, Robert. *Tahitians, Mind and Experience in the Society Isles.* Chicago: University of Chicago Press, 1973.

Liberman, Jacob. *Light: Medicine of the Future.* Santa Fe, N.M.: Bear and Company, 1991.

Lodge, David. *Paradise News.* London: Martin, Secker and Warburg, 1991.

London, Mrs. Jack. *The New Hawaii.* London: Mills and Boon, 1923.

Long, Max Freedom. *The Secret Science Behind Miracles.* Marina del Rey, Calif.: Devorss & Co., 1988.

Luomala, Catherine. *Voices on the Wind.* 1955. Reprint, Honolulu: Bishop Museum Press, 1986.

Malo, David. *Hawaiian Antiquities.* Honolulu: Bishop Museum Press, 1951.

McBride, L. R. *The Kahuna: Versatile Mystics of Old Hawaiʻi.* Hilo, Hawaiʻi: Petroglyph Press, 1972.

Melville, Leinani. *Children of the Rainbow.* Wheaton, Ill.: The Theosophical Publishing House, 1969.

Nakuna, Moses K. *The Wind Gourd of Laʻamaomao.* 2nd ed. Honolulu: Kalamaku Press, 1990.

Nisker, Wes. *Crazy Wisdom.* Berkeley: Ten Speed Press, 1990.

Oliver, Douglas. *Ancient Tahitian Society*, vol. 1. Honolulu: University of Hawai'i Press, 1974.

Park, Ruth. *My Sister Sif*. Melbourne: Penguin Books Australia, 1986.

Payne, Buryl. *Getting There Without Drugs*. London: Wildwood House, 1974.

Pila Chiles. *The Secrets and Mysteries of Hawaii: A Call to the Soul*. Deerfield Beach, Fla.: Health Communications, 1995.

Plato. *The Last Days of Socrates*. London: Penguin Books, 2003.

Pukui, Mary Kawena. *'Ōlelo No'eau. Hawaiian Proverbs and Poetical Sayings*. Honolulu: Bishop Museum Press, 1983.

Pukui, M. K., and S. Elbert. *Hawaiian Dictionary*. Hawaiian-English. English-Hawaiian. 5th ed. Honolulu: University of Hawai'i Press, 1989.

Pukui, M. K., S. Elbert, and E. T. Mookini. *Place Names of Hawai'i*. Honolulu: University of Hawai'i Press, 1974.

Pukui, M. K., E. W. Haertig, and C. Lee. *Nānā I Ke Kumu (Look to the Source)*, 2 vols. Honolulu: Queen Lili'uokalani Children's Center, 1972.

Reyes, Luis I. *Made in Paradise: Hollywood's Films of Hawai'i and the South Seas*. Honolulu: Mutual Publishing Press, 1995.

Rice, William Hyde. "Hawaiian Legends." In *Bernice Pauahi, Bulletin 3*. Honolulu: Bishop Museum Press, 1923.

Sahlins, Marshall. *Islands of History*. Chicago: University of Chicago Press, 1985.

Selye, Hans. *Stress Without Distress*. London: Hodder and Stoughton, 1974.

Sheldrake, Rupert. *The Presence of the Past: Morphic Resonance and the Habits of Nature*. Rochester, Vt.: Park Street Press, 1991.

———. *The Rebirth of Nature*. Rochester, Vt.: Park Street Press, 1994.

Sherman, William David. *Tahitian Journals*. London: Hearing Eye Press, 1990.

Schutz, Albert J. *The Voices of Eden: A History of Hawaiian Language Studies*. Honolulu: University of Hawai'i Press, 1994.

Smith, Allison A. Chun. "Kaho'olawe: The Sacred Isle." In *Hawai'i: New Geographies*, edited by D. W. Woodcock. Honolulu: Department of Geography, University of Hawai'i at Mānoa, 1999.

Thrum, Thomas. *More Hawaiian Folk Tales: A Collection of Native Legends and Traditions*. Chicago: A. C. McClurg and Co., 1923.

Turner, Victor W., and Edward M. Bruner, eds. *The Anthropology of Experience*. Urbana, Ill.: University of Illinois Press, 1986.

Valeri, Valerio. *Kingship and Sacrifice: Ritual and Society in Ancient Hawaii*. Chicago: University of Chicago Press, 1985.

Vitaliano, Dorothy. *Legends of the Earth: Their Geologic Origins*. Bloomington: University of Indiana Press, 1973.

Whorf, Benjamin. *Language, Thought, and Reality: Selected Writings of Benjamin Lee Whorf*. Cambridge: Technology Press of Massachusetts Institute of Technology, 1956.

Wichman, Frederick B. *Kauai: Ancient Place-Names and Their Stories.* Honolulu: University of Hawai'i Press, 1998.

Wolff, J. *Resident Alien: Feminist Cultural Criticism.* New Haven: Yale University Press, 1995.

Woolf, Virginia. *On Being Ill.* Ashville, Mass.: Paris Press, 2002.

Yardley, Laura Kealoha. *The Heart of Huna.* Honolulu: Advanced Neuro Dynamics, 1991.

Yeats, W. B. *Selected Poetry.* London: Pan Books, 1974.

Zambucka, Kristin. *'Ano 'Ano: The Seed.* Honolulu: Mana Publishing Co., 1978.

———. *The Mana Keepers.* Honolulu: Harrane Publishing Company, n.d.

Index